BAC PRO

PREMIÈRE TERMINALE professionnelles

planetwork

A. Cohen / A.-M. Neveu / F. Lebret / J. Martinez / sous la direction de B. Lallement

HACHETTE Technique

The authors of Planet Work would like to thank all the people who contributed towards the interviews for Street Talk: Shaun, Paul, Michael Garfield - The High-Tech Texan, Helen, Hannah, Graeme Mathy from Bournemouth Football Club, Louise from ASDA, Warren – The Cyclone Cowboy, David Johnson – a Sunday Times editor, Sara Evans – News International, Deborah Spencer, Louise – News International, Lindsay Moran and Leonardo from the Carlton Hotel, Bournemouth. Extra special thanks go to David Johnson and Valerie Sanson, without whose help in tracking down suitable professionals, we would probably still be looking. To all of you, your help and participation were priceless. We know your professional experience can only go towards encouraging and guiding all teenagers who use this book and who, hopefully, will follow in your footsteps. Thank you.

Couverture : François Supiot

Intérieur : Mongaui

Cartographie : Hachette

Dessins : Viravong

www.hachette-education.com
I.S.B.N. 2.01.18.0301.2

Planet Work

est une méthode destinée aux élèves de première et de terminale des baccalauréats professionnels.

Elle a pour objectifs :

- d'offrir un manuel qui réponde aux exigences du programme ;
- de maintenir la motivation des élèves en utilisant des supports authentiques et stimulants ;
- de proposer des activités variées et rigoureusement organisées pour aider les élèves à améliorer progressivement les savoir-faire fondamentaux.

Comme son titre l'indique, **Planet Work** est centré sur le monde du travail. Les élèves pourront appréhender les différents aspects de la vie professionnelle à travers les quatorze kits de l'ouvrage.

Le manuel se compose de 14 kits de 10 pages.

Speaking

Une page d'ouverture présente deux photos accompagnées de quelques questions permettant un travail d'anticipation sur le thème du kit.

STREET TALK

Un document enregistré, un entretien authentique avec des professionnels britanniques ou américains, constitue une première approche du thème.

Minimag

Des articles courts et faciles illustrent les différentes facettes du thème du kit. Ils sont accompagnés d'un appareil pédagogique de façon à pouvoir être appréhendés par les élèves de manière quasi autonome.

Reading

Un texte principal accompagné d'un guidage très détaillé entraîne les élèves à un travail de compréhension méthodique. Une phase d'observation et d'analyse de la langue, **Grammaire en contexte** introduit le fait de langue.

Language skills

- Une double page est consacrée à la présentation du fait de langue suivi d'exercices d'application **Entraînez-vous** et d'un rebrassage lexical **Jeux de mots**.
- Une troisième page comporte la rubrique **D'une langue à l'autre**, destinée à aplanir progressivement les difficultés de traduction, et l'**Atelier d'écriture**, dont l'objectif est d'améliorer l'expression écrite.

Planet Words

Cette page est consacrée au lexique utile du kit. Elle sert de référence et permet de le réviser. Des exercices sont proposés pour une meilleure appropriation de ce lexique.

Exam paper

Une évaluation clôt chaque kit. Généralement extraite d'un sujet d'examen, elle comporte des exercices de compréhension, de grammaire, de traduction et d'expression écrite, et met ainsi les élèves dans les conditions de l'épreuve.

Fiches

Des fiches méthodologiques et professionnelles ont pour objectif d'aider les élèves à prendre conscience de leurs stratégies d'apprentissage, et à faire face à des situations concrètes sur leur lieu de stage ou lors de leur vie professionnelle future.

- Un jeu "Get to the top".

Annexes

- Une fiche de conjugaison
- Une liste de verbes irréguliers
- Un tableau des prépositions
- Les mots de liaison et les adjectifs numéraux
- Des cartes : Royaume-Uni, États-Unis et pays anglophones.

Le manuel est accompagné d'un boîtier de 2 CD audio et d'un classeur de transparents.

- **Les CD audio** contiennent les interviews de la rubrique **Street Talk**, les résumés de ces interviews, les enregistrements des textes principaux et leurs résumés.
- **Le classeur** comporte des transparents et les grilles de compréhension accompagnant des documents enregistrés.

Planet Work propose 14 kits

Chaque kit comprend :

1. Speaking

En page d'ouverture, une première approche orale du thème du kit.

2. Minimag

STREET TALK

Une illustration du document sonore du CD audio, accompagnée d'un wordbox pour faciliter la compréhension orale.

Des textes courts et accessibles, accompagnés de questions.

3. Reading

Le texte principal, accompagné d'un guidage détaillé, permet un travail de compréhension approfondie.

4. Language skills

Une page de grammaire présentant un fait de langue de manière synthétique.

Language skills
L'expression du futur
Language skills kit 14

Une gamme d'exercices contextualisés pour mettre en pratique et consolider les points de grammaire.

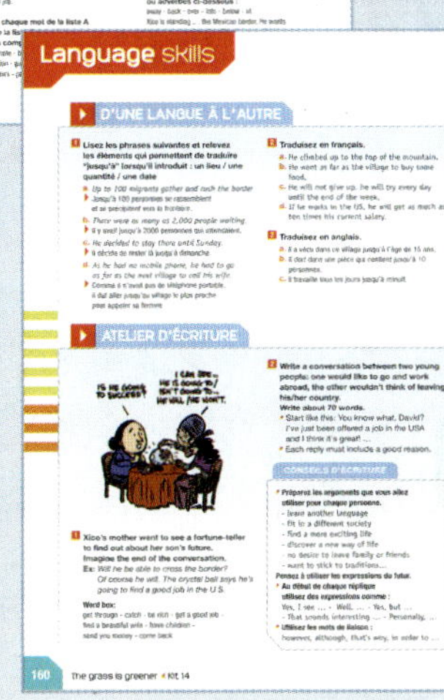
Language skills

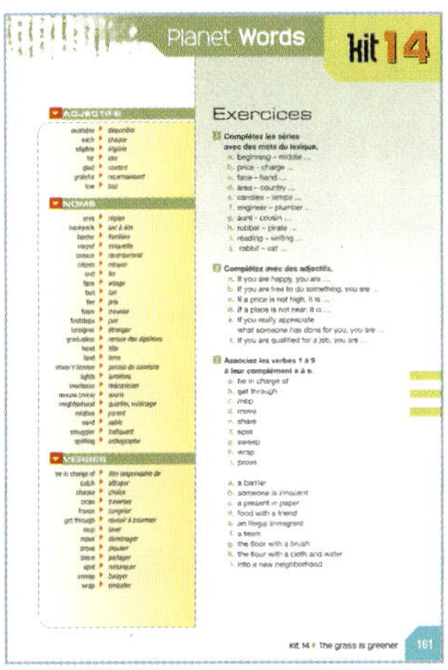
Planet Words kit 14
Exercices

5. Planet Words

Une page pour mémoriser et s'approprier le lexique du kit.

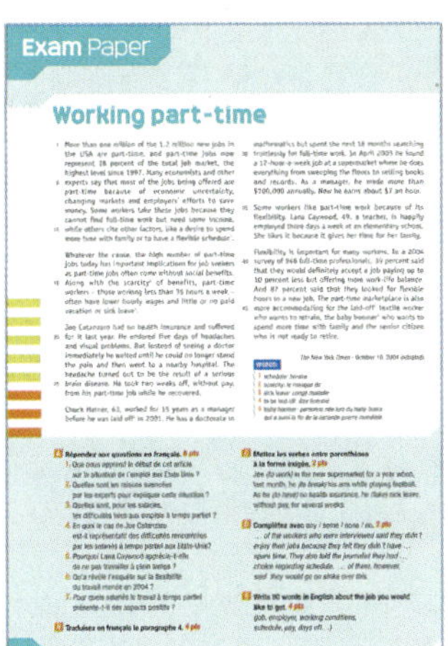
Exam Paper
Working part-time

6. Exam Work

Un sujet d'examen pour aider l'élève à se préparer à l'épreuve.

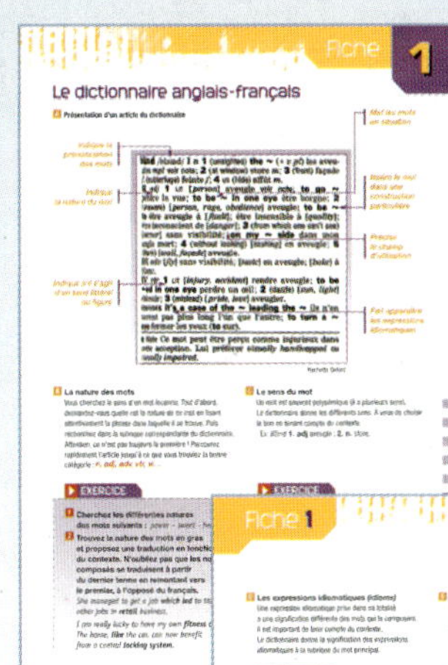
Fiche 1
Le dictionnaire anglais-français

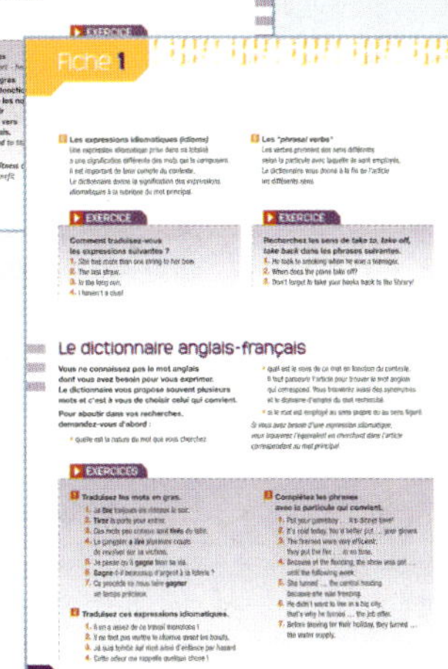
Fiche 1
Le dictionnaire anglais-français

Fiches Methodologiques

6 fiches de conseils pour aider l'élève à acquérir des méthodes de travail rigoureuses.

Des annexes

- une liste des verbes irréguliers
- une liste des prépositions
- une liste des mots de liaisons
- une liste des numéraux
- des cartes des pays anglophones, du Royaume-Uni et des États-Unis

Sommaire

Sommaire

L'épreuve écrite.

L'épreuve orale.

kit 1

© Taxi Getty

Odd jobs

© J.Wiedel Photolibrary/Alamy

Speaking

- Describe the girl and say what she is doing.
- Compare her to the youngsters in the small picture.
- How do you think they spend their free time?

STREET TALK

My trolley and me

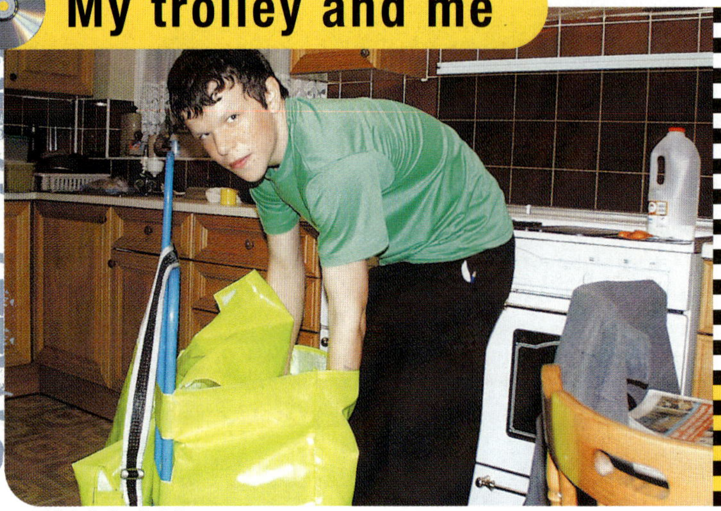

© Judy Martinez/Hachette

1 Listen to these words from the interview:

- paper round • leaflets
- businesses • extra • delivering
- stuff • strings • freezing

2 Listen to Shaun and fill in the questionnaire.

Shaun from Parkstone, U.K.

I Working in a charity shop

Delete | Answer | Answer all | Forward

Oxfam[1] experience

Princess *Post : 1 Week Ago - 11:45 AM - 03-07-2005*
I was just wondering if anyone has ever worked in Oxfam (or any other charity shop[2]) as a volunteer? Is it good experience, hard work, flexible, rewarding, etc? Some feedback would be so useful.

BlackHawk *Post : 11:54 AM Reply to Oxfam experience*
Working as a volunteer in a shop will give you valuable experience. You are also helping others. It adds experience to your CV. You deal with customers, handle cash, control stock and cash up. It is rewarding and flexible.

Junior *Post : 11:56 AM Reply to Oxfam experience*
You'll have the best time in the world. Go for it!

Josh *Post : 12:53 PM Reply to Oxfam experience*
I worked for Oxfam for about 6 months. It was fantastic. A great mixture of people and interesting work. It makes working in a job a lot easier + looks good on CV. Lunch and transportation are paid for.

Princess *Post : 02:58 PM*
Thanks for your help, excellent! I'm definitely going to work in a charity shop.

© Oxfam

WORDS:

1 Oxfam: *organisation caritative britannique*
2 Charity shop: *boutique vendant des articles d'occasion pour des organisations caritatives*

FEEDBACK

1 How are Princess and the other students communicating?
2 What does Princess need information for?
3 Did BlackHawk find working in a charity shop boring? Justify.
4 How could it help Princess in her future job hunt?
5 How would you describe Junior's advice: a little positive, enthusiastic, very enthusiastic?
6 Pick out all the positive words Josh used to talk about his experience at Oxfam.
7 What other important detail does he give about the job?
8 Is Princess going to follow the students' advice?

2 A sweet job

© C. Boisvieux/Hoaqui

Phoebe Kosman, 16, of West Barnstable, works at Kandy Korner on Main Street in Cape Cod[1]. She scoops[2] ice cream, cuts fudge, works as a cashier, stocks items, and makes small talk with tourists.

Kosman said she chose the job because she has friends who work there and enjoy it and because it's on Main Street. She works 20 hours a week and got the job by asking for an application. "You get to talk to a lot of people, many of whom are from interesting places with diverse backgrounds and have interesting stories to tell," Kosman said. "Also, you get to see the way kids' faces light up when they enter a candy store, and I like to make people happy," she said.

With jobs requiring little training and yet paying above minimum wage, Cape teens aren't having any problem finding jobs.

www.boston.com

WORDS:

1 Cape Cod: *une station balnéaire du Massachusetts*

2 scoops: *fait des boules (de glace)*

FEEDBACK

1 ▶ How old is Phoebe Kosman and where is she from?

2 ▶ What part-time job has she got?

3 ▶ Is her work monotonous? Justify.

4 ▶ Match the words with their French equivalents:

• fudge	*salaire*
• cashier	*caramel*
• wage	*caissière*

5 ▶ Pick out the reasons why she chose this job.

6 ▶ How do kids feel when they arrive at the shop? Why?

7 ▶ Why does she enjoy her job?

8 ▶ Find two advantages of odd jobs.

3 A job's a job

© R. Crandall/Cosmos

Another working teen is Jeff Quinn, 15, who works as a stock boy at Pet Supplies Plus in Cape Cod. "One day I was shopping there and they had a 'help-wanted' sign in the window, so I filled out an application and they hired me," he said. He works 24 hours a week, three days a week, for $5.75 an hour. Quinn said sometimes it interferes with his social life and schedule out of work. He said the main advantage of working at Pet Supplies Plus is just to have money. "The most frustrating part of the job is definitely mopping the floor, but I like stocking cans because it's easy. The really boring part is stocking sale items that weigh forty pounds." He said he might go back to the job next summer but wouldn't consider working there when school starts.

Quinn said what he really wanted to do this summer was to "watch television, relax, and hang out with my friends" adding that his dream job would be to work as a camp counselor.

www.capecodonline.com

FEEDBACK

1 ▶ How old is Jeff and where is he from?

2 ▶ What part-time job has he got?

3 ▶ How did he get the job?

4 ▶ How does his part-time job affect his private life?

5 ▶ What is the main advantage of his job?

6 ▶ What does he like in his job?

7 ▶ What does he dislike in his job?

8 ▶ Jeff said: "I wouldn't consider working there when school starts." Guess why.

9 ▶ What does he dream of doing for his holiday?

10 ▶ What would be his ideal job?

Comprehension

© B. Rieger/Hémisphères

Before you read

1. Describe the picture.
2. What is the man's job? Imagine the good and the bad points of his job. Would you like to do it?

Read the text

3. Say as much as you can about the main character: name, age, family, native country, job, country and city where she lives.
4. Which paragraphs contain information about:
   - the money she earns,
   - her physical appearance,
   - the description of her shoe stand,
   - her ambition,
   - her parents' attitude,
   - how she emigrated to the USA?
5. Now say if the text is about a shoe-shine girl:
   - working to pay for her studies;
   - working to send money to her family.

Read the first four paragraphs

6. Is Washington the only American city where you can find shoe-shiners? Justify.
7. How old was Paola when she came to the USA? Did she come illegally? Justify.
8. Was shoe-shining her first job? Justify. Who gave her the job?

Read the rest of the text

9. How many customers can she have at the same time?
10. Is her stand located in an isolated area of the city?
11. Pick out the good and the bad points of her job.
12. Are there many women doing her job? Justify.
13. What is her parents' attitude towards her?
14. Which sentence expresses Paola's real dream?
15. Find the equivalents for: *entrance-hall – domain – afraid – thinks*

ALLEZ PLUS LOIN

1 **Traduisez le mot composé** *shoe-shine girl.* Trouvez dans le texte un autre mot composé ayant le même sens. ▸ FICHE p. 75

2 **Décrivez l'endroit où Paola travaille** (§5). *Stand* est un mot transparent, *seat* est un nom de la même famille que *sit*; cherchez dans le dictionnaire les mots *brass*, *wood* et *rest.* Attention *rest* ici est un faux ami.
▸ FICHE p. 75

3 **D'après le contexte, quel est le sens de** *tip* ?
Vous savez qu'on parle de clients, que *tip* est précédé de *additional* qui est dérivé du mot transparent *addition.*

4 **D'après le contexte, quel sens peut avoir le mot** *rate*?
Lisez ce qui suit : *is three dollars and fifty cents.*

5 **Relevez le mot transparent de la même famille que** *man.*

RÉSUMEZ

1 **Écoutez l'enregistrement. Résumez en anglais en utilisant ces mots dans l'ordre.**
- Paola – shoeshiner – Washington
- comes – Brazil – college student
- needs – money – pay – studies
- works – uncle – lobby – government building
- job – can – tiring – likes
- says – has not faced – discrimination
- family – supports – proud
- goal – to earn – more tips – later – study – law

2 **Résumez en français en vous appuyant sur les questions suivantes.**
- D'où vient Paola Bernardez ?
- Qu'est-ce qui lui a permis de venir travailler aux États-Unis ?
- Comment gagne-telle sa vie ? Qui l'emploie ?
- De quoi rêve-t-elle ?

Grammaire en contexte

1. Le texte fait-il référence au passé ou au présent ?

2. Observez les énoncés suivants :

a) *That's why she's shining shoes.*

b) *Ms Bernardez shines anywhere between eight and forty-five pairs of shoes a day.*

- **Identifiez les formes verbales.**
- **Reliez chacun des énoncés à sa signification :**
  - il s'agit d'une action habituelle
  - il s'agit d'une activité temporaire

A shoe-shine girl from Brazil

Like any city, Washington D.C. has a lot of shoe-shiners. However, not many of them are tall, slender, stylishly dressed young women with flowing dark hair and a touch of make-up. Paola Adorno Bernardez, who came to the United States from Brazil, looks like a college student – which is what she would like to be. That's why she's shining shoes.

"I really want to go to college here. It's been my dream since I was a child. When I was eighteen, I started thinking about the idea of coming to the US. And, two years ago, I just came."

© P. De Wilde/Hoaqui

Ms Bernardez, who is now 22, came to the United States on a student visa. She spent the first ten months in America living with her uncle, earning some money by baby-sitting, and studying English.

"I finally asked my uncle for a job – he was the owner of this company – and he said, 'Well, if you have English already, you should start shining shoes.'"

Ms Bernardez's work station is a polished wooden stand with four high seats and brass foot rests. It's in the lobby of one of the many government buildings in the heart of Washington. Ms Bernardez says the rate for shoe-shines is three dollars and fifty cents, but her customers usually leave an additional – and sometimes substantial – tip.

"Now I earn exactly one thousand two hundred dollars monthly. But it depends on the season."

Ms Bernardez shines anywhere between eight and forty-five pairs of shoes a day. Although it can be tiring, she says she likes her job. "I can make so many friends and I can practise my English, I can talk with people. I love to talk about everything."

The vast majority of shoe-shiners in this country are male but Ms Bernardez says she hasn't really faced any discrimination, being a woman in a man's field. "And," she says, "my family supports me. Sometimes they feel proud. You know, they say 'Oh, my daughter, she is not scared, she is shining shoes just to pay for college.' The most important thing to them is that I'm working on my dreams."

Ms Bernardez hopes that her uncle, the owner of the shoe-shine business, will transfer her to a better location, perhaps Washington's Reagan National Airport, where she believes she would earn more in tips. Her long-term goal is to study international law. "I know it's going to take a long time, but I'm ready for that," she says.

Oksana Dragan, www.voanews.com

Le présent

Le présent simple V(-s)

Le symbole V(-s) représente le présent simple. L'énonciateur s'intéresse aux faits bruts et utilise V(-s) pour exprimer :

une caractéristique du sujet grammatical,
Ex: *Paola's friend teaches English.*
▸ L'ami de Paola enseigne l'anglais.

une vérité générale,
Ex: *The earth revolves round the sun.*
▸ La terre tourne autour du soleil.

une action habituelle,
Ex: *Paola shines shoes every day.*
▸ Paola cire des chaussures tous les jours.

une succession d'activités,
Ex: *She gets up, has breakfast, washes and leaves her flat.*
▸ Elle se lève, prend son petit déjeuner, se lave et quitte son appartement.

une référence à l'avenir (emploi du temps, horaire de trains, etc.).
Ex: *Tonight the shop closes at 8 p.m.*
▸ Ce soir, le magasin ferme à 20 heures.

Le présent *BE + V-ING*

Be* est conjugué au présent *(am, are, is)* + V-*ing
L'énonciateur donne son point de vue sur l'action et utilise *be* + V-*ing* pour :

une action en cours de réalisation,
Ex: *Look! She is shining a pair of green shoes!*
▸ Regarde ! Elle cire une paire de chaussures vertes !

une action temporaire,
Ex: *She is living in Washington at the moment.*
▸ Elle vit à Washington en ce moment.

une action prévue dans l'avenir,
Ex: *She is seeing her friend tomorrow.*
▸ Elle va voir son amie demain.
(L'énonciateur signale qu'il a l'intention de voir son amie demain.)

l'expression d'un certain agacement lorsque *be + V-ing* est associé à *always*.
Ex: *She is always smoking.*
▸ Elle n'arrête pas de fumer !
(L'énonciateur sous-entend qu'il est incommodé, agacé.)

Quelle forme choisir : *V(-S)* ou *BE + V-ING?*

Le présent simple
Ex: *Paola starts at 9 a.m.*
(L'énonciateur donne une simple information : heure à laquelle elle commence son travail.)

Le présent *Be + V-ing*
Ex: *It's 9 p.m. Paola is finishing up.*
(L'énonciateur ne se contente pas d'une simple information ; il commente le fait que Paola termine, donc elle est fatiguée.)

ENTRAÎNEZ-VOUS

1 Mettez ces verbes à la troisième personne du singulier et classez-les suivant la prononciation du « s » final : /s/, /ɪz/, /z/.
allow - become - cancel - control - create - encourage - live - own - park - reduce - reserve - share - use - walk

2 Écrivez des énoncés corrects.
Ex: he / go out / every day?
Does he go out every day?
a. she / not finish / before 9 p.m.
b. Betty / stay / at home every evening.
c. he / relax / whenever he is at home.
d. they / like / their new job?
e. Bob / start / at 8 a.m. every day?
f. Paola / not want / to shine shoes all her life.

3 Justifiez l'emploi des formes verbales en choisissant l'une des valeurs indiquées entre parenthèses.
a. Her uncle runs a shoe-shine business.
(caractéristique du sujet / référence à l'avenir)
b. The sun rises in the east.
(action temporaire / vérité générale)
c. Paola is seeing her family next month.
(action prévue dans l'avenir / action en cours de réalisation)
d. The last bus leaves at 10 p.m.
(horaires / action prévue dans l'avenir)
e. It is always raining in the evening!
(l'énonciateur est agacé / l'énonciateur est ravi)

4 Mettez les verbes entre parenthèses au présent (V(-s) ou *be* + V-*ing*).
a. Look at her! She … two pairs of shoes! (*shine*)
b. She … her job, although it … very tiring. (*like – be*)
c. What does she do exactly? First, she … each pair of shoes and then she … them. (*polish - shine*)
d. Her uncle's stand … early every morning. (*open*)

5 Traduisez.
a. Chaque jour, Paola parle anglais avec ses clients.
b. Cet homme essaie de partir sans payer. Regardez-le bien !
c. Très souvent, les clients laissent un pourboire.
d. Elle n'arrête pas de parler du Brésil.
e. Elle va étudier le droit international l'année prochaine.

JEUX DE MOTS

1 Complétez avec une de ces prépositions.
of – on – out – for (2 fois)
a. Paola asked her uncle … a job.
b. Like that she could pay … her studies.
c. She didn't want to depend … anyone.
d. She filled … a form and applied for the job.
e. Her parents were very proud ... her

2 Complétez avec un mot de liste ci-dessous.
already – since – that's why – between – like
a. Paola had … visited Washington before.
b. She thought it was … most cities in the USA.
c. She had wanted to go there … she was a child.
d. She studies … six and 8 hours a day.
e. … she'll soon be able to go to college.

3 Choisissez le verbe en italique qui convient.
a. Paola *practises/trains* her English with her American friends.
b. She *went/came* to live here in the USA five years ago.
c. She *starts/leaves* home at 6 a.m. in the morning.
d. However, she *wins/earns* a lot of money.
e. She'll be able to *go/come* to Brazil soon.

D'UNE LANGUE À L'AUTRE

1 Observez ces phrases et dites dans quelle phrase *like* est une préposition. Trouvez la nature de *unlike*.

a. *Her uncle's employees say they like their jobs.*
▸ Les employés de son oncle disent qu'ils aiment leur travail.

b. *Like many employees she wanted to work at the airport.*
▸ Comme beaucoup d'employés, elle voulait travailler dans l'aéroport.

c. *Unlike her parents, she was very ambitious.*
▸ Contrairement à ses parents, elle était très ambitieuse.

2 Traduisez les phrases suivantes.

a. Her hair is dark like her mother's.
b. Unlike most girls, she agreed to be a shoe-shiner.
c. Her customers like talking to her about her country.

3 Traduisez en anglais.

a. Comme son oncle, elle veut rester aux États-Unis.
b. Mais contrairement à son oncle, elle veut continuer ses études.

ATELIER D'ÉCRITURE

1 Complétez les énoncés en utilisant le word box :

Every day, Paola ...

It's 9 a.m. Paola is ...

Word box

- have breakfast – catch the bus – get up – arrive at work – have a shower
- welcome – prepare stand – talk to uncle – tell – ask

2 Say what is happening in the picture. Imagine what the boy normally does and write about his routine. (Write about 60 words)

Follow these steps:

- Paragraph 1: The boy in the picture…
- Paragraph 2: I imagine he normally…

CONSEILS D'ÉCRITURE

- **Pensez à utiliser le présent** *be* + V-*ing* **pour décrire ce que fait le jeune homme.**
- **Décrivez précisément ce que vous voyez :** *teenager / clothes / attitude / place / atmosphere…*
- **Pensez à utiliser le présent simple** (V-*s*) **et les marqueurs de temps :** *in the morning, at lunch time, in the afternoon, after dinner…*

ADJECTIFS

boring	*ennuyeux*
dark	*brun*
elderly	*âgé*
flowing (hair)	*flottant*
monthly	*mensuel*
polished	*ciré*
proud	*fière*
ready	*prêt*
rewarding	*gratifiant*
scared	*effrayé*
slender	*mince*
useful	*utile*
valuable	*précieux*

NOMS

cashier	*caissier*
college	*université*
dream	*rêve*
goal	*but*
item	*article*
location	*endroit, lieu*
make-up	*maquillage*
owner	*propriétaire*
rate	*taux*
schedule	*agenda, programme*
store	*magasin*
tip	*pourboire*
wage	*salaire*

VERBES

believe	*croire*
depend on	*dépendre de*
earn	*gagner*
enjoy oneself	*jouir de, s'amuser*
feel	*sentir, se sentir*
get a job	*trouver du travail*
hire	*embaucher*
handle	*gérer*
hang out	*traîner*
hope	*espérer*
interfere	*se mêler, intervenir*
relax	*se décontracter*
spend time	*passer du temps*
wonder	*se demander*

AUTRES

although	*bien que*
finally	*enfin*
first	*d'abord*
help-wanted	*cherchons personne*
stylishly dressed	*bien habillé*

Exercices

1 Complétez avec des adjectifs du lexique.

a. Mark's CV is not very interesting. It's …
b. Jenny is not blond. She's …
c. Mary thinks a lot of herself. She's …
d. This job is very satisfying. It's …
e. Emma is not fat. She's …

2 Trouvez l'intrus puis justifiez votre choix.

a. useful – valuable – rewarding – dark
b. stylishly dressed – slender – boring – flowing hair
c. although – relax – hang out – enjoy
d. tip – goal – wage – earn

3 Remplacez les mots et expressions soulignés par des équivalents.

a. Bill likes to <u>do nothing</u> in the park all day.
b. He prefers to <u>pass</u> his time chatting with friends.
c. His mother wants him to <u>find work</u>.
d. Bill does not want his mum to <u>intervene</u> in his life.
e. He says he can <u>manage</u> his life himself.

4 Associez les débuts de phrases 1 à 5 aux fins de phrases a à e.

1. I gave the waiter a tip…
2. The store will hire…
3. He sells…
4. She spends a lot of time…
5. The rate for the job…

a. …is $3 an hour.
b. …putting on her make up in the morning.
c. …because he was so polite.
d. …a new cashier.
e. …lots of items in his store.

5 Complétez avec les noms du lexique.

a. When she started working, she was offered $3,5 per hour, which was the going ...
b. But she sometimes earns a lot thanks to the … generous customers leave her.
c. She works for her uncle who is the … of the business.
d. Her real … is to become an international lawyer.
e. She hopes her … will come true.

Tree planting

Out of all the jobs I was considering, tree planting wasn't even on the list. Yet, after discussing it with other members who had already done it, I spent a whole season planting tree after tree. I found it a great way to earn lots of money while experiencing a new way of life with some fantastic people.

The planting camp I was on was quite large with 43 planters. I joined in the town of Prince George, British Columbia. There were lots of opportunities, and the planting companies were anxious to recruit.

The company took us by bus to the camp high in the Cariboo Mountains[1], a site I chose because of the spectacular scenery[2] and wildlife[3]. I started with spring planting and then went on to do some summer or 'hot' planting. We worked about 10 hours a day in 6-day shifts (some were longer, up to 14 days), we were paid around 30 - 40 cents a tree, depending on the type of ground being planted.

Some planters with lots of experience could manage to earn about $400 a day, but I could seldom get past $200 a day. This still enabled me to save about $1,000 for a 6-day week, as there was nothing to spend it on and camp costs were only $20 a day including the most fabulous meals – we had a wonderful Chinese cook.

Morning started with a refreshing shower beneath a waterfall before a Canadian style breakfast of hotcakes, bacon, eggs, sausage, toast with as much to eat as you wanted. It was then off to the planting areas with bags full of young trees and a planting dibble[4].

The heat at times was oppressive, and the work hard, but knowing how much I was earning seemed to make the day go quicker. At the end of the day there was a huge supper and then guitar music around the campfire – it cools off quickly in the mountains. Camp life was fantastic and just has to be experienced.

The amount of money you can now make from planting tropical trees is incredible and available to anyone willing to make the effort. It is so good that we have recently started doing it ourselves. We wish that such an opportunity had been around years ago – we'd all be millionaires now! And it's good for the environment, too.

Kim Johns

WORDS:

1 *Cariboo Mountains:* montagnes en Colombie Britannique (province du Canada)
2 *scenery:* paysage
3 *wildlife:* faune et flore
4 *dibble:* plantoir

A Répondez aux questions suivantes en français et justifiez vos réponses. 8 pts

a. Quels avantages l'auteur a-t-il tirés de son travail de planteur d'arbres pendant toute une saison ?
b. A-t-il eu des difficultés à se faire embaucher ?
c. Quelles étaient les conditions de travail ? (horaires journaliers, nombre de jours et salaire)
d. L'auteur faisait-il partie des gens qui gagnaient le plus? Pourquoi ?
e. Pourquoi a-t-il réussi à économiser 1000 dollars par semaine ?
f. En quoi le début de journée était-il particulièrement agréable pour l'auteur ?
g. Le travail de plantation d'arbres a-t-il uniquement un attrait financier ? A quoi ce travail contribue-t-il également ?

B Traduisez en français : «*The heat at times…*» «*…has to be experienced*». (lignes 31 à 36). 4 pts

C Construisez des phrases complètes. 2 pts

a. Planting trees / not be / tiring in the spring.
b. The narrator / have / a shower in the morning?
c. He / want / to experience a new way of life.
d. He / earn / enough money?

D Mettez les verbes au présent simple ou au présent *be+V-ing*. 2 pts

a. Where's your son. He ... trees in the mountains (plant).
b. Every day he ... the camp very early (leave).
c. I'm sure he ... a fantastic experience (have).

E Write a paragraph of 60 words to describe a summer day in a camping site (location, weather, other campers, meals, activities, campfires in the evening…). 4 pts

kit 2

© Stone/Getty

The right track

© The Photolibrary Wales/Alamy

Speaking

- Say where the man in the large picture is.
- Guess why he has chosen this job.
- Now describe the woman.
- Do you think it is easy to find the right job?

STREET TALK

A nice little business

© Judy Martinez/Hachette

Paul from Eastbourne, U.K.

1 Listen to these words from the interview.

• delivery work • lifeguard
• career • physical work • sign
• private hire • booking work
• save • wasting • trendy
• amount

2 Listen to Paul and fill in the questionnaire.

I Dai Rees, milliner[1]

© 3 Camerapress/Gamma

Career: I left school without O levels and cooked in a restaurant for 2 years. I then moved to a factory to train as a welder[2] as the money was better. I was made redundant and went to evening classes to do pottery. I went on to study design at the Royal College of art. My collections have been displayed in London, Paris and New York.

The job: It's not glamour all the way – it's hard work! I do a 17-hour day – it's my own business. There's also the administrative and PR[3] side of the job. My big luck was doing the accessories for Alexander McQueen for his Spring/Summer collection.

Low point: Never having a break and putting in so much work! Everyone assumes the job is glamorous but there's a lot of stress. Another low is when things are lost on shoots[4]. My hats are always adored and then they're gone!

Tips from the top: Never be afraid to ask. Be true to yourself.

BBC Interview

WORDS:

1 milliner: *modiste (créateur de chapeaux)*
2 welder: *soudeur*
3 PR: *relations publiques*
4 shoot: *séance de photos*

FEEDBACK

1 Did Dai have any qualifications when he left school? Justify.
2 What different things did he do? What profession did he finally choose?
3 Pick out a sentence showing that his collections are famous worldwide.
4 Why isn't his job "glamour all the way"? What does he have to do?
5 Why do you think his hats sometimes disappear on shoots?

2 Serena Jackson, nurse

© S. Touhig/Select

When I was little I loved acting. I had a difficult childhood and acting helped me forget my problems at home. I joined the local theatre group and became a professional actress. But when I was 25, I started to think I wasn't doing much with my life. Acting was great. I loved it, but I wanted to be myself, not someone else. I thought about all the things I could do instead – being a waitress for example. I tried it, but I really wasn't good at waiting on tables.

Suddenly I remembered when I was little I had a nurse's uniform. I was happy pretending to be a nurse. Perhaps I'd make a good real one. So, I went to nursing school. I couldn't give up acting completely as I had to pay my way through school. But once I graduated I stopped acting. That was five years ago and I've been nursing ever since.

Nursing changed my life. It taught me discipline and commitment. I was really happy.

Planet Work interview

FEEDBACK

1 ▸ Pick out the three different jobs Serena had and put them in the chronological order.

2 ▸ What happened when she was a child?

3 ▸ Why did she want to change jobs at the age of 25?

4 ▸ Was she good at her second job? Justify.

5 ▸ Why did she continue acting while she was studying?

6 ▸ What are the good points of the job she chose in the end?

3 Sam Lock, agricultural worker

© Photofusion/T.GE

Sam Lock originally wanted to be a vet but is now happily working on a farm in Somerset.

FEEDBACK

1 ▸ Say as much as you can about Sam: his native town, the schools he attended, the job he wanted to do when he was young.

2 ▸ How did he finish his secondary school?

3 ▸ How many jobs did he try between 1991 and 1992?

4 ▸ Why did he enjoy his studies at Cannington College?

I was born and went to school in Cardiff. When I was 15, I did my GCSEs[1] but I got very poor results. This stopped me from becoming a vet.

That summer we moved to Somerset. My mum's sister has a farm at Luccombe near Minehead and we moved into a farm cottage there. I joined the sixth form at Minehead School to retake my GCSEs but didn't enjoy it and left to be an au pair in Switzerland. Unfortunately that didn't work either because I got homesick. After that I did seven more jobs between 1991 and 1992.

By that time, my aunt's farm shop business was doing really well, so I asked them to employ me. They did, and I went to Cannington College to take an NVQ[2] in General Agriculture. I found it really interesting because I was learning about the job I was doing.

I'm now doing something I really enjoy.

BBC working life

WORDS:

1 GCSE: *General Certificate of Secondary Education*

2 NVQ: *National Vocational Qualifications*

Comprehension

Before you read

1. Describe the picture on page 25 and imagine this teenager's story.

Read the text

2. Which elements of your story are mentioned in Ben's story?
3. Match the words on the left with the corresponding information on the right.

Jamie Oliver •	• a teenager training in a restaurant
Ben Arthur •	• a famous British chef
GCSE •	• place of the restaurant
Fifteen •	• General Certificate of Secondary Education
East London •	• name of the restaurant

4. In which paragraphs do you find the following information?
   - The good and the bad points of the profession;
   - Ben's life before meeting Jamie Oliver;
   - what he learnt from him;
   - why Ben is proud *(fier)* of himself;
   - when he discovered the job he wanted to do.

Read the introduction

5. What do you know about the teenagers Jamie decided to train?
6. Pick out the word showing that a lot of people could see the training.
7. What was Jamie's challenge?

Read paragraphs 1 to 3

8. Why did Ben have no qualifications?
9. Did he go to the careers service to meet friends or to get some work experience?
10. Who does "them" in line 9 refer to?
11. Why did he say he was lucky?

Read the end of the text

12. Pick out elements showing that Ben feels better working in a kitchen than he felt at school.
13. Who helps him make progress?
14. Show that he is doing well compared to the friends he had when he was younger.
15. Why is Ben grateful *(reconnaissant)* to Jamie? Complete.
    - Jamie ... him
    - He explained to him ...
    - He encouraged him to ... and ....
    - Thanks to Jamie, Ben could make ...

ALLEZ PLUS LOIN

1 *Employee* est dérivé du verbe *employ* et signifie "quelqu'un qui est employé". Que veut dire alors *trainee* si *train* signifie "entraîner" ?

2 D'après le contexte que peut signifier l'adjectif *previous* (introduction) ? Nous savons que les jeunes ont entre 16 et 24 ans. ▶ **FICHE** p. 53

3 *I was hitting brick walls* (§1). Littéralement cela veut dire : Je heurtais des murs de briques. Qu'exprime cette expression : l'espoir ou le désespoir ?

4 *You don't want to let them down.* (§4). A quoi fait référence *them* ? Traduisez cette phrase en vous appuyant sur le contexte et les composants du verbe *let down.* ▶ **FICHE** p. 53

RÉSUMEZ

1 Ecoutez l'enregistrement et résumez en anglais.
- Jamie - famous - chef - decided - train - team - unqualified - youngsters - chefs - reality - show
- he - would - employ
- Ben - was - trainees
- Ben - left - without - qualification
- he - took part
- he - realized - cooking - perfect job
- he - worked - become - chef
- Jamie - taught - things
- thanks to - could - make - future

2 Résumez en français.
- Dites qui est Jamie Oliver et ce qu'il a décidé de faire pour les jeunes chômeurs.
- Que savez-vous du parcours de Ben avant sa rencontre avec Jamie ?
- Quelle est la situation de Ben aujourd'hui ?

Grammaire en contexte

1. Quel est le temps utilisé dans le paragraphe 2 à partir de *I went...*? **Justifiez.**

2. Observez la phrase suivante.

Jamie decided to train youngsters who were looking for something to do.

a) Repérez les formes verbales et identifiez-les.

b) Trouvez celle qui fait référence à une action en cours de déroulement dans le passé.

Ben's story

In 2003, Jamie Oliver (a famous British chef) decided to train a team of unemployed 16 to 24-year-olds. They had practically no previous experience of cooking. Jamie had 9 months to transform them, on TV, into top class chefs to staff his new restaurant, Fifteen, in East London. Ben Arthur was one of those trainees. Today he's a chef at Fifteen. This is his story.

I dropped out before I did my GCSEs and for the next few years felt like I was always hitting brick walls because I had no qualification.

I knew that education was important so I started looking for something that would give me some vocational training. I went to a local careers service and my lucky break came when Fifteen Foundation contacted them to find youngsters to take part in Jamie's show. I applied to become a chef.

I had never thought of cooking as a profession. But as soon as I walked into the interview, I thought, "yes I could do this, I could make this work." I realized it was a great opportunity.

Working in a kitchen is really very tiring, but it is exciting because, unlike school, you're actually making something that's appreciated. You can see yourself getting better and you have to put a lot of yourself into your work. Because everyone at *Fifteen* spends so much time helping you improve, you really work hard as you don't want to let them down.

When I go home to my mum's, I meet up with people I was hanging around with when I was younger. Some of them are still doing exactly what they were doing 5 years ago. I've got something to say when they ask me what I'm doing – I've got a story to tell.

© T.Allen/Axiomphoto

I have worked so hard to make this place work that I feel part of it is mine. Jamie didn't only train me; he showed me that a restaurant is a business. He made me realise I could open my own restaurant and make it work. Yesterday, I found myself chopping vegetables and making plans for the future. This is something I would never have done two years ago. Today, everything is possible.

www.channel4.com

Le prétérit

Le prétérit V-ed

Le symbole V-*ed* représente le prétérit. Attention, il s'agit d'un symbole, il ne faut donc pas ajouter *-ed* à tous les verbes.

Verbes réguliers : ils se terminent par *-d* ou *-ed*.

Verbes irréguliers : il s'agit de la 2e colonne de la liste p. 166

Ex: *Jamie Oliver* ***decided*** *to train young people.*
- Jamie Oliver a décidé de former des jeunes.

Ben ***went*** *to London in 2003.*
- Ben est allé à Londres en 2003.

L'énonciateur utilise V-*ed* pour exprimer un décalage par rapport au moment où il parle. Les activités mentionnées se situent dans le révolu, sans lien avec le présent.

Ex: *Ben* ***dropped out*** *of school last year.*
- Il a quitté l'école l'année dernière. (L'énonciateur met l'accent sur le révolu. Ben n'est plus à l'école.)

Les indications temporelles suivantes impliquent l'emploi de V-*ed* à cause de leur sens : *last year, yesterday, two days ago, etc*.

L'énonciateur utilise aussi V-*ed* pour parler de faits ou d'actions qui ne se situent pas dans le révolu, mais sont imaginaires.

Ex: *If he* ***got*** *his diploma, he would be pleased.*
- S'il obtenait son diplôme, il serait ravi.

Be au prétérit + V-ing

Be **est conjugué au prétérit (was, were), V-*ing* est invariable.**

L'énonciateur met l'accent sur le déroulement d'une action dans le passé. On commente ce que fait le sujet grammatical.

Ex: *Ben* ***was working*** *hard.*
- Ben travaillait dur. (L'énonciateur nous dit quelque chose sur Ben ; (par exemple, il était épuisé parce qu'il travaillait dur.)

L'énonciateur décrit une action en cours de réalisation dans le passé.

Ex: *Ben* ***was cooking*** *when Jill called him.*
- Ben cuisinait lorque Jill l'appela. L'énonciateur signale un événement dans le passé, V-*ed*, ayant pour cadre l'action en cours, *be* au prétérit + V-*ing*.

Used to + V

Cette forme verbale souligne la rupture avec le présent.

Ex: *When he was at school, Ben* ***used to quarrel*** *a lot with his friends.*
- Quand il était à l'école, Ben se disputait beaucoup avec ses amis. (Maintenant, ce n'est plus le cas.)

Would + V

Cette forme permet d'évoquer une habitude dans le passé. Cette habitude existe peut-être encore.

Ex: *When he was younger, he* ***would play*** *football on Saturdays.*
- Quand il était plus jeune, il jouait au football le samedi.

ENTRAÎNEZ-VOUS

1 Mettez ces verbes à la forme *V-ed* et classez-les suivant la prononciation du *-ed* final : /t/, /id/, /d/.

decide - want - play - walk - realize - think - appreciate - ask - work - drop - start - improve

2 Écrivez des énoncés corrects au prétérit en respectant la consigne entre parenthèses (+ = forme affirmative, – = forme négative, ? = forme interrogative).

Ex: *he / meet / the chef (?)*
Did he meet the chef?

a. he / enjoy / his training. (?)
b. he / work / every day / even / on Sundays. (+)
c. he / miss / his friends / at all. (–)
d. he / realize / it / be / a real opportunity. (+)
e. he / have / any plans / for the future. (?)
f. he / know / he / want / to make / his own way in life. (+)

3 Écrivez des énoncés cohérents en reliant les éléments 1 à 5 aux éléments a à e.

1. Did he find …
2. Just after the interview he realized …
3. When he visited his parents …
4. He was very grateful to Jamie …
5. He used to hang around with his friends …

a. … they were having dinner.
b. … when he was younger.
c. … because he taught him a lot of things.
d. … he was on the right track.
e. … the job tiring.

4 Mettez les verbes entre parenthèses au passé (V-*ed* ou *be* au prétérit + V-*ing*).

a. What ... Ben ... when Jamie...? *(do, come in)*
He ... a Japanese recipe *(prepare).*
b. ... he ... with the other trainees? *(get on well)*
c. He always ... to help them. *(try)*
d. What vegetables ... he when he ... his finger? *(chop, cut)*

5 Traduisez

a. J'ai commencé mon stage il y a deux ans.
b. J'avais 16 ans lorsque j'ai quitté l'école et je n'avais aucun diplôme.
c. Mes amis traînaient dans la rue quand je suis allé rendre visite à mes parents.

JEUX DE MOTS

1 Complétez le tableau

Nom	Adjectif	Adjectif contraire	Adverbe
fortune			
	real		
profession			
		uninteresting	
			possibly
			luckily

2 Classez ces adjectifs en deux catégories : mots à connotation positive et mots à connotation négative

tiring - hard - lucky - afraid - glamorous - poor - great - stressful

3 Complétez avec des adjectifs choisis dans l'exercice 2.

a. Ben dropped out because his school results were ...
b. He knew the training would be very ....
c. He also knew he was very ... to take part in the show.
d. Working all day was ... , but he never complained.
e. When he didn't know how to do things, he was never ... to ask
f. The day he became a chef was a ... day.

D'UNE LANGUE À L'AUTRE

1 Lisez les phrases suivantes et dites quels temps on utilise en français pour traduire le prétérit *V-ed*, et *be* au prétérit + *V-ing*.

a. *He left school when he was 16.*
▸ Il a quitté l'école à l'âge de 16 ans.

b. *He became a chef four years later.*
▸ Il est devenu chef cuisinier quatre ans plus tard.

c. *If he earned enough money, he would buy a restaurant.*
▸ Si il gagnait assez d'argent, il achèterait un restaurant.

d. *He was sleeping when his parents arrived.*
▸ Il dormait lorsque ses parents arrivèrent.

2 Observez l'emploi de *used to* + *V* et dites par quel temps on le traduit.

She used to work in a theatre, now she works in a hospital.
▸ Jadis elle travaillait dans un théâtre, maintenant elle travaille dans un hôpital.

ATTENTION

Ne confondez pas *used to* semi-modal avec *use* qui signifie "utiliser"

Ex: *She used her car to go to school.*
▸ Elle utilisait sa voiture pour aller à l'école.

3 Traduisez en anglais

a. J'ai demandé à ma tante de travailler à la ferme.

b. Je vivais dans une grande ville, et maintenant je vis à la campagne.

c. L'année dernière, j'utilisais le tracteur tous les jours.

ATELIER D'ÉCRITURE

1 Utilisez le prétérit *V-ed* et *be* au prétérit *+V-ing* pour compléter l'énoncé.

When James … at the restaurant, the …

Word box

- The chef, the cooks, the waiters, the manager, the customers.
- Peel vegetables, do the accounts, put flowers on the tables, prepare sauces, arrive, serve, welcome, talk.

2 Last summer you wanted some extra money. You looked around and were lucky enough to get a job. Write 60 words about it. Follow these steps:

- Say why you needed a job, what job it was, how you found it and how long it was for.
- Give details about your work: working hours, tasks, colleagues, atmosphere, etc.
- Explain the advantages and the disadvantages of the job.
- Say what you gained from your experience.

CONSEILS D'ÉCRITURE

- **Pensez à utiliser le prétérit.**
- **Rédigez des phrases simples.**
- **N'hésitez pas à utiliser le dictionnaire pour le lexique inconnu.**
- **Dans la conclusion, introduisez votre opinion avec** *I think that…*

ADJECTIFS

afraid (be)	*avoir peur*
glamorous	*superbe*
great	*génial*
homesick	*nostalgique*
poor	*pauvre*
previous	*précédent*
real	*réel*
redundant	*au chômage*
tiring	*fatigant*

NOMS

break	*pause*
childhood	*enfance*
designer	*styliste*
factory	*usine*
milliner	*modiste*
results	*résultats*
trainee	*stagiaire*
shoots	*photos*
staff	*personnel*
tips	*conseils*
waitress	*serveuse*
welder	*soudeur*
youngster	*jeune*

VERBES

act	jouer
apply	*poser sa candidature*
chop	*couper*
display	*exposer*
drop out	*quitter l'école sans diplôme*
employ	*employer*
enjoy	*aimer*
feel	*se sentir*
forget	*oublier*
give up	*abandonner*
graduate	*terminer ses études*
hang around	*traîner*
hit	*frapper*
improve	*améliorer*
join	*joindre, rejoindre*
move	*partir*
pretend	*faire semblant*
remember	*se rappeler*
train	*s'entraîner*

AUTRES

actually	*en fait*
instead of	*au lieu de*
still	*encore, toujours*
unlike	*contrairement à*

Exercices

1 Trouvez dans le lexique :

a. un synonyme de *teenager,*
b. les synonymes des verbes *like* et *show,*
c. les contraires des verbes *remember et graduate,*
d. l'équivalent de l'adverbe *in fact*.

2 Remplacez les mots en gras par des verbes du lexique en respectant la forme verbale utilisée.

a. He will always **keep in mind** his first meeting with Jamie.
b. He worked so much that his results were **getting better.**
c. The first weeks were very hard, but he never thought of **leaving.**
d. At the end of the year, he will **finish his studies**.
e. Then he will **go** to Manchester.
f. His young colleague will **come with** him.

3 Complétez avec des mots du lexique.

a. She decided to make hats … of doing pottery.
b. She was very happy being in fashion and did not regret her … job.
c. … her colleague who was always complaining, she adored her job.
d. She was very busy in London and never felt …
e. She was advised to … her hats in Paris boutiques.

4 Complétez avec des verbes du lexique.

a. Bob and Bill thought it was better to work than … the town centre doing nothing.
b. They decided to … to become masons.
c. So they had to ... going out every night.
d. Today they … very proud. They are qualified masons.
e. They are now going to … for a job in a big building company.

A would-be pilot

In a part of the world where so many young people never get off the ground, 17-year-old James Mokoena wants to be a pilot.

He will fly a fighter jet, but not just to wage aerial battles[1]. Africa is full of hungry people and people sick with malaria, he said. Many of them need a James Mokoena to bring them food and medicine.

"I haven't been in a plane," he said, but dismissively[2]. "I want to be in a plane for four, five years, and to know that I am in that plane – me. That I, James, am flying it."

He is standing outside his cement house, a four-room box on a dirt road in this township of about 30,000 on the Lesotho border. Inside is a single bed for him, three brothers and a sister. His mother is ill. His father never got past the sixth grade. Everything here fairly shouts that James's dream is folly.

Except James himself. Two years ago, having completed his elementary years at the township primary school, he walked the mile from Masjaing to Fouriesburg, the far wealthier[3] town on the other side of the highway. There, he announced that he wanted a better education than he could get at Masjaing's uninspiring local high school, from which few students ever graduate, and that he wished to enroll in the eighth grade[4].

"I asked him whether he realized there were school fees to be paid, and he said his father would pay them," said Irina Grice, the principal at Fouriesburg Intermediate School. "His father came, but oh, his clothes were torn, and he was very, very poor."

But the father said, 'The child chose, and he wants to be in this school'."

One in three of South Africa's 37 million blacks live in townships like Masjaing, slums[5] built to keep them away from white people when they were not mining whites' coal or cleaning whites' houses. Of those township dwellers over age 15, well over half are jobless. Of those with jobs, about 6 in 10 earn less than $250 a month. The townships are poverty traps[6] in a nation where the rich-poor gap is among the widest on earth.

Michael Wines
The New York Times
April 30, 2005

WORDS:

1 wage aerial battles: *mener des batailles aériennes*
2 dismissively: *d'un air dédaigneux*
3 wealthier: *plus riche*
4 eighth grade: *niveau 4 ème*
5 slums: *bidonvilles*
6 trap: *piège*

A Répondez en français aux questions suivantes en utilisant uniquement les informations contenues dans le le texte. Composez des phrases complètes et justifiez toujours vos réponses. 8 pts

a. Quelle est l'ambition de James ? Pourquoi choisit-il ce métier ?
b. Donnez autant d'informations que possible sur son lieu d'habitation et sa famille.
c. Dans quel but s'est-il rendu à Fouriesburg ?
d. Cette école est-elle gratuite ?
e. Son père s'oppose-t-il à sa décision ?
f. Quel est le pourcentage de noirs habitant dans des ghettos ?
g. Sont-ils très touchés par le chômage?
h. Toute la population d'Afrique du Sud vit-elle aussi mal ?

B Traduisez en français : "*Two years ago …*" "… *the highway*" (lignes 18 à 22). 3 pts

C Trouvez les questions correspondant aux réponses en gras. 2 pts

a. **Two years ago**, James walked from Masjaing to Fouriesburg.
b. He decided to go to Fouriesburg **because he wanted a better education**.
c. His father met **the principal of the school**.
d. The school was **one mile** from Masjaing.

D Mettez les verbes à la forme qui convient. 2 pts

a. Last year, he (*choose*) to go to a new school and (*have*) to walk miles to get there.
b. James's mother (*cook*) dinner when he (*tell*) her about his important decision.

E Imagine James's life in his new school far from his family. Write 80 words about it. Mention the positive and the negative sides of his decision. 5 pts

Le dictionnaire anglais-français

A Présentation d'un article du dictionnaire

Met les mots en situation

Indique la prononciation des mots

blind /blaɪnd/ **I** *n* **1** (unsighted) **the ~** (+ *v pl*) les aveugles *mpl* voir note; **2** (at window) store *m*; **3** (front) façade *f*; (subterfuge) feinte *f*; **4** US (hide) affût *m*.
II *adj* **1** LIT [*person*] aveugle voir note; **to go ~** perdre la vue; **to be ~ in one eye** être borgne; **2** (unaware) [*person, rage, obedience*] aveugle; **to be ~ to** être aveugle à [*fault*]; être insensible à [*quality*]; être inconscient de [*danger*]; **3** (from which one can't see) [*corner*] sans visibilité; **on my ~ side** dans mon angle mort; **4** (without looking) [*tasting*] en aveugle; **5** (blank) [*wall, façade*] aveugle.
III *adv* [*fly*] sans visibilité; [*taste*] en aveugle; [*bake*] à blanc.
IV *vtr* **1** LIT [*injury, accident*] rendre aveugle; **to be ~ed in one eye** perdre un œil; **2** (dazzle) [*sun, light*] éblouir; **3** (mislead) [*pride, love*] aveugler.
IDIOMS **it's a case of the ~ leading the ~** ils n'en savent pas plus long l'un que l'autre; **to turn a ~ eye** fermer les yeux (**to** sur).

■ Note Ce mot peut être perçu comme injurieux dans cette acception. Lui préférer *visually handicapped* ou *visually impaired*.

Hachette Oxford

Indique la nature du mot

Insère le mot dans une construction particulière

Précise le champ d'utilisation

Indique s'il s'agit d'un sens littéral ou figuré

Fait apparaître les expressions idiomatiques

B La nature des mots

Vous cherchez le sens d'un mot inconnu. Tout d'abord, demandez-vous quelle est la nature de ce mot en lisant attentivement la phrase dans laquelle il se trouve. Puis recherchez dans la rubrique correspondante du dictionnaire. Attention, ce n'est pas toujours la première ! Parcourez rapidement l'article jusqu'à ce que vous trouviez la bonne catégorie : *n, adj, adv, vtr, vi…*

C Le sens du mot

Un mot est souvent polysémique (il a plusieurs sens).
Le dictionnaire donne les différents sens. À vous de choisir le bon en tenant compte du contexte.
Ex: *Blind* **1. adj** aveugle ; **2. n.** store.

EXERCICE

1 **Cherchez les différentes natures des mots suivants :** *power – sweet - head.*

2 **Trouvez la nature des mots en gras et proposez une traduction en fonction du contexte. N'oubliez pas que les noms composés se traduisent à partir du dernier terme en remontant vers le premier, à l'opposé du français.**

She managed to get a job ***which led*** *to three other jobs in* ***retail*** *business.*

I am really lucky to have my own ***fitness centre****.*
The home, ***like*** *the car, can now benefit from a central* ***locking system****.*

EXERCICE

Traduisez les phrases suivantes.

1. *The tip is included in the price.*
2. *He was suspended by his finger tips from the window frame.*
3. *The book gave him useful tips about car maintenance.*
4. *Tipping rubbish in the canal is forbidden.*

D **Les expressions idiomatiques *(idioms)***

Une expression idiomatique prise dans sa totalité a une signification différente des mots qui la composent. Il est important de tenir compte du contexte. Le dictionnaire donne la signification des expressions idiomatiques à la rubrique du mot principal.

EXERCICE

Comment traduisez-vous les expressions suivantes ?

1. She has more than one string to her bow.
2. The last straw.
3. In the long run.
4. I haven't a clue!

E **Les "*phrasal verbs*"**

Les verbes prennent des sens différents selon la particule avec laquelle ils sont employés. Le dictionnaire vous donne à la fin de l'article les différents sens.

EXERCICE

Recherchez les sens de *take to, take off, take back* dans les phrases suivantes.

1. He took to smoking when he was a teenager.
2. When does the plane take off?
3. Don't forget to take your books back to the library!

Le dictionnaire anglais-français

Vous ne connaissez pas le mot anglais dont vous avez besoin pour vous exprimer. Le dictionnaire vous propose souvent plusieurs mots et c'est à vous de choisir celui qui convient.

Pour aboutir dans vos recherches, demandez-vous d'abord :

- quelle est la nature du mot que vous cherchez.
- quel est le sens de ce mot en fonction du contexte. Il faut parcourir l'article pour trouver le mot anglais qui correspond. Vous trouverez aussi des synonymes et le domaine d'emploi du mot recherché.
- si le mot est employé au sens propre ou au sens figuré.

Si vous avez besoin d'une expression idiomatique, vous trouverez l'équivalent en cherchant dans l'article correspondant au mot principal.

EXERCICES

1 **Traduisez les mots en gras.**

1. Je **tire** toujours les rideaux le soir.
2. **Tirez** la porte pour entrer.
3. Ces mots peu connus sont **tirés** du latin.
4. Le gangster **a tiré** plusieurs coups de revolver sur sa victime.
5. Je pense qu'il **gagne** bien sa vie.
6. **Gagne**-t-il beaucoup d'argent à la loterie ?
7. Ce procédé va nous faire **gagner** un temps précieux.

2 **Traduisez ces expressions idiomatiques.**

1. Il en a assez de ce travail monotone !
2. Il ne faut pas mettre la charrue avant les bœufs.
3. Je suis tombé sur mon amie d'enfance par hasard.
4. Cette odeur me rappelle quelque chose !

3 **Complétez les phrases avec la particule qui convient.**

1. Put your gameboy ... It's dinner time!
2. It's cold today. You'd better put ... your gloves.
3. The firemen were very efficient: they put the fire ... in no time.
4. Because of the flooding, the show was put ... until the following week.
5. She turned ... the central heating because she was freezing.
6. He didn't want to live in a big city, that's why he turned ... the job offer.
7. Before leaving for their holiday, they turned ... the water supply.

kit 3

© Age/SDP

GEEKS

© TPH/SDP

Speaking

- Describe the pictures.
- Compare the way the two people are working in the pictures.
- Give some of the advantages and drawbacks of computers.

STREET TALK

The high-tech Texan

© Esbin-Anderson/AgeFotostock/Hoa-qui

Michael, the high-tech Texan, USA.

1 Listen to these words from the interview.

• passionate • obviously • based • electronics • engineering • innovations • personal digital assistant • surrounded • influence • educate • fortunate • modest • communicator • instilled • security system • temperature

2 Listen to Michael and fill in the questionnaire.

I Ice cream at midnight

One rainy night, Krissy Canavan, a 21-year-old Columbia University student, wanted an ice cream. So she went online, and soon ice cream was delivered to her door by CU Snacks.

CU Snacks was started by Brandon to serve his peers[1]. His dad lent him a laptop and his mum gave him a freezer. At the click of a mouse, CU Snacks delivers items[2] from freshly baked cookies to deodorant.

Using the Web cuts costs and increases efficiency. Fellow students act as Web developers very cheaply. Orders come in through the Web site, so there are no staff telephone lines, and there is no storefront to maintain. Customers pay online using debit or credit cards.

CU Snacks sells close to 50 different drinks and 30 types of ice cream, frozen foods and pharmacy items. Delivery people are paid by the hour. They wait for orders to come in, then deliver by bicycle. It's an easy way for students to get snacks when the stores are shut.

© CuSnacks

David Wald on his delivery tour.

Prices are a bit higher than those local retailers charge[3], but there is no minimum order size and delivery is free.

On the first night, CU Snacks received about 25 orders for products like soda, juice and chips. Now they're getting 30 to 50 each night.

Rachel METZ
The New York Times

WORDS:

1 peers: *étudiants*
2 item: *article*
3 charge: *font payer*

FEEDBACK

1 What is CU Snacks? Who are its clients?
2 Who created it? Did CU Snacks require much equipment to get started? Justify.
3 Find the differences between a traditional business and CU Snacks. Which one is cheaper to run?
4 Pick out all the different items clients can order.
5 Why does CU Snacks work more at night?
6 Is CU Snacks a successful business? Justify.

2 My cellphone, my life

© photopqr/ledauphinelibere/A.Surel/Maxppp

We aren't there yet. Despite the technical advances, I can't completely run my life on my cellphone/PDA[1].

Okay, it helps me manage things. I can do email, anywhere. I can take, send, watch and listen to movies and audio. That is all very nice.

But it's the next generation that excites me and makes me very, very curious.

This is what I want to be able to do on my next PDA/phone.

1. Store at least a gigabyte of information.
2. Use a USB port to copy any standardized files to or from my computer.
3. Call a number or use bluetooth to replace my credit or debit cards.
4. Watch training videos in Mpeg4. If my car breaks down I want to be able to watch a video on how to fix it.
5. Store all my receipts in the phone in case there is a problem.
6. Store ALL my IMs and Text Messages.
7. Download tickets to events. When I go to the show I just let them scan my phone. I don't need a ticket.

   I may call it my phone, but in reality, it's my portable transaction device. It's a digital world, everything's possible!

WORDS:

1 PDA: Personal Digital Assistant

FEEDBACK

1 ▸ What does the narrator mean when he says "we aren't there yet?"

2 ▸ Say what the narrator can do with his own cellphone.

3 ▸ Say what the author would like to be able to do on a new phone.

4 ▸ How could a cellphone help you if you have a problem with your car?

5 ▸ What is the advantage of having a sophisticated cellphone if you decide to go to a show?

6 ▸ Pick out the expressions that correspond to the following definitions:

a) A unit used to measure memory on your computer.

b) A way to connect peripheral devices to computers.

c) Technology for sending information from one device to another over a short distance without wires.

d) A portable assistant that contains your diary and addresses.

e) A film format to watch video on your phone or computer.

f) The abbreviation for instant messages.

7 ▸ What can you do on your phone? Would you like to have a phone like the one described above? Give reasons for your answers.

Comprehension

© Y. Fonck/Hoaqui

Before you read

1. Describe the pictures.
2. Say what you can do with a computer.
3. Have you ever communicated with someone through your computer? If so, do you enjoy communicating like this or do you prefer traditional face-to-face communication? Justify.
4. Read the heading and guess what the text is about.

Read the text

5. Check your answers to see if you guessed correctly.
6. Give as much information as you can about the members of the family (their names – the town, state and country where they live – what their house looks like – the children's ages – the parents' workplace)
7. Say in which paragraphs you find information about:
   - the advantages of chatting on line,
   - the activities that can be done through a computer,
   - the drawbacks of technology.

Read paragraphs 1 to 4

8. Pick out elements showing that the family does not communicate face-to-face.
9. Pick out the activities that people usually do through their computers, then the unusual activities of the Schwartz family.
10. Pick out the advantages of communicating on-line according to Ms Schwartz.

Read the end of the document

11. Which sentence in paragraph 5 contradicts the idea that "technology in the home can isolate kids"?
12. Pick out two advantages of technology in paragraph 6.
13. How does the family communicate when the father travels?
14. Does Mr Schwartz think that communication in the future will be better or worse?

ALLEZ PLUS LOIN

1 Que qualifie l'adjectif *cozy* (ligne 5) ? D'après le contexte, est-il un adjectif appréciatif ou dépréciatif ? Donnez le sens possible de cet adjectif.

2 Dites si le nom *chores* (ligne 15) fait référence à une activité agréable ou pénible.

3 Donnez l'exemple qui indique que l'internet est un moyen de communication fiable. (§4)

4 D'après le contexte, *deepen communication* (ligne 29) voudrait-il dire réduire la communication ou l'approfondir ?

5 Traduisez les mots composés suivants : *family chats, household management, family conflict, face-to-face interaction, four-way instant-message chats.*
Attention à l'ordre des mots ▸ **FICHE** p. 53

RÉSUMEZ

1 **Ecoutez l'enregistrement et résumez en anglais.**
- family - typical
- home - computers - communicate
- usually - the Internet - do shopping - send
- the Schwartzes - household management - practical jokes
- reduce - conflict
- in addition - technology - deepen - communication
- travel - chat - hotel

2 **Résumez en français.**
- Citez trois avantages et deux inconvénients du mode de communication utilisé par la famille Schwartz.

Grammaire en contexte

1. **Observez les énoncés a, b et c et dites à quoi correspond l'absence ou la présence du déterminant :**
   - pluriel de « *a* » devant un nom dénombrable pluriel ?
   - présentation d'un élément nouveau ?
   - élément connu ?

   a) The family's six networked computers (§2)
   b) A recent visit with the Schwartzes (§5)
   c) They have strong relationships (§5)
2. **Trouvez 3 déterminants possessifs dans le paragraphe 4 et justifiez leur emploi.**
3. **Dans le paragraphe 2, repérez la construction exprimant la réciprocité.**

The high-tech family

A Schwartz family conversation sounds much like any other. Greg - "Can I use the phone?" Lauren - "No. I'm talking to Cindy." Greg - "Tell me when the phone's free."

The only difference is they can't see or hear each other. They're not even on the same floor. Instead, they're instant messaging each other on two of the family's six networked computers.

Behind the modest façade of Sandy and Jeff Schwartz's cozy two-story house in Palo Alto, California, a tech revolution is under way[1]. The couple and their children, Greg, 17, and Lauren, 14, are pushing the usual use of family technology – shopping, doing homework, sending e-mail to far away friends and relatives – to include intimate family chats, gift giving, household management and even practical jokes.

© D. Crété/Sunset

Ms Schwartz says chatting online reduces family conflict. Instead of yelling room to room to get the kids to do their chores, she engages in "Internet nagging[2]". If the kids forget a chore, their mother's instant messages are on record. When Ms Schwartz thinks she's assigned jobs and hasn't, the computer reveals her lapse[3].

Critics say heavy technology use in the home can isolate kids and reduce face-to-face interaction with adults. But a recent visit with the Schwartzes suggested no such problems. With both parents working at home, they have strong relationships and lots of time together at breakfasts, after-school snacks and family dinner. The kids are active and involved: Greg is an Eagle Scout and rock climber; Lauren, a young political activist, loves acting and playing the guitar.

In a healthy family like the Schwartzes, technology seems to deepen communication, and even facilitate expression for the children. When Mr Schwartz travels, the family finds four-way instant-message chats superior to the telephone. On business trips he logs on from the hotel where he is staying. The family holds several conversations at once.

As much fun as they're having now, the Schwartzes are even more optimistic about the future. "By the time I'm a grandparent," Mr Schwartz says, "our ability to stay in touch as families is going to be awesome[4]."

Sue Shellenbarges
www.scoutingway.com

WORDS:
1 under way: *en marche*
2 nagging: *harcèlement*
3 lapse: *erreur*
4 awesome: *géniale*

I - La détermination

Les articles

Il existe trois articles en anglais : *a* / *an* - *Ø* - *the*.

L'article *a* / *an*

Il permet de présenter un élément d'information nouveau. L'énonciateur sous-entend que ce dont il parle n'est pas connu de la personne à qui il s'adresse.

***A* / *an* s'emploie uniquement devant un dénombrable singulier.**

Ex: *Greg has found a website for his sister.*
▸ Greg a trouvé un site pour sa sœur.
(Sa sœur ne connaît pas le site.)
He received an e-mail.
▸ Il a reçu un message

L'article zéro (ou Ø)

Avec les noms indénombrables (toujours au singulier) lorsqu'ils ne sont pas déterminés :

Ex: *The Internet facilitates **Ø** communication.*
▸ L'Internet facilite la communication.
(Il s'agit de la communication en général.)

Avec les noms dénombrables au pluriel, ce qui équivaut à *a* / *an* au pluriel :

Ex: *When he travels, Mr. Schwartz sends **Ø** messages from his hotel.*
▸ Quand il voyage, M. Schwartz envoie des messages de son hôtel.

L'article *the*

***The* fait référence à du connu ou du déjà vu.**

Ex: *Lauren thinks **the** website Greg has found is very interesting.*
▸ Lauren pense que le site trouvé par Greg est très intéressant.
(Il ne s'agit pas de n'importe quel site mais de celui trouvé par Greg.)

Les déterminants possessifs

I	→ ***my***	*we*	→ ***our***
you	→ ***your***	*you*	→ ***your***
he/she/it	→ ***his/her/its***	*they*	→ ***their***

Ils peuvent remplacer un article.

Ex: ***Their** house is very modern.*
▸ Leur maison est très moderne.
The house is very modern.
▸ La maison est très moderne.

On choisit le déterminant possessif en fonction du possesseur (contrairement au français).

Ex: ***Her** computer is sophisticated.*
▸ Son ordinateur est sophistiqué.
(Il s'agit de l'ordinateur de Mme Schwartz.)

Ex: ***His** bedroom is in a mess!*
▸ Sa chambre est en désordre !
(Il s'agit de la chambre de Greg.)

II - Les pronoms

Les pronoms possessifs

mine – yours – his / hers / its – ours – yours – theirs

Ils ne sont jamais suivis d'un nom puisqu'ils remplacent un nom.

Ex: *His computer is too old. **Mine** is better.*
▸ Son ordinateur est trop vieux. Le mien est mieux.

Les pronoms réfléchis

myself – yourself – himself / herself / itself – ourselves – yourselves – themselves

Les pronoms réfléchis renvoient au sujet du verbe.

Ex: *He is enjoying **himself**.*
▸ Il s'amuse.
*They are enjoying **themselves**.*
▸ Ils s'amusent.

Les pronoms réciproques

each other – one another

Ils impliquent une interaction entre au moins deux personnes :

Ex: *Greg and Lauren helped **each other**.*
▸ Greg et Lauren se sont entraidés.

ENTRAÎNEZ-VOUS

1 Complétez avec *a* / *an*, *the* ou *Ø*.

a. Yesterday, … man knocked at the door and said he wanted to see Mr Schwartz.
b. … man came in and started talking about … computers.
c. He said he wanted to show Mr Schwartz … very sophisticated computer.
d. Actually, … computer was smaller than … shoebox.
e. Mr Schwartz said that … advanced technology did not concern him any more.

2 Complétez avec un déterminant possessif ou un pronom possessif.

a. "What do you think of … new printer? I bought it yesterday in the shop next to my sister's flat."
b. "It looks great. But where is … old printer? Could you give it to me? … has broken down."
c. "That would have been a great idea but … sister has just taken it because … was too old: it was an ink-jet printer."
d. "You know what? You could go to the shop where I bought … The sales begin tomorrow."

3 Utilisez un pronom réfléchi.

a. She asked … why the data had disappeared.
b. Greg has managed to solve his problem. He is proud of … .
c. "Are you enjoying …?" their mother asked.
d. "We have done it …! I am glad it is over."
e. "I made … a cup of tea! I felt so tired!"

4 Utilisez un pronom réfléchi ou réciproque.

a. When Lauren went to university, Greg was bored and they wrote to … .
b. Betty could not help looking at … in the mirror. She wanted to be perfect for her party.
c. Betty did not come to Lauren's party. They no longer speak to … .
d. Greg's friends said they did not enjoy … because the music was boring.
e. Lauren and Greg helped … to clean the house because it was such a mess.

5 Traduisez.

a. L'homme qui est venu hier est le père de Brian.
b. Il voulait voir son fils car ils ne se parlent plus.
c. Brian a arrêté ses études la semaine dernière et sa mère est inquiète.
d. Il a trouvé un emploi dans un grand magasin mais la vie ne sera pas facile.

JEUX DE MOTS

1 Reliez les mots des colonnes A et B pour faire des mots composés cohérents.

A	B
on-line	activities
after-school	climber
household	use
rock	shopping

2 Complétez avec la préposition appropriée choisie dans la liste ci-dessous.

between - on - in - from - at

a. The family lives ... the same house, but not ... the same floor.
b. The parents work ... home.
c. When their father is abroad he e-mails his family ... his hotel.
d. The Schwartz family does not think that e-mail reduces communication ... people.

3 Complétez avec les mots de liaison suivants.

if - when - instead of

a. ... communicating on the phone, the family uses the computer.
b. ... he travels, Mr Schwartz connects with his family from his hotel room.
c. ... we communicate through e-mail only, we will certainly feel very isolated.

D'UNE LANGUE À L'AUTRE

1 Relevez les articles indéfinis et les adjectifs possessifs et dites ce que vous remarquez en ce qui concerne leur traduction en français.

a. Greg wants to become a professional climber.
▸ *Greg veut devenir alpiniste professionnel.*

b. By the time I am a grandparent, everything will be different.
▸ *Quand je serai grand-père, tout sera différent.*

c. He was walking with his hands in his pockets.
▸ *Il marchait les mains dans les poches.*

2 Que remarquez-vous concernant la traduction en anglais des articles définis ?

a. La technologie isole les jeunes et réduit la communication.
▸ *Technology isolates young people and reduces communication.*

b. La famille resta à la maison le dimanche.
▸ *The family stayed at home on Sunday.*

3 Traduisez en français.

a. Lauren would like to be an actress.

b. She enjoyed debating major issues with adults.

c. Every Saturday she would leave home with her cap on her head and her tennis racket in her hand.

4 Traduisez en anglais.

a. Les jeunes aiment la technologie.

b. Mon frère veut devenir programmeur en informatique *(computer programmer)*

ATELIER D'ÉCRITURE

1 Make up the conversation using these prompts. Add all the necessary elements.

Delete | Answer | Answer all | Forward

- **Ms. Schwartz → Greg:**
clean / living-room?
- **Greg → Ms Schwartz:**
No, not yet. … vacuum-cleaner / broken. I / do / housework later.
- **Ms. Schwartz → Lauren:**
you / buy / wine / recipe?
- **Lauren → Ms Schwartz:**
I / buy / bottle / Italian wine but / not find / one you wanted.
- **Ms. Schwartz → Lauren:**
Don't forget /prepare / cake / Dad / his birthday. What about / make / chocolate cake / you / prepare / last week?

2 Do you use a computer at school, at work or at home? What do you do with it? Do you think it is really useful? Write an essay of 70 words.

- First start with a general idea about computers.
- Then, speak about the work you do at school (or at work) on computers.
- Next, say if you have got a computer at home and how you use it (homework, e-mail, games, etc.).
- Finally, give your opinion about computers.

CONSEILS D'ÉCRITURE

- **Pensez à utiliser le présent simple.**
- **Énumérez deux ou trois tâches que vous faites sur l'ordinateur à l'école ou en stage.**
- **Dites comment vous utilisez l'ordinateur.**
- **Pour donner votre opinion, utilisez :** *personally - as far as I am concerned - in my opinion…*

ADJECTIFS

awesome	*génial*
cozy	*confortable*
free	*gratuit*
frozen	*congelé*
healthy	*sain, en bonne santé*
heavy	*lourd*
networked	*en réseau*
on-line	*en ligne*
rainy	*pluvieux*

NOMS

ability	*capacité*
cellphone	*téléphone cellulaire*
chatting	*bavardage*
chores	*corvées*
customer	*client*
delivery	*livraison*
efficiency	*efficacité*
events	*événements*
freezer	*congélateur*
gift	*cadeau*
household	*ménage*
items	*articles*
laptop	*ordinateur portable*
nagging	*harcèlement*
order	*commande*
reality	*réalité*
retailer	*détaillant*
snack	*casse-croûte*
staff	*personnel*
store	*magasin*

VERBES

chat	*bavarder*
deepen	*approfondir*
deliver	*livrer*
download	*télécharger*
facilitate	*faciliter*
increase	*augmenter*
isolate	*isoler*
lend	*prêter*
log on	*se connecter*
order	*commander*
store	*grand magasin*
yell	*hurler*

AUTRES

behind	*derrière*
despite	*malgré*
several	*plusieurs*
soon	*bientôt*

Exercices

1 Complétez avec les mots suivants :
on-line – laptop – soon – delivery – order – rainy – free – cozy

a. Just imagine! I am watching TV in my … flat and outside the weather is …. Suddenly, I feel like eating some ice cream. I switch on my …, go … and … my favourite ice cream.

b. Very …, the boy who delivers the ice cream is at the door with my chocolate ice cream. Isn't it great? Prices are a little bit higher but the … is … .

2 Associez les mots suivants à leur synonyme.

1. chatting	a. keeping information
2. yelling	b. receiving data
3. logging on	c. talking
4. downloading	d. shouting
5. storing	e. connecting

3 Complétez avec des mots du lexique se terminant en *-er*.

a. A … is somebody who sells goods.
b. A … is somebody who buys goods.
c. You can … goods on the Internet. It's very easy!
d. A few minutes later, somebody can … them.
e. You can also store food in your …

4 Complétez avec les noms du lexique.

a. I love shopping in this store. The ... is always welcoming.
b. You can see that they don't consider their work as a series of ... .
c. They help you find the different ... you are looking for.
d. In the ... department they are really nice. They explain how each device works.
e. If you don't know what ... to give someone for their birthday, go there.
f. They have a real ... to give you good advice.

Ambulance blogger **tells all**

I've never met Tom Reynolds, yet I know more about this semi-anonymous London ambulance worker than I know about most of my own work colleagues.

Tom is passionate about his job as an ambulance man. And for the last three years Tom, a blogger, has been sharing his diary online with thousands of other people.

Each day, Tom can get up to 11,000 hits from people eager to read about day-to-day life in a London ambulance, his views on NHS[1] reforms or his contempt[2] for people who misuse the service.

But what made him decide to invite the rest of the world into his life?

"I have always been interested in computers and I saw that people were writing blogs and I thought that I would have a go.

Some people write a personal journal, but I like the idea that other people are hearing me when I complain.

I never thought it would take-off, as I never thought I was a good enough writer.

I just enjoy writing and talking to other bloggers and people who have used the ambulance service."

Tom mainly writes about his own experiences, what he calls his 'daily grind'[3] and the patients he meets each day.

"I love the ambulance service and I think it is the best job in the world. I work outside and I work helping people.

Whether they are genuinely ill or not we are able to calm them down and get them the right treatment. At the end of the day I can go home and think that I have done a good job."

One of the difficult things for Tom in his diary was maintaining the anonymity of his patients. His employers know he writes the log[4] and it is monitored[5].

He said: "Basically I try not to give any identification, I do not give any locations, no names and no photos. I am constantly aware that my bosses are reading the website so I do have to moderate my language and make sure I am responsible for what I write".

His audience ranges from[6] ambulance service users to fellow crew members, who will often give their own comments on issues he has raised, such as his fears for the future of the ambulance service.

By Jane Elliott
BBC News Online

WORDS:

1 NHS: *assurance sociale britannique*
2 contempt: *mépris*
3 daily grind: *le boulot quotidien*
4 write the log: *tenir un journal*
5 monitored: *suivi, contrôlé*
6 range from …to: *aller de …à*

A Répondez en français. 8 pts

a. Pourquoi la journaliste dit-elle qu'elle connaît mieux Tom Reynolds que la plupart de ses collègues ?
b. Le journal en ligne de Tom Reynolds intéresse-t-il les autres internautes ? Pourquoi ? Quels sujets y évoque-t-il ?
c. Pourquoi préfère-t-il tenir un journal en ligne plutôt qu'un journal intime ?
d. Donnez trois raisons pour lesquelles Tom aime son métier.
e. Quelles précautions Tom Reynolds prend-il lors de la rédaction de son journal en ligne ?

B Traduisez en français : "*I am constantly aware that … .*" (lignes 40 à 47). 4 pts

C Complétez avec *the* - *a*/*an* ou *Ø*. 2 pts

She has been writing … blogs for one year now. As … student she likes discussing about … problems she can have at … college or with her boyfriend. She finds it exciting to read … blog written by somebody with … different opinion or … interesting new idea.

D Complétez avec un pronom réfléchi ou réciproque. 2 pts

a. Tom, do you enjoy … when you write blogs?
b. Yes, I do. I have a lot of friends now on the internet and we help … in everyday life.
c. Do bloggers consider … as famous people?
d. No, they don't try to impress … . They only want to share experiences.

E Write a paragraph of 00 words In English to answer the following questions. 4 pts

Why do you think people write blogs? Why do other people read them? What about you? Are you a blogger too? Why or why not?

kit 4

© Prod DB 20th Century Fox-Davis-Revolution Studios/DR/TCD

Fair play

© Enigma/Photo12.comAlamy

Speaking

- Describe the people in the large picture.
- According to you, who are the three men in the background?
- Say what the woman is doing. Is this a usual job for a woman? Why or why not?
- Do you think some jobs are reserved for men and others for women?

STREET TALK

An unusual job for a lady

◂ **Helen** from Eastbourne, U.K.

© Helen/Hachette

1 **Listen to these words from the interview.**

• approved • surrounded
• fault • apprenticeship
• male-dominated

2 **Listen to Helen and fill in the questionnaire.**

Laila Ali, a female boxer

© AP/Sipapress

Laila Ali, Muhamed Ali's daughter.

What advice would you give young women interested in the male-dominated world of sports?

Laila: Personally, I don't really focus on the fact that it's male-dominated. Today, we can practically do what we want. If you are ready to work hard and be the best that you can, then you will probably be a success. The world of boxing is a little behind every other sport as far as accepting women is concerned. So, you have to make sure you work with somebody who takes you seriously and who guides you along the right way.

What do you say to critics who say that what you do isn't ladylike?

Laila: People don't really say that to me too much. What I get usually is, 'You're so pretty, why do you box?' I'm so used to that now that it just goes in one ear and out the other. You see, it's what I want to do. People aren't comfortable with it, but I feel most comfortable in the ring. I can't imagine anything different. I just love to fight.

FEEDBACK

1 ▸ What do you know about Laila's family? What's her job?
2 ▸ What does Laila feel about doing a man's sport?
3 ▸ What must women do to succeed in sport?
4 ▸ What kind of coach must female boxers choose?
5 ▸ Do people understand female boxing? Does Laila care about it?
6 ▸ Pick out two sentences showing that boxing is exactly the right job for Laila.

2 Spider woman

© Photonica/Getty

Mumbai's Suhag Khemlani is India's first woman professional window-cleaner.

She went to London for a training course. "The training was tough[1]. All cleaning work must be completed before the offices open. We were expected to be on the job at 4 a.m. whether it was raining or freezing."

The training involved everyday chores like cleaning, polishing and emptying garbage bins. Initially the men were amused and surprised to see a teenager learning window-cleaning. Today a senior official at her company says, "I feel it is in her bones to be a window-cleaner."

However, Suhag realized buildings needed more than traditional window cleaners. They needed the services of Spidermen. "Spidermen slide[2] down exteriors with a rope[3] tied to their waists[4] to clean the façades of high buildings. It needs courage and stamina[5] and attitude to do that. I wanted to introduce Spidermen in India and in my company and I thought I must first become a Spiderwoman myself."

She became India's first Spiderwoman. Today her company has Spidermen in most cities.

Planet Work interview

WORDS:

1 tough: *dur*
2 slide: *glisser*
3 rope: *corde*
4 waists: *tailles*
5 stamina: *endurance*

FEEDBACK

1 ▸ Give Suhag's nationality and job.
2 ▸ Where did she learn her job?
3 ▸ Why did the employees have to be on the job at 4 a.m.?
4 ▸ What exactly did they do every day?
5 ▸ What sentence shows that there weren't many girls on the training course?
6 ▸ What are Spidermen able to do?
7 ▸ What qualities are required to become a Spiderman?
8 ▸ What did Suhag decide to do before introducing Spidermen in India? Has she succeeded? Justify.

3 A man in a woman's world

More and more males are choosing to become secretaries. Sarah Eldoori, Public Relation manager at Office Angels, states that 25 per cent of the workers on her books are men, 10 per cent more than a year ago. "People's attitudes are changing; maybe ten years ago male secretaries would face ridicule and discrimination, but not now."
Steven France, 25, works as a personal secretary at the Central Office of Information. "I was the only man in a room with 13 women. They said I was the first man to come into their office for 15 years. They'd been working there all their lives and kept on asking me why I had become a secretary. In their day a man would never be a secretary. They all agreed it was a sign of the times."
Male secretaries may no longer be unusual but they still have a long way to go before they can be regarded as the norm.

www.office-angels.com

FEEDBACK

1 ▸ What is the article about?
2 ▸ Pick out elements from the text showing that people's attitudes are changing.
3 ▸ Say as much as you can about Steven France.
4 ▸ Are his colleagues used to having a man in their office? Justify.
5 ▸ What is people's attitude towards male secretaries today?

Comprehension

© Rex Interstock/Sunset

Before you read

1. Describe the pictures and make a list of words you expect to find in the document.

Read the document and check

2. Say which paragraph(s) :
   - deal with Dave's story;
   - deal with Chris's story.
3. Is the document about:
   - American fathers who look after children professionally;
   - the difference between American dads and American mums?
   - the difficulties American fathers have with their kids.

Read the text again

4. Find two expressions in the text meaning the same as "looking after children".
5. Why did Dave start babysitting?
6. What unusual (*inhabituelle*) decision did Dave make when his wife was expecting a baby?
7. Are the eight children he looks after his own?
8. Give information about Chris Grimes:
   - where he is from;
   - when he started his business;
   - what the name of his business is;
   - if he had had any training before opening his center;
   - how he came to do this job;
   - how many children he looks after.
9. According to Grimes, who has social prejudices: fathers or mothers? Justify.
10. What did Dave look like when he started his new job?

ALLEZ PLUS LOIN

1 Décomposez le mot *daycare center* (ligne 11) et donnez une traduction possible.

2 D'après le contexte que peut vouloir dire *run a center*, on dit aussi *run a shop*, *run* a-t-il son sens habituel ?

3 *Once* veut dire une fois. On trouve le mot *one* dans *once*. Quel serait logiquement le sens de *twice* ?

4 Vous ne connaissez pas ce verbe *apologize* (ligne 29), mais si vous lisez bien ce qui suit "*I'm sorry...*", vous pouvez rapidement en deviner le sens. ▸ **FICHE** p. 53

RÉSUMEZ

1 Ecoutez l'enregistrement et résumez en anglais.
- more and more - fathers - becoming daycare dads
- Dave - started - babysitting - when- young - helped mum run a nursery
- when - got married - had - children - decided - stay - home - work - daycare dad
- Chris - left - job - opened - daycare center - because - not happy - daughter's two daycare centers
- now - with - new job - make - money - look after - child
- he - surprised - see - fathers - don't like - men - care for - kids

2 Résumez en français.
- Donnez les raisons pour lesquelles Dave et Chris ont décidé d'ouvrir une garderie.
- Dites si leur fonction est bien perçue par les parents.

Grammaire en contexte

1. **Dans le § 4,** repérez deux adjectifs destinés à comparer deux éléments ou deux groupes d'éléments.
   - Décomposez chaque construction.
   - Que compare-t-on ?
2. **Dans l'introduction,** repérez les deux comparatifs irréguliers
   et dites à quels adjectifs ils correspondent.
3. **Dans le § 4,** trouvez deux adjectifs destinés à distinguer un ou plusieurs éléments par rapport à l'ensemble de la catégorie.
   - Décomposez chaque construction.

Daycare dads

More and more dads are caring for their own kids at home and some are also parenting the kids of other more traditional fathers. How do these dads feel about caring for other families' kids? Do they run centers better or worse than women?

Dave Maxson of Westminster is a daycare dad. He grew up in a neighborhood[1] where he couldn't find a job. So he decided to babysit and help his mom run a nursery. When his wife, Cathy, got pregnant, he decided to stay home. He now cares for eight children, two of whom are his.

Chris Grimes of Des Moines, Iowa, took up the daycare business after 6 years working in a soybean factory. Unhappy with his daughter's two bad daycare centers he found himself taking childcare classes at a local college and discovered he "really liked being a parent." He wanted to spend more time with his daughter. The only way he could do this and make money was to open his "Tiny Days Daycare Center." Now in his 3rd year of business, he has six kids including his three and a half year-old daughter. He's had the same kids since he opened three years ago.

© Prod DB 20th Century Fox-Davis-Revolution Studios/DR/TCD

Grimes has found that, when it comes to discrimination, the dads rather than the moms give him the most trouble. In one case, a mother interviewed him twice, and liked what she saw. Grimes was sure she would send him her child. However, on the third visit, the husband came along and abruptly asked him questions about insurance. Although Chris had what was required, the husband just left, with his wife apologizing on the way out saying "I'm sorry, he is like that." They never called back.

Discipline is no problem for Dave Maxson. When he started, he had a "biker look", weighed 245 pounds and had a full beard. Now he has lost the beard and 85 pounds. Although he looks smaller and less imposing than before, he still has a firm voice due to his father's military style upbringing. The kids pay attention when he speaks. Who is the most difficult kid in his day-care center at the moment?"My daughter is the worst child I have!"

by Peter Baylies

WORDS:

1 neighbourhood: *quartier*
2 upbringing: *éducation*

La comparaison

Les comparatifs

Lorsque l'énonciateur emploie un adjectif au comparatif, il compare deux éléments ou deux groupes d'éléments.

LE COMPARATIF DE SUPÉRIORITÉ

Adjectif court (une ou deux syllabes) :
adjectif + *er* + *than*

Ex: *Dave looks* ***younger than*** *Chris.*
▸ Dave a l'air plus jeune que Chris.

Adjectif long (plus de 2 syllabes) :
more + adjectif + *than*

Ex: *His life is* ***more interesting*** *now.*
▸ Sa vie est plus intéressante maintenant.

LE COMPARATIF D'ÉGALITÉ

as + adjectif + *as*

Ex: *Men are* ***as patient as*** *women.*
▸ Les hommes sont aussi patients que les femmes.

Ex: *He thinks that fathers are* ***not as open-minded as*** *mothers.*
▸ Il pense que les pères n'ont pas l'esprit aussi ouvert que les mères.

LE COMPARATIF D'INFÉRIORITÉ

less + adjectif + *than*

Ex: *My job is* ***less boring than*** *yours.*
▸ Mon métier est moins ennuyeux que le tien.

AUTRES COMPARAISONS

- **De plus en plus**

Adjectif court : adjectif + *er* + *and* + adjectif + *er*
Ex: *Their children are getting* ***happier and happier.***
▸ Leurs enfants sont de plus en plus heureux !

Adjectif long : *more and more* + adjectif
Ex: *My job gets* ***more and more tiring*** *every day.*
▸ Mon travail est chaque jour de plus en plus fatigant.

- **L'accroissement parallèle**

the + comparatif, *the* + comparatif
Ex: ***The longer*** *he stays with his children,* ***the happier*** *he feels.*
▸ Plus il passe de temps avec ses enfants, plus il est heureux.

Les superlatifs

Lorsque l'énonciateur emploie un adjectif au superlatif, il distingue un ou plusieurs éléments dans la catégorie.

LE SUPERLATIF DE SUPÉRIORITÉ

Adjectif court : *the* + adjectif + *est*

Ex: *Susan is* ***the nicest*** *kid in the center.*
▸ Susan est la plus gentille du centre

Adjectif long : *the most* + adjectif

Ex: *My daughter is* ***the most demanding*** *kid in the class.*
▸ Ma fille est l'enfant la plus exigeante.

COMPARATIFS ET SUPERLATIFS IRRÉGULIERS

Adjectif	Comparatif	Superlatif
good	*better*	*the best*
bad	*worse*	*the worst*
far	*farther*	*the farthest*
	further	*the furthest*

COMPARATIFS ET SUPERLATIFS IRRÉGULIERS

Les adjectifs se terminant par une consonne suivie de "y" : y devient i

Ex: *funny* *funnier* *the funniest*

Les adjectifs se terminant par une consonne précédée d'une voyelle : redoublement de la consonne.

Ex: *big* *bigger* *the biggest*

ENTRAÎNEZ-VOUS

1 Dans les énoncés ci-dessous, dites si :

a. l'énonciateur compare deux éléments ou deux groupes d'éléments ;

b. l'énonciateur distingue un élément ou plusieurs éléments

1. Dave is happier than his wife.
2. Dave says he is the happiest man in the world.
3. It is more interesting to care for children than work in a factory.
4. He thinks it is the best job in the world.
5. His friends think he looks less strong than his brother.
6. Some people think that men are not as caring as women.

2 Complétez avec *as* ou *than*.

a. Caring for kids is not more difficult for men … for women.

b. Some people think men are less patient … women!

c. Working at home can be as hard … working in an office.

d. Some women think it is more pleasant to work outside … stay at home.

e. Working with adults is more interesting … staying with kids all day long.

3 Utilisez un comparatif.

< pour infériorité / > pour supériorité

a. Do you think window-cleaning is … mountaineering? (> dangerous)

b. No, it isn't. It is just … because you work when people sleep at night. (> tiring)

c. Being a woman window-cleaner is probably … being a day care dad. (> exciting)

d. However, traditional window cleaners are usually … I am. (< athletic)

e. I love this job : it is … cleaning the windows at home! (< boring)

4 Ecrivez des énoncés cohérents en reliant les éléments ci-dessous.

1. Male secretaries
2. Some people think secretarial work
3. The most important thing
4. Steven feels happier now

a. is less interesting for men than for women.

b. because he has been accepted by the other secretaries.

c. are as serious as female secretaries.

d. is to feel happy in your workplace.

5 Traduisez.

a. Il a l'air plus jeune !

b. Son travail est de plus en plus intéressant.

c. Dave est aussi âgé que Chris.

d. Dave pense qu'il est l'homme le plus heureux du monde.

e. Plus il est patient avec les enfants, plus ils sont calmes

JEUX DE MOTS

1 Donnez les contraires des mots suivants.

easy – same – dirty – last – best – common

2 Complétez ces séries.

a. ear, nose, …, …, …

b. first, second, …, …, …

c. practically, comfortably, …, …, …

d. biker, worker, …, …, …

3 Associez un mot de chaque liste pour faire des mots composés que vous traduirez.

- car - training - childcare - insurance - window
- company - cleaner - factory - classes - course

4 Complétez avec la préposition qui convient.

a. He usually starts … 9 p.m.

b. He does not work … Saturdays.

c. He gets on well … the kids.

d. Parents are happy … him.

e. They keep asking him questions … their children.

f. They worry a lot … them.

g. … some fathers, only women are able to care for children.

Language skills

D'UNE LANGUE À L'AUTRE

1 Observez les phrases suivantes et dites quelle forme prend l'adjectif *old* au comparatif et au superlatif quand on parle des membres d'une même famille.

a. *Jane is the eldest of their four children.*
▶ Jane est l'aînée de leurs quatre enfants.

b. *They have two sons.*
Their elder son works in a daycare center.
▶ Ils ont deux fils.
L'aîné travaille dans une garderie.

2 Que remarquez-vous concernant la traduction du comparatif dans cette phrase?

Suhag has got two brothers.
She gets on well with the younger one.
▶ Suhag a deux frères.
Elle s'entend bien avec le plus jeune.

3 Traduisez

a. His elder sister has just found a job.
b. His parents are visiting their eldest son next week.

4 Traduisez

a. He thinks that his daughter is getting nicer and nicer.
b. He feels more and more relaxed.
c. He notices that fewer and fewer parents complain about his work.

5 Observez les phrases a et b et leur traduction, puis traduisez les phrases 1 et 2.

a. *The cooler he is, the fewer problems he has with children.*
▶ Plus il est calme, moins il a de problèmes avec les enfants.

b. *The less he shouts, the better results he gets.*
▶ Moins il crie, meilleurs sont les résultats (qu'il obtient).

1. *The more children he has, the happier he is.*
2. *The less he sees his parents, the better he feels.*

ATELIER D'ÉCRITURE

© John Walmsley

1 During the holidays the headmaster renovated the local primary school and bought lots of new material. Two parents compare the school before and after. Imagine their comments:

Ex: The school looks cleaner than before.
It's not as dirty as before.
There is/there are …

Word box:
- computers, tables, screens, computer games, on-line lessons, teaching material, walls, screens
- windows, big, beautiful, clean, dirty, small, useful, old-fashioned, modern, pleasant, well-equipped

2 Should men work in nurseries or infant schools? Justify in 80 words. Follow these steps:
- Start with a general idea about the absence of men in nurseries.
- Then find one or two reasons why men don't work in nurseries.
- Next, give two or three advantages.
- Finally, give your personal opinion.

CONSEILS D'ÉCRITURE

- **Pensez à utiliser des articulations logiques pour :**
  - énumérer vos arguments :
    first - second - moreover - finally…
  - opposer vos arguments :
    but - however - nevertheless…
- **N'oubliez pas d'introduire votre opinion personnelle à l'aide de :**
  In my opinion - personally - I think that - as far as I am concerned…

ADJECTIFS

male-dominated	*masculin*
own	*propre (à soi)*
sure	*sûr*
pregnant	*enceinte*
required	*requis*
tough	*dur*
unusual	*inhabituel*

NOMS

advice	*conseils*
beard	*barbe*
biker	*motard*
bone	*os*
chores	*corvées*
course	*cours*
ear	*oreille*
factory	*usine*
garbage bin	*poubelle*
guts	*courage*
high-rise	*tour*
lawn	*pelouse*
neighborhood	*voisinage*
ring	*ring*
rope	*corde*
soybean	*soja*
stamina	*endurance*
upbringing	*éducation*
waist	*taille*

VERBES

apologize	*s'excuser*
become	*devenir*
care for	*s'occuper de*
empty	*vider*
expect	*s'attendre*
feel	*sentir, se sentir*
fight	*se battre, combattre*
focus on	*porter son attention sur*
freeze	*geler*
grow up	*grandir*
look	*paraître*
slide	*glisser*
tie	*attacher*
take over	*prendre*
weigh	*peser*

AUTRES

although	*bien que*
however	*cependant*
twice	*deux fois*

Exercices

1 Complétez avec des noms du lexique.

a. Cars are made in a ...
b. Boring tasks are called ...
c. A climber ties a ... round his waist.
d. A very tall building is called a ...
e. Rubbish is put in a ...
f. A series of lessons is called a ...
g. If you are very courageous, people say you have got the ...
h. Boxers compete in a ...
i. Grass grows on a ...
j. The place where people live together is their ...
k. Santa Claus always wears a long white ...

2 Complétez avec le mot entre parenthèses qui convient.

a. 1. It is very ... for a man to do this job. (unusual, unusually)
b. He is very ... in caring for children. (interesting, interested)
c. ... he is young, he is very competent. (however, although)
d. He ... older with this beard. (looks at, looks)
e. He feels ... in the center. (comfortably, comfortable)
f. Children must ... when they are rude. (apologize, excuse)

3 Complétez avec des verbes du lexique.

a. I ... to be accepted by male workers.
b. I don't want to ... with them.
c. I do sport regularly to ... good.
d. I would love to ... a Superwoman.
e. That's why I ... on my job.

A manny

Male nannies, or mannies, have become increasingly fashionable. Even famous actresses, like Liz Hurley, are now using their services. Working mothers want someone who can play football with their sons, while single mothers are seeking masculine role models for their children.

'A lot of working women are absolutely up for male au pairs,' said Maggie Dyer, who has 10 men out of 300 au pairs on the books of her London Au Pair and Nanny Agency.

'If someone nasty[1] rings the doorbell or there is a crisis with the plumbing, a male au pair is more likely to be able to cope. Whenever a family has a successful male au pair, when he leaves they won't hear of having a girl.'

Dyer has a male nanny from New Zealand on her books who is instantly hired whenever he becomes available, but says few men apply. 'It's really sad, when male teachers in primary schools are now common.'

Chris Meeks, a former factory worker, agrees. When he was made reduntant, he became a childminder and is now working with his wife – a childminder for nearly two decades – at their home in Hertfordshire.

'I never think about going back now,' said Meeks, a member of the National Childminders Association. 'Before, I was making pieces for airplanes and you never saw where they went. Now I can see how the children come on. At the end of the day, you feel worthwhile[2].'

A father of seven grown-up children, he is trained in first aid and child development and is good at nappy changing. He hates being the only man on training courses, but there are now enough fathers at the school gates for him to blend in[3].

He feels that more men would be attracted if childcare was recognised as a career. 'Younger fathers will stay at home and look after their own children now, but not somebody else's. But I think, as the years go by, that will probably change.'

WORDS:
1 nasty: *louche*
2 worthwhile: *utile*
3 blend in: *se mêler*

A Répondez aux questions suivantes en français et justifiez vos réponses. 8 pts

a. Quelles catégories de mères recherchent des hommes pour garder leurs enfants et quels avantages y voient-elles ?
b. Quel genre d'agence Maggie Dyer dirige-t-elle ?
c. Citez deux problèmes concrets que les garçons au pair peuvent résoudre en plus de leurs tâches habituelles.
d. Y-a-t-il beaucoup d'hommes qui travaillent dans l'agence de Maggie ?
e. Quelle décision Chris Meeks a-t-il prise lorsqu'il a perdu son emploi ?
f. Pourquoi préfère-t-il son travail actuel à son ancien métier ?
g. Comment acquiert-il les compétences nécessaires pour ses nouvelles responsabilités ?

B Traduisez en français : *"He feels that…." "…will probably change."* (lignes 36 à 40). 3 pts

C Complétez avec *"as"* ou *"than"*. 2 pts

a. Baby sitting is more interesting … working in a factory.
b. Male childminders are less popular … female childminders at the moment.
c. Yet, they are more efficient … most girls at coping with problems in the house.
d. And they can be as caring … women with young children.

D Mettez les adjectifs entre parenthèses au comparatif ou au superlatif. Ajoutez les éléments nécessaires. 2 pts

a. In general women are (*attracted to childcaring*) men.
b. However men are sometimes (*successful*) women.
c. Some mothers think mannies are (*good*) nannies to look after their boys.
d. More and more young fathers think that childminding is (*rewarding*) job!

***E Write a paragraph of 50 words about the advantages and drawbacks of being an au pair.* 5 pts**

Les mots inconnus

La langue anglaise a subi l'influence du français au XIème siècle, lors de la conquête normande. Le français est resté la langue officielle jusqu'au XIVème siècle. Il en subsiste donc de nombreuses traces dans l'anglais d'aujourd'hui.

Transparence et ressemblance

De nombreux mots sont semblables en anglais et en français.

Ex: *nation, fiancé, continent, nature, international...*

Certains mots anglais appartiennent à la même famille que leur équivalent français. Ils sont issus d'une même origine, mais certaines voyelles ou consonnes sont différentes.

Ex: *Parliament, totally, princess, calm, stupid...*

1 Traduisez les phrases suivantes.

1. Suddenly she entered.
2. He was an imposing person.
3. Discipline is no problem for him.
4. There is a nature reserve in this place and the animals are protected.

Les indices grammaticaux

L'environnement du mot

En observant ce qui précède ou ce qui suit un mot, mais aussi sa place dans la phrase, vous pouvez deviner si c'est un adjectif, un adverbe, un nom ou un verbe. Cela vous aide à trouver sa signification.

Ex: *To cross the border, they pay smugglers a lot of money.*

En raison de la place qu'il occupe dans la phrase, "smugglers" ne peut être qu'un nom. Il signifie "passeurs".

2 Donnez la nature des mots en gras et leur sens possible.

1. The migrants **wrapped** their feet in carpet material.
2. In Chicago, you **definitely** need a car to go to work.
3. The visas go to regions with low **rates** of immigration.
4. He did not get on with his **former** employer.
5. It is a very big firm, its annual **turnover** exceeds £7million.

Les préfixes et les suffixes

La connaissance des préfixes et des suffixes est une aide précieuse à la compréhension d'un mot.
▸ fiche dérivation.

Ex • *He became homeless after he lost his job.*
home-less: sans abri
• *I disagree with you.*
dis-agree: ne pas être d'accord

Les mots accolés

On peut aussi découper un mot pour deviner ce qu'il veut dire.

Ex: He was wearing a backpack. (backpack est composé de back qui signifie dos et pack un sac backpack : sac à dos)

Ces mots ont été jadis des mots composés, juxtaposés, ou reliés par un tiret. Mais l'usage fréquent de ces mots ensemble a fini par les accoler pour n'en faire qu'un seul.

Ex: - *bed-room* ▸ *bedroom*
- *baby-sitter* ▸ *babysitter*
- *phone card* ▸ *phonecard.*

3 Traduisez les mots en gras en les découpant

1. The twins often help with the **housework**.
2. As they were too noisy, the children were sent to their **playroom**.
3. He lives on the **outskirts** of London.
4. Look at that person in the **foreground** of the picture (*fore* vient de *before*).
5. This hat looks different in **daylight**.
6. Protect your eyes with **sunglasses**.
7. She was offered a pair of **earrings** for her birthday.
8. He visited a forest of **evergreen** trees.
9. A few children were **barefoot**, but most wore sandals.
10. The store was looking for an experienced **salesperson**.

Les indices contextuels

La présence de synonymes, d'antonymes, de définitions sont autant d'aides à la compréhension d'un mot.

Ex: *She spent her day cleaning, mopping, polishing.* (*mopping* est une tâche semblable à *cleaning* et signifie "éponger")

L'élucidation d'un mot se fait aussi grâce à la connaissance de la situation et de ce qui logiquement peut être attendu à un endroit donné du texte.

4 Devinez le sens du mot en gras et dites si vous êtes aidé(e) :

- **par la présence d'un synonyme, d'un antonyme, d'une définition ;**
- **par la connaissance de la situation ;**
- **par la logique.**

1. He counsels teenagers on all things cool and **hip**.
2. When you **blend** eggs with butter, you mix them together.
3. She thought she would be **homesick**. In fact she didn't miss anything at all.
4. He sells all sorts of **items**, clothes, shoes, pans...
5. His customers came from different **backgrounds**. Some were quite rich, others were **penniless**.
6. The really boring part of the job is stocking items that **weigh** forty pounds.
7. He was jobless and spent his time **hanging out** with his friends.
8. You think he works hard, actually he is very **lazy**.
9. I couldn't **give up** my job as I had to pay my way through school.
10. Many townwhip **dwellers**, people who live in townships, are unemployed.
11. The people were **roaring** and shouting and screaming and jumping up and down.

5 Dites si les pointillés correspondent à un nom, un adjectif, un verbe ou un adverbe, puis complétez la phrase de la manière la plus appropriée.

1. Studying abroad was a ... change for me.
2. I used to be ..., but now I feel very confident.
3. I have ... left my parents.
4. When you live abroad, you must adapt to a new ...
5. You have to ... differences.
6. I ... travel alone, but next week I'll travel with a friend.

Les faux amis

Il existe cependant des faux amis. La logique vous aidera à les débusquer.

6 Traduisez les mots en gras.

1. She was making a strawberry **pie** for her mother's birthday.
2. If you don't wear your helmet, you risk an **injury**.
3. I thought he was her father, he was **actually** her husband.
4. The **journey** to London took an hour only.
5. Drinking and driving is a real **hazard** for your safety.
6. He was punished because he was **rude** to his teachers.

kit 5

© Anzenberger/Cosmos

A gap year

© P.Bessard/REA

Speaking

- Look at the large photo. Guess where the scene takes place.
- Describe the two people in the foreground. In the small picture, say where these people are and what they are doing.
- Is it a good idea to study in a foreign country? Why?

STREET TALK

A year off after school

© Pallava Bagla/Corbis - Judy Martinez/Hachette

1 Listen to these words from the interview.

passionate • obviously • electronics • engineering • innovations • personal • digital assistant • surrounded • influence • educate • fortunate • communicator • based • instilled • modest • security • system • temperature.

2 Listen to Hannah and fill in the questionnaire.

◂ Hannah from London, U.K.

I My Erasmus year

© J. Wiedel/Photo12.com/Alamy

I spent my Erasmus[1] year in the small town of Poitiers, France. Having lived in Bristol for the previous two years, it was a bit of a shock to arrive in a place containing fewer than 80,000 people. I could not imagine living there for one whole year. I was the first international student to arrive and I spent most of my first week walking alone down Poitiers's narrow streets and sitting in cafés.

This continued for about a week until I met another Erasmus student, a girl from Barcelona. She invited me to a party and I met about sixty students from all over Europe. It was a tremendous relief[2].

The academic side of things was enjoyable. It was a little bit difficult to keep up with lectures in French at first but then your ear gets used to it. And it is so satisfying to say 'I'm doing this in French!'

On the financial side of things it was the least stressful year of my degree[3]. In fact, due to the generous grants[4] from the Erasmus programme I ended up making a profit from my year abroad as I took on a small job in a bar while I was there. I went travelling with the leftover money.

Overall, it is an experience that has changed me quite a lot. I am more self-confident and can do things on my own. If you're thinking about doing an Erasmus year, then do so. You may come out with a network of friends you can visit all over the world.

Jonathan AGER. www.erasmus.ac.uk.

WORDS:

1 Erasmus: *programme européen pour les étudiants qui veulent étudier à l'étranger*
2 relief: *soulagement*
3 degree: : *diplôme*
4 grants: *bourse*

FEEDBACK

1 ▸ Where did Jonathan come from? How did he feel when he arrived in Poitiers? Why?
2 ▸ Pick out the sentence showing that he got bored the first two weeks.
3 ▸ When was he able to make new friends?
4 ▸ What did Jonathan think of lectures in French at the beginning?
5 ▸ Did he have any financial problems while he was studying in Poitiers? Justify?
6 ▸ How did he manage to save money for travelling?
7 ▸ What did he gain from his Erasmus experience? Does he recommend it or not?

2 Shanty town football

© S.Cunningham/Photo12.com/Alamy

I went to Costa Rica during my gap year intending to do the typical backpacker[1] 'thing' of turtle beaches, scuba diving, volcanic springs and Caribbean surfing. But how quickly my experience changed when I decided to catch some afternoon sun at a park in the capital city, San Jose! Little did I know I'd be asked to join in a game of football with the shanty town[2] children! With no understanding of Spanish and very limited footballing skills, I rose to the challenge, took on the Ticos and had my best experience by far!

Playing 'shanty town' football with the local children made me realise how much fun you could have and what close friendships you could make with people from a completely different culture, even though I didn't speak a word of their language! I was also surprised at how skilful so many of the boys and girls were, despite most of them only having a pair of old school shoes to play in! Not only was it great fun, it was very eye-opening too.

Costa Rica is breathtaking! The diversity of its wildlife and awesome landscapes, combined with the warmth of the friendly locals, has made it a country that I'll never forget... and one I will always want to return to. As for playing sports overseas, I loved it so much that I am now spending the summer in South Africa with Gap Sports Abroad, playing and coaching sports to township[3] children!

Jolyon OFCHARD-LISLE. www.payaway.oc.uk.

WORDS:

1 backpacker: *routard*
2 shanty towns : *bidonville*
3 townships: *ghettos en Afrique du Sud*

FEEDBACK

1 ▸ Where and when did Jolyon go backpacking?
2 ▸ What surprising thing was he asked to do in San Jose?
3 ▸ Why was it a challenge for him? Give two reasons.
4 ▸ What benefits did he draw from it?
5 ▸ What did he notice about the boys and girls?
6 ▸ What sentence shows that it was an enriching experience?
7 ▸ Pick out all the positive words about Costa Rica.
8 ▸ How has this experience changed Jolyon's summer plans?

Comprehension

© photo12.com/Alamy

Before you read

1. Describe the picture above. What do you think the girl is doing in Asia?
2. Would you like to do the same? Why?

Read the text

3. What does the text mainly deal with:
   - the positive points of studying abroad;
   - the positive and the negative points of studying in a foreign country;
   - the difficulties of travelling alone?
4. Compare Katherine's life and personality before and after studying abroad.

Read paragraphs 1 and 2

5. Had Katherine and her parents ever been abroad on holiday? Justify.
6. Quote the simple daily tasks she was able to do abroad.
7. What was she really proud of?
8. Find words synonymous with: on my own - holidays - important.

Read the rest of the document

9. Pick out the advantages she mentions about travelling.
10. What qualities are needed to enjoy travelling?
11. Which continents did she visit? Which didn't she visit?

ALLEZ PLUS LOIN

1 Les mots *attend* et *college* (§1) sont des faux amis. Relisez. Demandez-vous quel est l'âge de Katherine et déduisez le sens de *college*.
▸ **FICHE** p. 53

2 Essayez de traduire *modern-day explorer*
▸ **FICHE** p. 75

3 *I was able to "make it" on my own abroad.* Traduisez la phrase en précisant le sens de *make*. Appuyez-vous sur le contexte.

4 Donnez deux phrases qui indiquent que les voyages l'ont rendue plus tolérante.

RÉSUMEZ

1 Ecoutez l'enregistrement et résumez en anglais.
- before - studies - abroad - Katherine - shy - who - no international experience
- protected - girl - abroad - on her own - change - life
- but - made it - more competent
- the more - the stronger
- thanks to travelling - new places - people - things
- travelling - helped - confident - tolerant

2 Résumez en français.
- Pourquoi cette année à l'étranger a-t-elle constitué un gros changement pour Katherine ?
- Qu'a-t-elle gagné sur le plan personnel ?
- Pourquoi les voyages qu'elle a effectués seule ont-ils été particulièrement enrichissants ?

Grammaire en contexte

1. Dans le paragraphe 4, trouvez :
a) un quantifieur exprimant une certaine quantité.
b) un quantifieur (présent deux fois) exprimant une grande quantité.

2. Dans l'énoncé : *"I hadn't had much international experience"* (§ 1),
a) Repérez le quantifieur.
b) Que remarquez-vous concernant le nom qui le suit ?

Studying abroad

Before studying abroad, I had never been away from home alone for more than a few weeks. Some children go to camp, I didn't. I did not even move away from home to attend college, and I had never lived abroad. I hadn't had much international experience apart from a few short family vacations. Obviously, studying abroad was a huge step and change for me because I was pretty sheltered growing up. I had no idea what the world outside of the U.S. was really like; I felt like a modern-day explorer or adventurer starting out to see the world.

It may sound a little ridiculous, but I was very proud of myself. I was able to make it on my own abroad. I used to be shy and, little by little, I was competent enough to perform any simple, daily tasks like going to the market, using public transportation, and navigating through the city without getting lost.

The more I travelled, the more confident I felt. I was living, studying, travelling and exploring safely and successfully all on my own. I was actually enjoying myself in another country, in another culture, and in another language.

Travelling also greatly helped me grow and become much more independent. Travelling opens you up to so many new places, people and ideas. Travelling is the adventure part of studying abroad: what you learn in the classroom comes to life and is put into practice. Travelling also requires some adaptation and tolerance. Not many things are the same abroad. Not only do you have to adapt to foreign environments, lifestyles, and customs, you have to tolerate these differences and work toward seeing them in a more positive light.

I frequently travelled alone in Spain and visited a lot of other European and Scandinavian countries. I also travelled to Morocco in North Africa. Thanks to all these travel experiences I found out more about myself. It was challenging to travel on my own, but I feel stronger now. I know I can get along with any person I meet in the future. I hope I have become a more tolerant person who finds difference not bad, but rather just different and interesting.

Katherine C. Fitz Simons Graduate Student,
B.A. Spanish, Journalism University of Southern California

Les quantifieurs indéfinis

Ils désignent une quantité plus ou moins importante ou un nombre plus ou moins grand.

La totalité

***All* s'emploie avec un nom indénombrable donc singulier ou dénombrable pluriel.**

Ex: *Katherine lost **all** her money but not **all** her papers!*
▶ Katherine a perdu tout son argent mais pas tous ses papiers !

Une grande quantité

***Much* s'emploie avec un nom indénombrable.**

Ex: *Katherine didn't have **much** money.*
▶ Katherine n'avait pas beaucoup d'argent.

***Many* s'emploie avec un nom dénombrable pluriel.**

Ex: *Did she have **many** friends?*
▶ Avait-elle beaucoup d'amis ?

***A lot of* s'emploie avec un nom indénombrable ou dénombrable pluriel, plutôt à la forme affirmative.**

Ex: *She had **a lot of** work to do and **a lot of** books to read.*
▶ Elle avait beaucoup de travail à faire et beaucoup de livres à lire.

Une petite quantité jugée suffisante

***A little* s'emploie avec un nom indénombrable.**

Ex: *I just need **a little** time.*
▶ J'ai juste besoin d'un peu de temps.

***A few* s'emploie avec un nom dénombrable pluriel.**

Ex: *I spent **a few** weeks in the city.*
▶ J'ai passé quelques semaines dans la ville.

Une petite quantité jugée insuffisante

***Little* s'emploie avec un nom indénombrable (singulier).**

Ex: *I had so **little** time that I decided to travel by bus.*
▶ J'avais si peu de temps que j'ai décidé de voyager en bus.

***Few* s'emploie avec un nom dénombrable pluriel.**

Ex: *Few people can understand me.*
▶ Peu de gens peuvent me comprendre.

Une quantité jugée suffisante

***Enough* s'emploie avec un nom indénombrable (singulier) ou dénombrable pluriel.**

Ex: *I didn't have **enough** money to travel.*
There weren't enough jobs.
▶ Je n'avais pas assez d'argent pour voyager. Il n'y avait pas assez d'emplois.

Une certaine quantité

***Some* s'utilise dans :**

- **les énoncés affirmatifs**

Ex: *I met **some** very nice people.*
▶ J'ai rencontré des gens très sympathiques.

- **les énoncés interrogatifs quand l'énonciateur est certain de l'existence du nom ou quand il attend une réponse positive.**

Ex: *Would you like **some** more fish?*
▶ Voulez-vous encore un peu de poisson ?
(L'énonciateur propose du poisson car il est certain d'en avoir et s'attend à ce que son invité accepte son offre.)

***Any* s'utilise dans :**

- **les énoncés interrogatifs**

Ex: *Have you got **any** plans for tomorrow?*
▶ Avez-vous des projets pour demain ?

- **les énoncés négatifs**

Ex: *I don't have **any** plans.*
▶ Je n'ai aucun projet.

- **les énoncés affirmatifs**

***Any* ne fait plus référence à une quantité mais se traduit par "n'importe lequel", "n'importe laquelle", etc. Il est accentué.**

Ex: *I will accept **any** suggestion.*
▶ J'accepterai n'importe quelle suggestion.

Une quantité nulle

***No* s'emploie avec un nom indénombrable ou dénombrable pluriel.**

Ex: ***No** pets and **no** noise in mosques!*
▶ Pas d'animaux et pas de bruit dans les mosquées !

ENTRAÎNEZ-VOUS

1 Dites si les mots en gras sont des noms dénombrables (D) ou indénombrables (I).

a. Il don't have much **time**.
The bus will leave in a few **minutes**.
b. Did you manage to put all your **things** in your **backpack**?
c. Do you want some **apples** and some more **water**? You know it's a long journey.
d. I have enough **food** and I have two **magazines**.

2 Choisissez le quantifieur qui convient.

a. I had so … things to do. *(much / many)*
b. First, I had to find a place to sleep and I thought … cheap hotel would do. *(any / no)*
c. Next, I had to change … money. *(some / any)*
d. Then, I thought I could spend … hours in my room. The journey had been very tiring. *(a little / a few)*
e. Finally, I met … other students in the evening. We decided to see each other the next day. *(some / any)*

3 Complétez avec *much* / *many* / *a little* / *little* / *a few* / *few*.

a. I remember I slept very … hours that night. Sometimes, you are too tired to sleep.
b. It took me very … time to walk to the bar. It was only 5mn away.
c. When I arrived, only … students were there.
d. There was so … traffic in the street that I thought the others were late.
e. So, I asked for … more tea

4 Complétez avec *some*, *any* ou *no*.

a. What are you going to do? Have you got … idea?
b. I am going on an Erasmus course for a year in Poitiers. Come and see me if you have … time.
c. I have … intention of travelling next year.
d. I don't have ... money.
e. I'm looking for … odd job to pay for my studies.

5 Traduisez.

a. Je n'ai jamais assez de temps pour jouer au football.
b. J'ai peu de travail aujourd'hui.
c. J'ai rencontré beaucoup de gens sympathiques.
d. Certains paysages vous coupent le souffle.
e. Toutes mes expéditions ont été intéressantes. Je sais que je peux voyager dans n'importe quel pays.

JEUX DE MOTS

1 Complétez le tableau.

Noms	*Adjectifs*	*Adverbes*
pride		
	competent	
strength		
warmth		
surprise		
		differently
		skillfully
	practical	
adventure		

2 Complétez ces phrases avec des mots choisis dans le tableau

a. The people from Costa Rica welcomed me with great ... .
b. The boys were quick and played ... .
c. Their life was really ... from mine.
d. Although they were quite thin, they were actually ... .
e. It was ... to see that they never complained.
f. I enjoyed the ... so much that I decided to spend my vacations with poor children.

Language skills

D'UNE LANGUE À L'AUTRE

1 Observez les phrases suivantes et dites pourquoi l'expression "de moins en moins" est traduite de deux façons différentes.

a. *Fewer and fewer teens write letters.*
▶ De moins en moins de jeunes écrivent des lettres.

b. *It takes less and less time to send and receive messages.*
▶ Cela prend de moins en moins de temps d'envoyer et de recevoir des messages.

2 Traduisez en français.

a. Parents think that children have less and less energy.
b. Fewer and fewer young people are attracted to manual jobs.
c. Very few want to work as plumbers or builders.

3 Observez les phrases suivantes.

a. I knew very little about their living conditions.
b. But I noticed that too many people were unemployed.
c. I was surprised to see so many boys playing football in their school shoes.

Quels sont les adverbes qui modifient les quantifieurs ? Proposez une traduction pour chacune des phrases.

4 Traduisez en français.

a. You can come any time you want.
b. Ask anyone, everybody knows where the store is located.
c. I was surprised to see so many boys playing.
d. You can take any of these bags, they are all the same price.

ATELIER D'ÉCRITURE

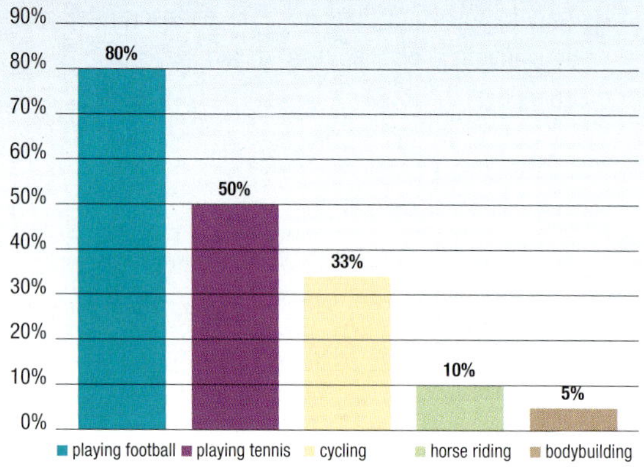

1 Look at the graph and say what sports students enjoy doing in their spare time. Use : many, half, one third, some, a few, a lot of.

Ex: *In their spare time … (of) students enjoy(s) ….*

2 Answer the following question in 80 words. What country would you choose if you could go and study abroad?

- First, say what country you would choose.
- Then, explain why you are attracted to this country.
- Next, mention the advantages you would get from this experience.
- Finally, give your opinion about international or European study programmes in general.

CONSEILS D'ÉCRITURE

- **Utilisez des quantifieurs pour évoquer les atouts du pays que vous avez choisi :** *a lot of, many , much…*
- **Introduisez votre opinion par :** *as far as I am concerned, I think/feel, personally, in my opinion…*

ADJECTIFS

awesome	*merveilleux*
alone	*seul*
breathtaking	*à couper le souffle*
daily	*quotidien*
enjoyable	*agréable*
eye-opening	*qui ouvre les yeux*
foreign	*étranger*
huge	*énorme*
left over	*restant*
previous	*précédent*
proud	*fier*
ridiculous	*ridicule*
tremendous	*énorme*
self-confident	*sûr de soi*
sheltered	*protégé*
shy	*timide*
skilful	*adroit*
stressful	*stressant*
strong	*fort*

NOMS

backpacker	*routard*
gap	*fossé*
grant	*bourse d'études*
landscape	*paysage*
lecture	*cours, conférence*
lifestyle	*style de vie*
network	*réseau*
relief	*soulagement*
side	*côté*
shanty town	*bidonville*
task	*tâche*
township	*ghetto noir*
warmth	*chaleur*
wildlife	*faune*

VERBES

coach	*entraîner*
get along with	*s'entendre avec*
get used to	*s'habituer*
grow up	*grandir*
intend	*avoir l'intention*
hope	*espérer*
keep up with	*suivre*
make it	*réussir*

AUTRES

actually	*en fait*
despite	*en dépit de*
frequently	*fréquemment*
obviously	*évidemment*
all over the world	*dans le monde entier*

Exercices

1 Complétez avec des noms du lexique.

a. Thanks to my year abroad, I now have a … of friends from all over the world.
b. I had to attend … in French.
c. It was so tiring that weekends were a real …
d. Playing football with … kids was a revelation to me.
e. The … between poor and rich people in this country is huge.

2 Trouvez les synonymes des mots suivants.

a. often
b. pleasant
c. in the whole world
d. enormous
e. train (to)

3 Complétez avec des adjectifs.

a. I have never travelled …
b. At the beginning, living on my own was a bit …
c. I used to be very … ; now I feel very confident.
d. I enjoyed going to my … classes.
e. I have learnt a lot from travelling. It is really an … experience.

4 Complétez avec des mots du lexique.

a. Visiting a … country is very enriching.
b. Without the Erasmus …, he would never have been able to pay for his studies in France.
c. Katherine thought she would be very unhappy, … she was enjoying herself very much.
d. … the culture differences, she got on very well with the Spaniards.
e. She admired the country and its various …
f. But travelling also has its negative …

A window on the world

Visit any British town or city that attracts tourists from late spring to the end of the summer, and you are guaranteed to come across a group of excitable foreign students over here to learn English. Language schools run courses all year round, but the summer months are traditionally their busiest. All those students have to live somewhere, of course, and a placement with a local family is the best way for them to develop their language skills.

"The children gain a lot from the experience," says Mandy Winder of Brighton. She and her husband Michael have taken students from the local educational institutes for the past 12 years. "I have bought my children a globe, and the first thing Emily, 10, and Megan 7, do when a new student arrives is to find out where he or she comes from."

The practical side of taking in a student is simple. Basics required are a reasonably-sized furnished room with a desk and chair and use of a bathroom. Mandy certainly tries to make her guests feel part of her family. "We all eat together – that's when most of the talking gets done – and I try to make them feel at home. I ask them to tell me what foods they like and don't like." In return for their hospitality, the host family receives about £70 to £80 per week.

Introducing a stranger into family life can cause a few problems. There are a few complaints. Mandy said that a few years ago she was watching a television programme when the foreign student picked up the remote control and switched over without asking. She remembers Japanese girls who came with strict guidelines[1] not to talk to men. "They would chat to me, but hardly talk to my husband. Another drawback of taking in students comes when they leave. If they've been with us for a long time, the children can find it hard when they go," says Mandy.

So, is playing the host a worthwhile[2] experience? In general, yes, especially if you have a big house with rooms to escape to. You have to be relaxed to do it – there are a lot of people who wouldn't want someone else in their home. Mandy Winder agrees: "The children have benefited from it enormously. They've learnt how to live with other people and they're very aware that we're not the only people in the world. Educationally, their geography has improved and they've had a bit of a head start[3] by hearing other languages being spoken".

Telegraph Weekend

WORDS:
1 guidelines: *directives*
2 worthwhile: *qui vaut la peine*
3 head start : *avance, avantage*

A Répondez en français aux questions suivantes, en utilisant uniquement les informations contenues dans le texte. Composez des phrases complètes et justifiez toujours vos réponses. 8 pts

1. À quel moment de l'année de jeunes étrangers affluent-ils dans les villes touristiques de Grande Bretagne ? Dans quel but ?
2. Quelles sont les conditions matérielles requises des familles anglaises qui souhaitent accueillir un étudiant étranger ?
3. Que fait Mandy pour favoriser l'accueil des jeunes étrangers dans sa famille ?
4. Citez deux exemples de difficultés que l'accueil d'un jeune étranger peut entraîner.
5. Quels avantages les enfants de Mandy retirent-ils de l'accueil de jeunes étrangers ?

B Traduisez en français le second paragraphe du texte: *"The children gain a lot ..." "... where he or she comes from"* (lignes 10 à 15). 4 pts

C Recopiez le paragraphe suivant en mettant les verbes entre parenthèses à la forme exigée par le contexte. 2 pts

My name is James. I'm a student and I would like to be a French teacher. I *(love)* travelling and last year I *(stay)* with a French family for three months. It *(be)* a great experience! At the moment I *(take)* my final exams. If I pass them, I'll spend my summer holidays in the south of France again.

D Complétez les phrases avec des mots choisis dans la liste ci-dessous. 2 pts

much / many / few / a few / little / a little

1. Why do so ... students come to the south of England in the summer?
2. Host families can only take in ... guests at a time.
3. The children make too ... noise in this family.
4. He got up late! He has got ... time left for his breakfast now.

E Imagine you are going on a language course in Britain. Would you like to stay in a host family? Give your reasons in 80 words in English. 4 pts

kit 6

© DPPI/Sipapress

Is sport work?

© D.Cransby/Photo12.com/Alamy

Speaking

- Guess who the people in the large photo are.
- Look at their faces and say what has just happened.
- Now, look at the small picture and say as much as you can about the man.
- Do you think it is easy to become a professional sportsman? Justify.

STREET TALK

The best job in the world

© Judy Martinez/Hachette

1 Listen to these words from the interview.

- level • dream • privileged
- involve • physically demanding
- break in • defence • brilliant.

2 Listen to Graeme and fill in your questionnaire.

Graeme, Bournemouth Football Club, UK.

I My team

By Dougray Scott, actor

© J.Sullivan:/Photo12.com/Alamy

I was born and brought up in Fife[1], so I should support a Fife team, not an Edinburgh team like Hibs[2]. But you support the team your dad takes you to see, don't you? I was brought up with the great Hibs teams of the past. It's unbelievable now, but Hibs had reached the semi-final of the first-ever European Cup in 1956. When I went to football as a small lad[3] aged five or six, it was magic. It was a thing of beauty. When I watch football, I'm lost in the game. I forget about everything else. Even if it's a rubbish game, I still love it. I love the fact that in football anything can happen. Even when you're 4-1 down with 10 minutes to go, you think: 'We could get three goals in 10 minutes.' So, I'm the eternal optimist.

Acting doesn't get me as passionate. I love acting and I take my work incredibly seriously, but I prefer football. If I had the choice of an evening with Robert De Niro or Alex Ferguson[4], it would be Alex Ferguson every time. In August 2001 the international premiere of my film, *Enigma,* in Edinburgh, clashed with Rangers[5] v[6] Hibs. I arrived at the cinema with Kate Winslet but slipped out[7] after 15 minutes to watch the game in a pub across the road. There are some more important things in life than acting.

WORDS:

1 Fife: *une ville écossaise*
2 Hibs or Hibernian: *un club de foot en Ecosse*
3 lad : *garçon*
4 A. Ferguson: *coach de Manchester United*
5 Rangers: *une équipe de foot écossaise*
6 V: *versus (contre)*
7 slip out: *s'éclipser*

FEEDBACK

1 What's Dougray Scott's job and where was he born?
2 Did he support the football team of his town? Why?
3 Why did Hibs have a good reputation in the past?
4 Find two expressions showing that football is something very special for Dougray.
5 What does he like in the sport?
6 Pick out the sentence showing that his passion for football comes first.
7 Which important events coincided in August 2001? What did he decide to do?

2 A professional baseball player

Curtis Pride plays in the Major League Baseball Players Association.
He is a deaf player who graduated from High School and then got a Bachelor's degree in Finance.

What advice would you give to a student who wants to be a baseball player?

Curtis: Always make education your number one priority. While I am always proud when I am introduced as a deaf player who made it to the major leagues, I am even more proud when I am introduced as a major league player who also has a college degree.

Describe your typical day.

Curtis: During the season my daily routine is pretty much the same. For a night game, I relax at home until noon, eat a light lunch and then head to the stadium at 3 p.m. where I work out. During the off season, I work out every day to stay in shape. I also like to do speeches and school appearances. It gives me a great feeling when I see that my story can be an inspiration to others trying to overcome adversity to achieve a dream.

Interview deafness.about.com

© J. Zelansky/Icon SMI/DPPI

FEEDBACK

1 ▸ What is Curtis Pride's job?
2 ▸ What physical problem does he have?
3 ▸ Did he study at university?
4 ▸ What advice does he give to students who want to go professional?
5 ▸ How does he like to be introduced? Why?
6 ▸ Does he stop doing sport completely during the off season? Justify.
7 ▸ How does he share his experience with young people?

Comprehension

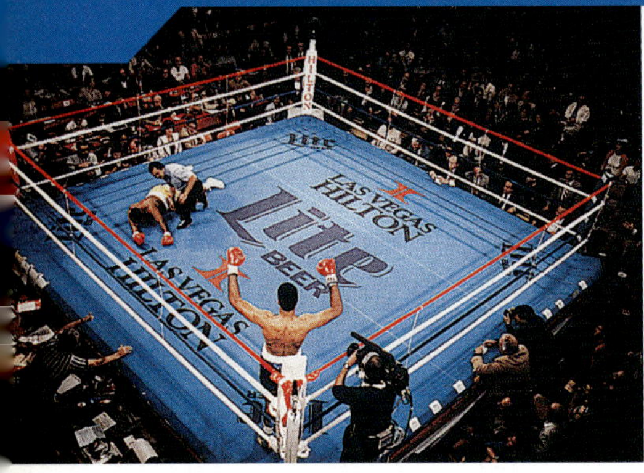

© All Sport/Vandystadt

Before you read

1. Describe the pictures.
2. Do you think kickboxing is a hard sport? Justify.
3. Imagine the various reasons why someone would like to become a professional kickboxer.

Read the heading and subheading

4. Do you think the text is pessimistic or optimistic? Pick out negative or positive elements to justify.

Read the text quickly

5. Give as much information as you can about the main character: name, age, nationality, religion, parents' situation.
6. Say in which paragraphs you find information about:
   - the reason why Harun fights,
   - the places where matches are held,
   - the Malaysian authorities' decision.

Read the first three paragraphs

7. Which elements imply that the environment is really poor?
8. Is he seeking fame or does he just want to earn a little money? Justify.
9. What decision did the Malaysian authorities make? Is it justified? Say why.
10. Why do young Malaysians want to compete?

Read the end of the text

11. Pick out elements showing that matches are illegal.
12. Is the law actually enforced (*appliquée*)? Justify.
13. Did Harun go to secondary school?
14. Choose the right answer. Why has Harun never had a girlfriend?
    - because he is unattractive
    - because he has no money

ALLEZ PLUS LOIN

1 Quel mot (ligne 1) indique qu'il y aura plus d'un match ?

2 D'après le contexte (*awaiting his turn*) que peut signifier *shadow boxing*?
Est-il en train de boxer réellement contre quelqu'un?

3 *A talisman containing a scroll. Talisman* est un mot transparent. Imaginez ce qu'il peut contenir.

4 *However* (ligne 19) est un adverbe qui exprime l'opposition. Donnez les deux idées qui s'opposent.

5 D'après le contexte *lack of opportunity* précédé de *poverty, illiteracy* signifie-t-il qu'il y a des possibilités pour ces jeunes Malaysiens ou qu'il n'y en a pas.

RÉSUMEZ

1 Ecoutez l'enregistrement et résumez en anglais.

- Harun – waiting – turn – kickbox
- if – wins – match – dollars – parents – buy – fish – vegetables
- Thai kickboxing – dangerous
- competitors – killed – ring
- so – government banned
- but – young Malaysians – boxing – because – earn a living – rural regions
- Harun – thinks – if – wins – will earn
- then – get married

2 Résumez en français.

1. Donnez la raison pour laquelle Harun se bat.
2. Pourquoi les autorités malaysiennes ont-elles interdit les matches?
3. Dans quelle mesure la victoire peut-elle transformer la vie de Harun?

Grammaire en contexte

- **Dans le premier et le dernier paragraphe, relevez un énoncé comportant une hypothèse et une conséquence.**
- **Repérez les formes verbales indiquant la conséquence et identifiez-les.**
- **Quel mot indique qu'il s'agit d'une hypothèse ?**
- **Traduisez ces énoncés en français et comparez les formes verbales utilisées dans chacune des deux langues.**
- **D'un point de vue chronologique, à quel moment renvoient ces énoncés ?**

Fighting to survive

Kickboxing is a tough way to make a little money.

Harun Bin Shaari is shadow-boxing, awaiting his turn in the ring. The 22-year-old Malaysian kickboxer is sitting in a small tented area near a makeshift[1] ring. Bin Shaari ties a talisman containing an Arabic scroll to his arm for good luck. If he wins the match, the $130 prize money will allow his parents – poor plantation workers – to buy fish and vegetables to supplement their regular diet of rice. But victory is not ensured: his opponent, a Thai kickboxing champion, is taller, stronger and more experienced.

© D.White/Photo12.com/Alamy

The Malaysian version of Thai kickboxing was once[2] so dangerous that competitors were sometimes killed in the ring. For that reason, the "sport" was banned in Northern Malaysia decades ago.

However, growing numbers of young men are signing up to compete because, they believe, there are no other ways to earn a living. "I fight for money to survive," says Bin Shaari.

It's not difficult to set up a match. In farmers' fields, with the tacit complicity of local authorities, rings are erected. Poor farmers and businessmen make bets on matches that range from $10 to $1,300. "It's all secret, from friend to friend," says one kickboxing trainer.

WORDS:

1 makeshift: *improvisé*
2 once: *autrefois*
3 nevertheless: *néanmoins*
4 destitute: *sans ressources*
5 grade school: *école primaire*

The number of kickboxers is small under a thousand but is nevertheless[3] a symbol of the poverty, illiteracy and lack of opportunity in Malaysia's rural regions.

Bin Shaari's mother and father are destitute[4]. Bin didn't make it past grade school[5] and has never found a conventional job. Despite movie-star looks, he has never had a girlfriend, either.

"Maybe, he says, if I win enough in the next two years, I will get married."

Adapted from *Newsweek*, December 2000

L'expression de l'hypothèse

Pour exprimer une hypothèse, on emploie une subordonnée introduite par *if*, *when*, *as soon as* ...

Elle est suivie ou précédée d'une proposition principale exprimant la conséquence qui découle de cette hypothèse.

Ex: *If he wins the match, he will get money.*

▸ S'il gagne le match, il recevra de l'argent.

"S'il gagne le match" : proposition subordonnée exprimant une hypothèse, "il recevra de l'argent" : proposition principale exprimant la conséquence qui découle de cette hypothèse.

Il y a une gradation dans la possibilité que cette hypothèse et cette conséquence se réalisent.

Des chances de réalisation importantes

***If*, *when*, *as soon as* + *V*(*s*) dans la subordonnée, *will* +*V* dans la principale**

If

Ex: *If he becomes a champion, his life will change.*

if + V-s — *will + V*

▸ S'il devient un champion, sa vie changera.

When

Ex: *When I have enough money, I will buy a car.*

V-Ø — *will + V*

▸ Quand j'aurai assez d'argent, j'achèterai une voiture. (Il faut d'abord que je possède assez d'argent pour que je puisse acheter une voiture.)

As soon as

Ex: *As soon as I have my driving licence, I will drive to Italy.*

V-Ø — *will + V*

▸ Dès que j'aurai mon permis de conduire, j'irai en Italie en voiture. (Le permis de conduire est nécessaire à la réalisation de mon projet : partir en Italie.)

Les chances de réalisation sont tout à fait possibles.

ATTENTION

***When* et *as soon as* sont employés dans des énoncés permettant de se projeter dans l'avenir mais sont immédiatement suivis de *V*(-*s*). Il n'en est pas de même en français.**

Ex: *When I **have** enough money, I will get married.*

▸ Quand **j'aurai** de l'argent, je me marierai.

Ex: *As soon as **I get** the prize, I will stop boxing.*

▸ Dès que **j'aurai** le prix, je m'arrêterai de boxer.

Des chances de réalisation moins importantes

***If* / *when* / *as soon as* / + *V-ed* dans la subordonnée, *would* +*V* dans la principale**

Ex: *If Ben came early, I would see him.*

V-ed — *would + V*

▸ Si Ben arrivait tôt, je le verrais.

V-*ed* ne fait pas référence au passé mais à du non-réel.

On peut avoir aussi :

Ex: *If Ben came early, I could see him.*

▸ Si Ben arrivait tôt, je pourrais le voir.

could exprime une capacité que n'exprime pas *would*.

Les chances de réalisation sont peu importantes, mais encore possibles.

Des chances de réalisation nulles

***If* / *as soon as* / *when* + *had* + *V-en* dans la subordonnée, *would*+ *have*+ *V-en* dans la principale**

Ex: *If Ben had come early, I would have seen him.*

had + V-en — *would have + V-en*

▸ Si Ben était arrivé tôt, je l'aurais vu.

On pourrait aussi avoir :

Ex: *If Ben had come early, I could have seen him.*

▸ Si Ben était arrivé tôt, j'aurais pu le voir.

L'hypothèse ne s'est pas réalisée, et la conséquence non plus. Cette forme peut exprimer un regret, car les événements ne se sont pas produits.

ENTRAÎNEZ-VOUS

1 Choisissez la bonne fin de phrase.

a. If he loses the match, *he will be sad / he would be sad / he would have been sad.*

b. If he had a lot of money, *he would not have fought / he will not fight / he would not fight.*

c. If kickboxing were not so dangerous, *it would not be banned / it will not be banned / it would not have been banned.*

d. If he had had better results at school, *he will have a conventional job / he would have had a conventional job / he would have a conventional job.*

2 Mettez les verbes entre parenthèses à la forme correcte.

a. If the weather is fine, we (*go*) to the beach.

b. I would go to Malaysia if I (*can*).

c. If he was strong enough, he (*practise*) kickboxing.

d. If he had had enough money, he (*buy*) a convertible.

3 Écrivez des énoncés cohérents en reliant les éléments 1 à 5 aux éléments a à e.

1. If he had not eaten so much…
2. He would watch the match…
3. We will leave…
4. They will practise kickboxing…
5. I would cycle to school…

a. …when they are old enough.
b. …if I had a helmet.
c. …he would not have been ill.
d. …if he did not have any homework to do.
e. …as soon as the match is finished.

5 Traduisez en anglais.

a. Dès qu'il arrivera, nous partirons pour le stade.

b. Je pratiquerai le kickboxing quand je serai plus grand.

c. Si j'avais eu peur pendant le match, je te l'aurais dit.

d. Viendra-t-il si je lui demande ?

JEUX DE MOTS

1 Trouvez dans le texte page 69 les synonymes des mots suivants.

hard – adversary – forbidden – poor

2 Trouvez les noms correspondant aux adjectifs suivants. Utilisez votre dictionnaire si nécessaire.

illiterate – tough – poor – young – dangerous – victorious – strong – secret

3 Complétez le paragraphe suivant.

Harun is a bit afraid, his match is approaching. He kisses his talisman for g… l…. He is looking at his o… who looks much s… than him. Harun does not like boxing, the sport is really d…, that is why it was b… in the country. But illegal matches still t… place in r… areas.

Harun f… to e… a little money and h… his p… parents.

4 Complétez avec des mots transparents du texte page 69.

a. Don't tell anybody what I said. It's …

b. The Statue of Liberty is a … of the United States.

c. Keep this rabbit foot in your pocket. It is a … which will bring you luck.

d. Kickboxing is a way for young men to … in Thailand.

D'UNE LANGUE À L'AUTRE

1 Observez la traduction des phrases suivantes et dites ce que vous remarquez concernant les temps employés en anglais et en français.

a. *If Harun wins the prize, he will be able to help his parents.*
▸ Si Harun gagne assez d'argent, il pourra aider ses parents.

b. *He will buy fish and vegetables as soon as he gets the $130 prize money.*
▸ Il achètera du poisson et des légumes dès qu'il recevra les 130 dollars du prix de la victoire.

2 Traduisez en français.

a. If the law is enforced, matches will disappear.
b. If Harun stays in the village, he will have to work on a plantation like his parents.
c. If he finds a good job, Harun will stop fighting.
d. As soon as he has enough money, he will get married.
e. If he had any children, they would be educated.
f. He will support his parents when he can.

3 Traduisez en anglais.

a. Quand il sera riche, il achètera une maison.
b. Il aura un entraîneur dès qu'il pourra.

ATELIER D'ÉCRITURE

1 Write a paragraph about this young boy's dreams. We've started it for you. Use the wordbox to help you.
If I had a lot of money, ...

Word box:
• sports car – big house – good time – beach – charity – expensive restaurants – other countries
• travel – spend – sunbathe – visit – donate – help

2 Answer the following question in 80 words. Would you like to be a professional sportsperson?

Follow these steps.
• First say what sport you would like to do.
• Then imagine what your daily routine would be like.
• Answer these questions:
How long would you spend training everyday?
Would you travel a lot?
What would you do in your free time?
What people would you meet?
• Write about the advantages and the drawbacks of this job,
• Finally, give your personal opinion about professional sportspeople in general.

CONSEILS D'ÉCRITURE

• **Vous devrez inclure dans votre essai des propositions introduites par *if*. Aidez-vous de la page 70 de votre manuel.**

• **Pour parler de votre vie quotidienne, utilisez des marqueurs de temps** *(in the morning, then, later)* **et des adverbes de fréquence** *(often, regularly, usually)*

ADJECTIFS

deaf	*sourd*
destitute	*sans ressources*
makeshift	*impovisé*
proud	*fier*
tough	*dur*

NOMS

decade	*décennie*
degree	*diplôme*
field	*champ*
goal	*but*
illiteracy	*illétrisme*
lack	*manque*
lad	*garçon*
opponent	*adversaire*
poverty	*pauvreté*
prize	*prix*
rubbish	*déchets*
scroll	*parchemin*
team	*équipe*

VERBES

achieve	*atteindre, réaliser*
act	*jouer*
allow	*permettre*
ban	*interdire*
bet	*parier*
born (be)	*naître*
bring up	*élever*
earn	*gagner (de l'argent)*
ensure	*garantir, assurer*
erect	*ériger*
forget	*oublier*
graduate	*terminer ses études*
grow	*pousser*
kill	*tuer*
overcome	*surmonter*
reach	*atteindre*
shadow-box	*boxer à vide, sans adversaire*
support	*soutenir*
win	*gagner (un prix)*

AUTRES

despite	*en dépit de*
during	*pendant*
either ... or	*soit... soit*
else	*autre*
even	*même*
maybe	*peut-être*
nevertheless	*néanmoins*
once	*une fois, autrefois*

Exercices

1 Complétez les phrases ci-dessous avec des noms de la liste.

lack – teams – poverty – goal – degree – decades – illiteracy

a. In a lot of developing countries, people suffer from … and … of opportunity.
b. For … now governments have built schools to combat …
c. Educating the most people is their main ….
d. … of teachers give lessons to rural children.
e. Very few students have a college ….

2 Trouvez dans la liste les verbes qui peuvent avoir les noms 1 à 10 pour complément.

Ex: … ***a lesson*** ▸ ***learn a lesson***

1. … a goal
2. … a tall building
3. … an appointment
4. … one's family
5. … money
6. … children
7. … a difficulty
8. … a prize
9. … on matches
10. … smoking

3 Complétez les phrases avec des mots de la rubrique "Autres".

a. … the summer season Curtis works out every day.
b. … he played two matches on the same day.
c. … when he is tired, he keeps on training.
d. … his busy timetable, he makes speeches in schools.
e. He doesn't know what … he can do to encourage children.
f. … he is quite optimistic.

Exam Paper

Netball in my life

I've always played sport. I am a semi-professional netballer[1], playing for the Australian Team and captaining the Queensland Firebirds. Add this to my Aboriginal heritage and my work within Aboriginal communities[2] and I guess it was only natural that I would end up working in the field of sport and recreation for Indigenous people. When I first left school I did a few different jobs, mainly in the clerical[3] and banking industry.

I am now employed by the National Aboriginal Sports Corporation Australia (NASCA) as the National Netball Development Manager. This job is excellent as it marries my sport with my job perfectly.

My job is not the normal 9 to 5 position. I work from home and my hours vary depending on where I am and what commitments[4] I have with netball. My work involves traveling throughout Australia to Indigenous and non-Indigenous communities and schools to conduct netball clinics[5] and identify talented players. Other parts of my job include coordinating netball carnivals and events, coordinating overseas tours for the Australian Indigenous Netball team and coaching the teams while on tour, liaising[6] with sponsors and partners and mentoring[7] players and students. I have no typical week, it's always different depending on where I am or what's on. It's a full-time job but it's great because I can work around my own training time.

The negative sides of my job are no different from those in other jobs. I don't like working weekends and sometimes my social life suffers due to my training and playing commitments and the odd hours I work. Traveling can be tiring and some of the more remote areas don't have the facilities for me to train. These, however, are insignificant compared to the good things about my job! I get to meet some interesting and high-profile people including Cathy Freeman[8] and the Prime Minister. I've appeared on television on Gladiators and the Footy Show. I have traveled to some great places throughout Australia and the world. Of course, I also find it very rewarding working with and for Aboriginal people and talking to various groups about my work and the issue of reconciliation.

Sharon Finman

WORDS:

1 netball: *sport proche du basketball*
2 Aboriginal communities: *communautés Indigènes d'Australie*
3 clerical: *de bureau*
4 commitments: *engagements, responsabilités*
5 clinics: *centre médical*
6 liaising: *travaillant en liaison*
7 mentoring: *aidant, guidant*
8 C. Freeman: *athlète aborigène, championne olympique du 400m à Sydney*

A Répondez en français aux questions suivantes et justifiez vos réponses. 8 pts

1. Quelles sont les deux fonctions de Sharon Finnan dans le domaine sportif ?
2. Pourquoi dit-elle qu'il est naturel qu'elle s'occupe des indigènes de son pays?
3. Quel poste occupe-t-elle dans la NASCA?
4. Citez quatre de ses activités dans cette organisation.
5. Qu'a-t-elle la possibilité de faire en plus de son travail ?
6. Le travail de Sharon est-il routinier ? Justifiez votre réponse à l'aide d'informations contenues dans le texte.
7. Citez trois éléments positifs de ce travail.

B Traduisez le début du dernier paragraphe : *"The negatives sides of my job ... the facilities for me to train".* (lignes 29 à 34). 4 pts

C Mettez les verbes entre parenthèses au temps qui convient. 4 pts

1. She will start her training as soon as she ... *(finish)* coaching her team.
2. If she identifies a talented player, she ... *(ask)* him to come for an interview.
3. If she found generous sponsors, life ... *(be)* easier for her team.
4. When she ... *(meet)* the Prime Minister, she won't forget to mention Aboriginal people's problems.

D Answer the following questions in English in about 80 words. 4 pts

Is it easy or difficult to earn a living through sport today?
Give examples to support your views.

La dérivation

Un mot anglais peut ne comporter que la racine.

Ex: *friend, rain, drive, firm...*

Parfois il comporte un préfixe ou un suffixe, ou les deux à la fois.

Ex: *dislike, vocational, uneasily.*

1 Identifiez le préfixe, la racine et le suffixe dans les mots suivants.

1. *skilfully*
2. *professionally*
3. *physically*
4. *shopping*
5. *rewire*
6. *unkind*
7. *application*
8. *recruitment*
9. *glamorous*
10. *uninspiring*

Les préfixes

Les préfixes ne modifient pas la catégorie grammaticale.

Ex: *responsible / irresponsible* (adjectif)
like / dislike (verbe)
employment / unemployment (nom)

Les préfixes changent le sens des mots.

• **un-**, **dis-**, **im-**, **ir-**, **non** ***expriment le contraire.***

Ex: *comfort* ▸ *discomfort*
possible ▸ *impossible*
agree ▸ *disagree*
smoker ▸ *non smoker*

• **mis**, ***indique une erreur.***

Ex: *pronounce* ▸ *mispronounce*

• **over**, ***indique un excès.***

Ex: *fed* ▸ *overfed* (suralimenté)

• **under**, ***exprime l'insuffisance.***

Ex: *fed* ▸ *underfed* (sous alimenté)

2 Trouvez les contraires des mots suivants. Vérifiez dans le dictionnaire si nécessaire.

1. *understand*
2. *friendly*
3. *skilled*
4. *qualified*
5. *patient*
6. *visible*
7. *violent*
8. *approve*

Les suffixes

Ils modifient la catégorie du mot. Ils transforment un verbe en nom, un nom en adjectif, un adjectif en adverbe, ou un adjectif en nom.

• **er**, ***transforme un verbe en nom.***
Ex: *drive* ▸ *driver*

• **ful**, ***transforme un nom en adjectif.***
Ex: *help* ▸ *helpful*

• **ly**, ***transforme un adjectif en adverbe.***
Ex: *slow* ▸ *slowly*

• **less**, ***transforme un nom en adjectif (sens privatif).***
Ex: *home* ▸ *homeless*

• **able**, ***transforme un verbe en adjectif.***
Ex: *drink* ▸ *drinkable*

• **ness**, ***transforme un adjectif en nom.***
Ex: *happy* ▸ *happiness*

3 Complétez avec le mot qui convient.

1. He is not a ... manager.
(tradition - traditional - traditionally)
2. He runs his shoe-business ... .
(success - successful - successfully)
3. The office is equipped with ... armchairs.
(comfort - comfortable - comfortably)
4. The company needs competent ... .
(programmes - programmers)
5. Everybody likes him because he is very ... .
(help - helpful - helpfully)

6. The manager … asked him a lot of questions.
(abrupt - abruptly)
7. His job consisted in measuring the food quality and the … of the store.
(clean - cleanly - cleanliness)
8. The company offers its employees an … trip to Nevada.
(annual - annually)
9. They spend an … week together.
(enjoy - enjoyable - enjoyably)
10. He couldn't do anything to help them.
He was actually ….
(power - powerful - powerless)

LES MOTS COMPOSÉS

On dit qu'on est en présence d'un mot composé lorsque deux mots sont accolés, juxtaposés ou reliés par un tiret.

Ex: *shoeshop, computer keyboard, mother-tongue*

C'est toujours le dernier mot qui est le mot principal.
Le ou les éléments qui le précèdent le qualifient. Comme des adjectifs, ils sont placés avant le nom et sont en général invariables.

Pour traduire un mot composé, on commence toujours par le dernier mot, on remonte et on finit par le premier.

4 Repérez le mot principal.

1. phonecard
2. Chicago baseball team
3. rush hour traffic
4. soybean factory
5. pottery evening classes
6. plane factory
7. biker look
8. movie star
9. address book
10. labour market

5 Complétez en formant un mot composé.

1. a dish of potatoes is a …
2. a dress for a party is a …
3. a collector of stamps is a …
4. a story about ghosts is a …
5. a race of cars is a …
6. a brush for painting is a …
7. a cleaner of streets is a …
8. the manager of a company is a …

6 Associez deux mots de la liste pour former des mots composés qui correspondent aux traductions ci-dessous.

- *turnover - extra - programmers - computer*
- *buildings - entrance - screen - firm*
- *laptop - equipment - door- income*
- *dream - office - company - job*

1. l'équipement de bureau
2. les bâtiments de la société
3. l'écran de l'ordinateur portable
4. le chiffre d'affaires de l'entreprise
5. la porte d'entrée
6. des programmeurs d'informatique
7. un métier de rêve
8. un revenu supplémentaire

7 Traduisez.

1. a rental service
2. a clothes shop
3. a fashion designer
4. a fashion victim
5. a car race
6. a race car
7. a bus driver
8. a three-week holiday
9. pocket money
10. bank account

8 Relevez les mots composés contenus dans ce paragraphe et traduisez-les.

. Microsoft plans to create a telephone service.
. Microsoft is preparing to enable computer users to make a normal phone call from their PC.
. The computer giant has increased its presence in the fast-growing internet phone sector by purchasing leading player Teleo for an undisclosed sum.

kit 7

© M.Peterson/REA

Selling matters

© C.Haller/REA

Speaking

- Describe the two pictures (where? who? what?)
- Where do you prefer doing your shopping: in a big store, or in a small shop? Why?
- What qualities are required to be a good salesperson? Give examples.

Happy to help

STREET TALK

© Judy Martinez/Hachette

1 **Listen to these words from the interview.**

• train • check outs • customer-friendly • taken over • Walmart • huge • polite • eye contact • item • free of charge • replacement

2 **Listen to Tricia and fill in the questionnaire**

Tricia from ASDA, Boscombe, U.K.

I My forehead is for sale

Are you looking to buy some advertising space for your business at a reasonable price? Try someone's forehead!

Andrew Fischer, 20, became famous nationwide when he was the first person to turn himself into an advertising billboard[1] in early January. He earned $37,375 for the use of his forehead space. It read "Snore Stop," a snoring[2] remedy. "People will always comment on something out of the ordinary," Fischer said. "People like weird."

On hearing about Fischer's success, a local couple in Oshkosh put their foreheads and their car up for sale as advertising space for 30 days on an auction Web site[3] last week. They received more than $102 from the Northwestern to advertise the magazine on their foreheads.

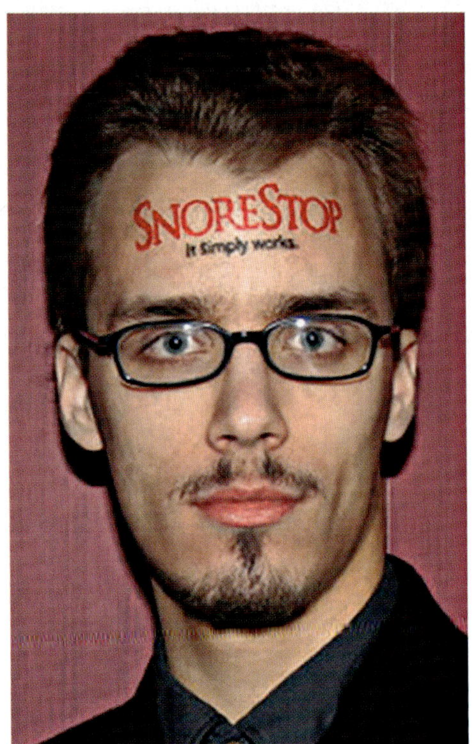

© EPA/Sipa

A New Yorker, Joe Tamargo, 31, has decided to permanently tattoo ads to his body. He has even set up a Web site, livingadspace.com, where anyone can advertise to make extra cash by selling ads on their body, clothing, pets, car, house, or anything else they can think of.

Caycee Hess, *The Advance Titan*
February, 2005

WORDS:

1 billboard: *panneau d'affichage*
2 snoring: *ronflement*
3 auction web site: *site de ventes aux enchères en ligne*

FEEDBACK

1 ▸ Look at the photo. On what part of the boy's body can you see the advertisement?
2 ▸ What new advertising space does the journalist suggest to business people?
3 ▸ Why did A. Fischer become famous in January 2005? What did he advertise? Was it worth it? Justify.
4 ▸ What does "weird" mean: funny / strange / dangerous?
5 ▸ How does Andrew explain his popularity?
6 ▸ What did one couple do after hearing about Andrew's success?
7 ▸ What has Joe Tamargo decided to do to make money?
8 ▸ Do you think many people will visit his web site? Justify.

2 Sam, the selling specialist

Macy's is the world's largest department store. Read what selling specialist Sam has to say.

Why did you join Macy's and why have you stayed?

Sam: I came because I've always had a passion for helping people and Macy's seemed like a great place for me to fulfill[1] that role. I will always love retail and working at Macy's. I've stayed here because it's a great place to work with wonderful people.

What do you enjoy most about what you do and what are your overall job responsibilities?

Sam: I enjoy interacting with the different people. I love helping the customers find the things that they are looking for. I am a selling specialist, so my job responsibilities are to sell and promote my product line.

What does it take to be a good salesperson?

Sam: I think you have to provide the customer with the best possible service. That's why a customer will come back here rather than go to another store. We all basically sell the same things – it's the service that makes the difference.

What is the hardest thing about working at Macy's?

Sam: Well, the hours are long and you are on your feet most of the time. The other hard thing for me was the strict dress code. You really have to look good if you want to work here. And then there are the customers. Some can be more difficult to deal with than others. But they train us to stay calm, cool and collected[2].

WORDS:
1 fulfill: *remplir*
2 collected: *serein*

© R.Levine/Photo12.com/Alamy

FEEDBACK

1 ▸ Look at the photo, read the introduction and say what Sam's job is and what kind of place he works in.
2 ▸ What has Sam always loved doing?
3 ▸ Can he do it at Macy's? Justify.
4 ▸ Find the reason why Macy's is Sam's ideal workplace?
5 ▸ What does Sam particularly enjoy in his job?
6 ▸ As a selling specialist, what does his job consist in?
7 ▸ According to Sam on what condition will the customers come back to his store?
8 ▸ Sam gives two reasons why his job is hard. What are these reasons?
9 ▸ Why are salespeople usually able to deal with difficult customers?

Comprehension

© C.Haller/REA

Before you read

1. Describe the pictures.
2. What do people usually go to this sort of department store for?
3. Read the title. Is a shopper:
   - someone who does shopping;
   - someone who owns a shop?
4. Imagine the reason why some people are called 'mystery-shoppers'.

Read the text

5. Check your answer to question 4.
6. Say in which paragraphs you find:
   - a mystery-shopper's feelings;
   - the reasons why companies recruit mystery-shoppers;
   - the names of some of these companies;
   - the reasons why Kashlak does this job;
   - what the work of a mystery-shopper consists in.

Read paragraphs 1 to 5

7. Pick out the different places Tina may visit as a mystery-shopper. And in each place say what she has to check.
8. Quote the four qualities that Tina has to assess in the different places she goes to.
9. What are the qualities of a good mystery-shopper?
10. Does Kashlak work full-time as a mystery-shopper? Justify.

Read the end of the text

11. Explain the role played by mystery-shopping companies.
12. For what reason is McDonald's going to recruit mystery-shoppers?
13. Are the companies that need mystery-shoppers' services big or small? Justify.
14. Who does a company owner now call to have information about his business? Why?
15. Why should company owners be well informed?

ALLEZ PLUS LOIN

1 Relevez dans les cinq premiers paragraphes tous les mots qui expriment le mystère.

2 Traduisez (§ 6) le mot composé qui donne des précisions sur la société *TrendSource*. ▸ **FICHE** p. 75

3 Relevez les deux verbes qui signifient "évaluer, mesurer".

4 Lisez la dernière phrase du document et essayez de traduire *mistreated* en vous demandant quel est le sens du suffixe *-mis* ▸ **FICHE** p. 75

RÉSUMEZ

1 Ecoutez l'enregistrement une fois et résumez en anglais.
- mystery-shopper – consists in – customer service – cleanliness – product quality
- then – provides – company
- mystery-shopper – discreet
- spy – company
- mystery-shopping – usually – part-time
- companies – need – shoppers – objective – going on – businesses

2 Résumez en français.
1. Dites en quoi consiste le travail des clients espions.
2. Quelles qualités doivent-ils posséder ?
3. Quel type de sociétés les recrute ? Dans quel but ?

Grammaire en contexte

1. Relevez les modaux dans les énoncés suivants :
- You may find Tina Kashlak at a restaurant. (§1)
- You must be discreet. (§3)
- You can't be at every store all the time. (§8)
- In the past the owner would pick up the phone. (§8)

2. Par quoi les modaux sont-ils suivis ?

3. Quelle est leur valeur ?

a. une habitude dans le passé
b. une impossibilité
c. une éventualité
d. une obligation

Mystery-shoppers

You may find Tina Kashlak at a restaurant – she may be secretly timing the number of minutes it takes the server to deliver her food. Or you may see her at an all-night supermarket, making sure the parking lot is well-lit at night. Then again, you may see her in a clothing store, pretending to search for just the right dress. In fact her true mission is to assess the friendliness of the clerks.

© H.King/Corbis

Tina Kashlak is a mystery-shopper. Like thousands of service-industry spies she is paid to detail her shopping experiences for company managers. Although she looks like an ordinary shopper, her mission is to anonymously rate businesses on customer service, cleanliness, management and product quality.

"I feel a little bit like a private investigator," says Kashlak, who has been mystery-shopping for about five years. "It's something I don't talk about with many people. You must be discreet and maintain your anonymity".

Kashlak, of Orlando, Fla., does mystery shopping part-time, like most secret shoppers. She has a full-time job in the retail industry but really enjoys mystery-shopping when she is free. It provides extra income and she finds being 'a spy' really exciting.

Secret shoppers work freelance. They are recruited by mystery-shopping companies who train them to provide feedback.

Rodney Moll is president of TrendSource, a 13-year-old, San Diego-based mystery-shopping company that arranges some 100,000 shopping trips a year. Clients include Taco Bell, Kentucky Fried Chicken, Pizza Hut, Coca-Cola, Blockbuster Entertainment, Daimler Chrysler and J. Walter Thompson advertising.

McDonald's restaurants announced recently that they would start employing mystery-shoppers to assess service, cleanliness and food quality in an attempt to revive slow sales.

"If you own a thousand stores," Moll says, "you can't be at every store all the time. In the past the owner would pick up the phone, call a store and say, 'Hi, Mr. Manager, how is everything going?' And the manager would tell you that everything was all right. We provide objective information about what's really going on in the field. Company owners spend millions of dollars on advertising. If their customers are mistreated, they should know."

By Kathryn REM

Les modaux

can, may, must, will, shall, could, might, would, should

Qu'est-ce qu'un modal ?

Avec un modal, l'énonciateur donne son avis sur la relation entre le sujet grammatical et le verbe.

Valeur 1 : Un modal permet à l'énonciateur de porter un jugement sur le sujet grammatical.

Ex: *On Mondays, Tina can work as a spy.*
▶ Le lundi, Tina peut exercer le métier d'espionne. (elle en a la possibilité)

Valeur 2 : Un modal permet à l'énonciateur de prendre position sur les chances de réalisation d'une action.

Ex: *The manager may lie if I call him.*
▶ Il se peut que le gérant mente si je l'appelle. (Le propriétaire n'en est pas sûr).

Généralités sur l'emploi des modaux

- **Ils ne prennent pas de –s à la 3ème personne du singulier.**
- **Ils n'ont pas d'infinitif : to ~~can~~**
- **Ils sont toujours suivis d'une base verbale.**
- **Ils ne prennent pas de *do* / *does* / *did* aux formes interrogatives et négatives.**
- **Formes négatives contractées :**

Ex: *cannot* ▶ *can't* *must not* ▶ *mustn't*

Les modaux - valeur 1

a) La capacité (pouvoir ou savoir) :

• ***can, cannot* / *can't* au présent**

Ex: *Tina can assess the different places she visits.*
▶ Tina sait évaluer les différents endroits dans lesquels elle se rend.

• ***could, could not* / *couldn't* au passé**

Ex: *Tina said she could handle the job.*
▶ Tina a dit qu'elle était capable de faire le travail.

b) La permission : *can* / *may*

Ex: *You can / may start spying.*
▶ Vous pouvez commencer à espionner.

c) L'obligation : *must*

Ex: *But you must be discreet!*
▶ Mais vous devez être discrète !

d) Le conseil : *should*

Ex: *You should wear a wig.*
▶ Vous devriez porter une perruque.

e) L'interdiction : *mustn't*

Ex: *You mustn't tell anyone about your job.*
▶ Vous ne devez parler à personne de cet emploi.

Les modaux - valeur 2

Les chances de réalisation vont du quasi-certain au presque impossible : *must* - *should* - *will* - *may* - *could* - *might* - *can't*

Ex: *Tina **must** be at the restaurant now.*
▶ Tina doit être au restaurant en ce moment.

Ex: *Tina **may** be at the restaurant now.*
▶ Il se peut que Tina soit au restaurant en ce moment. (c'est possible)

Ex: *Tina **could/might** be at the restaurant now.*
▶ Il se pourrait que Tina soit au restaurant en ce moment. (on peut l'imaginer)

Ex: *Tina **can't** be at the restaurant now.*
▶ Il est impossible que Tina soit au restaurant en ce moment. (ce n'est pas possible)

Les substituts des modaux

Puisque les modaux ne sont utilisables qu'au présent et au prétérit, il faut avoir recours à des substituts.

a) La capacité ou l'incapacité : *be able to.*

Ex: *He is not **able to** manage the store.*
▶ Il n'est pas capable de diriger le magasin.

b) La permission ou l'interdiction : *be allowed to* / *not be allowed to.*

Ex: *The manager will **be allowed to** stay.*
▶ Le gérant aura l'autorisation de rester.

c) L'obligation ou l'absence d'obligation : *have to* / *not have to*

Ex: *You will **have to** be more strict.*
▶ Il vous faudra être plus strict.

ENTRAÎNEZ-VOUS

1 Mettez les énoncés suivants à la forme négative puis à la forme interrogative.

a. She can meet unfriendly clerks.
b. She will write a report later.
c. Company owners should know about problems.
d. Owners would like objective information.

2 Dans les énoncés ci-dessous, repérez les modaux et donnez leur valeur.

éventualité • conseil • impossibilité • obligation

a. On Mondays, Tina can't see her family.
b. The owner might visit a store if he has doubts.
c. You must care about cleanliness. It's very important!
d. They should inform the owner.

3 Complétez avec *can*, *can't*, *must*, *mustn't*, *should* et *shouldn't*.

a. I … see you today. With all my work, my agenda is full.
b. But you … have some rest. It's absolutely necessary!
c. How … you say that?
d. You … have two jobs at the same time!
e. Perhaps I … think about it.
f. It's impossible! You … accept these working conditions.

4 Complétez avec les modaux suivants : *would*, *can't*, *may* et *must*.

a. The owner … visit this clothing store. It depends on Tina's report.
b. The owner … visit this clothing store. Tina's report is alarming.
c. The owner … visit this clothing store. He has got a bad cold.
d. The owner … visit this clothing store if he had some time.

5 Choisissez la forme qui convient.

a. You … come early. The shop opens in an hour. (mustn't / don't have to)
b. The manager … tell the truth if there were not so many conflicts within the company. (can / would be able to)
c. I'd like to … visit all my stores. But it's impossible, that's why I hire mystery shoppers. (can / be able to)

6 Traduisez.

a. Tina devra être discrète dans son nouvel emploi.
b. Je sais, je devrais porter des lunettes !
c. Puis-je vous téléphoner après ma visite chez Taco Bell ?
d. Les chiens ne sont pas autorisés dans ce magasin.

JEUX DE MOTS

1 Trouvez dans le texte p. 81 les équivalents des mots ci-dessous :

waiter – look for – sales assistant – customer – engaged – proprietor

2 Le nom *friendliness* est formé à partir de l'adjectif *friendly* et du *suffixe -ness*. Sur le même modèle, trouvez les noms correspondant aux adjectifs suivants : *rude / dirty / calm*.

Utilisez les adjectifs ou les noms obtenus pour compléter les phrases :

a. The manager was shocked at the salesgirl's …
b. The secret shopper found the restaurant a … place. She wouldn't recommend it!
c. The young assistant is always so … She can deal with the most difficult customers!

3 Complétez les phrases avec les mots du texte.

a. Before sending them on mission, mystery-shopping companies t… secret shoppers.
b. Mystery-shoppers can visit many places in the r… industry.
c. They p… useful information for the shop owners.
d. Shop owners need to understand why the s… go up or down in their stores.
e. If you've got free time, mystery-shopping will bring you some extra i…

D'UNE LANGUE À L'AUTRE

1 Observez les phrases suivantes et leur traduction et repérez comment on a traduit les modaux.

a. *The customers must be warmly welcomed.*
▸ Il faut accueillir les clients chaleureusement.

b. *The mystery-shopper will have to be discreet.*
▸ Il faudra que le client espion soit discret.

c. *This job may be well paid.*
▸ Il se peut que ce travail soit bien payé.

d. *The manager might be away next week.*
▸ Il se pourrait que la patron soit absent la semaine prochaine.

2 Traduisez en français en utilisant des tournures impersonnelles.

a. The shop owner may ask you to come for an interview.
b. The new sales assistant will have to be trained.
c. Customers might be surprised by the staff turnover.
d. A mystery shopper mustn't arouse suspicion from employees.

3 Traduisez en anglais.

a. Il faudra que les clients soient servis rapidement.
b. Il se peut qu'il vende sa vieille voiture sur Internet.
c. Il ne faut pas accepter de telles conditions de travail.
d. Il se pourrait que les ventes soient meilleures cette année.

ATELIER D'ÉCRITURE

© J.L.Leblanc/Stockphoto/REA

1 Complete the conversation between Kashlak and Jenny, a newly-recruited mystery-shopper. Use *should, must, can, shall, ...*

Kashlak: *You know you shouldn't wear eccentric ...*
Jenny: *Of course not. What do you suggest? What ... I wear?*
...

2 Answer the following questions in 80 words.
What do you think of people who turn themselves into advertising billboards? Would you be ready to do the same? Why?

Follow these steps:
- Introduce the subject.
- Then give the advantages people can expect from this experience.
- Next say whether you could do it or not and explain why.
- Finally, say what you think of advertising.

CONSEILS D'ÉCRITURE

- **Respectez le plan proposé.**
- **Utilisez les modaux dans la seconde étape de votre essai :** *can, may, must, might, will.*
- **Dans la troisième partie, donnez au moins une raison pour justifier votre position.**

ADJECTIFS

early ▶ *tôt*
free ▶ *libre, gratuit*
hard ▶ *difficile*
weird ▶ *étrange*
well-lit ▶ *bien éclairé*

NOMS

attempt ▶ *tentative*
auction ▶ *vente aux enchères*
billboards ▶ *panneaux d'affichage*
cleanliness ▶ *propreté*
customer ▶ *client*
department store ▶ *grand magasin*
dress code ▶ *code vestimentaire*
forehead ▶ *front*
friendliness ▶ *gentillesse*
full time ▶ *temps plein*
income ▶ *revenu*
part time ▶ *temps partiel*
retail shop ▶ *commerce de détail*
sales assistant ▶ *vendeur(se)*
shopper ▶ *acheteur*
space ▶ *espace*

VERBES

advertise ▶ *faire de la publicité*
assesss ▶ *évaluer*
deal with ▶ *avoir affaire à*
deliver ▶ *livrer*
earn ▶ *gagner de l'argent*
fulfill ▶ *accomplir, réaliser*
include ▶ *comprendre, inclure*
look for ▶ *chercher*
look ▶ *avoir l'air*
make sure ▶ *s'assurer*
own ▶ *posséder*
pretend ▶ *faire semblant*
provide ▶ *fournir*
rate ▶ *évaluer*
search ▶ *chercher*
sell ▶ *vendre*
set up ▶ *créer, monter (une entreprise)*
snore ▶ *ronfler*
train ▶ *former*
turn oneself into ▶ *se transformer en*

AUTRES

although ▶ *bien que*
in the field ▶ *sur le terrain*
most of ▶ *la plupart de*
rather than ▶ *plutôt que*

Exercices

1 Trouvez dans le lexique les contraires des mots suivants *ordinary* / *dark* / *late* / *busy* / *easy*. Utilisez les contraires pour compléter les phrases.

a. Some customers like to arrive … at the supermarket.
b. She wants other people to look at her, that's why she wears … clothes.
c. Do you find it … to deal with difficult customers?
d. People will feel safer if the supermarket car park is … .
e. She doesn't have much … time to do her shopping.

2 Associez les mots de la colonne A à ceux de la colonne B pour faire des mots composés.

A.	B.
- advertising	- boy
- dress	- service
- after sales	- shop
- retail	- billboard
- sales	- assistant
- delivery.	- code.

3 Utilisez les mots du lexique pour compléter ce paragraphe.

There's a lot to do in a retail shop. The owner and the … arrive early at the shop. First they check the … of the place, then they make sure they can … customers with all their products. They also change the … to inform clients about new products or special discounts. Soon it's time to open the shop: clients will come because they appreciate the sellers'… as well as the quality of their products.

4 Complétez avec les verbes du lexique..

a. What do you do to ... a living?
b. I ... household goods in a big store.
c. It's not an easy job.You must always ... smart.
d. You must also be able to ... all kinds of customers.
e. You must ... your boss is always pleased with your work.
f. One day I hope I will ... my own shop.

Shopping on-line

"If only the Internet had been around when my children were growing up," says Sandie Hurford, a 49-year-old mother of four. "Women today have never had it so good. I've bought so many pairs of football boots and school uniforms that I've had my surfeit of[1] shopping. I find shopping on-line much less of a chore[2]." In fact, the more Mrs Hurford shops on-line, the more she likes it. "I work, so I don't want to spend my time queuing up to get into shops or car parks. The Salisbury's delivery charge is only £5, and for the pleasure of not having to go for a trolley load of groceries, that is the most tremendous bargain ever."

Meanwhile, Mrs Hurford's boss, John Maslen, 32, likes the Internet for window shopping. "Even if I don't buy anything, I tend to surf, especially for computers and travel. I now see the Internet, rather than the high street, as my first resource for shopping."

A study from Sussex University reports that women have become fast and efficient shoppers on-line. They don't waste time browsing[3]. They just get on with the job.

Men are starting to browse for pleasure. They find buying on-line more enjoyable because it removes much of the pain: no driving into town, no hassle[4] about where to park. Men also prove to be the secret Internet spenders. A recent survey reveals that men are seven times more likely than women to spend up to £1,000 online, while one man in 20 admits to having splurged[5] £5,000 or more on items such as cars and luxury holidays.

Conventional shopping roles are now being reversed and sons are teaching their mothers how to shop."Using price-comparison sites is something my 17-year-old son has taught me," Mrs Hurford says.

The Internet has the power to change lives for the better. Mark Sykes, a 32-year-old IT consultant[6], is typical: "I get better value shopping on-line and it's less hassle. It's also more of a pleasure, and it's more relaxing." He's not the only one to have discovered this, as Peter Green confirms: "During the past three months, I've bought DIY[7] materials, an oven, a fridge, CDs, wine and books. I'd buy everything online if I could."

Sunday Times, February 29 2004 (adapted)

WORDS:

1 I have had my surfeit of … : *J'ai eu plus que ma part de …*
2 a chore : *une corvée*
3 to browse : *surfer (d'un site à l'autre)*
4 hassle : *tracas*
5 to splurge (money) : *dépenser sans compter*
6 IT consultant (Information Technology): *spécialiste en informatique*
7 DIY : (Do It Yourself) : *le bricolage*

A Répondez en français aux questions suivantes. 8 pts

1. Quel est le regret de Sandie lorsqu'elle évoque ses achats d'autrefois ? **1 pt**
2. Pour quelles raisons aime-t-elle maintenant acheter sur Internet ? **1,5 pt**
3. Comment John Maslen utilise-t-il Internet ? Quels sont ses centres d'intérêt ? **1 pt**
4. Que révèle une étude de l'université du Sussex concernant le comportement d'achat sur Internet des femmes ? **1 pt**
5. Qu'en est-il du comportement masculin en ce qui concerne les achats sur Internet ? **1,5 pt**
6. Qui des hommes ou des femmes dépense le plus sur Internet ? Justifiez votre réponse avec des exemples. **1 pt**
7. Donnez le point de vue de Mark Sykes sur les achats sur Internet. **1 pt**

B Traduisez en français *"Conventional shopping …" "… Mrs Hurford says"*. (lignes 32 à 35). 4 pts

C Recopiez le paragraphe suivant en mettant les verbes entre parenthèses à la forme exigée par le contexte. 4 pts

Barbara seems almost programmed to enjoy (shop). (motivate) by pleasure, she usually (do) it for fun or on impulse. When she (meet) her husband five years ago, Barbara (not know) how to shop on-line. Since then, she (spend) more and more time on the Internet. Now, she likes (browse) for pleasure, and (feel) more relaxed.

D Write 80 words in English about the advantages and / or the risks of shopping on-line. 4 pts

© D.Bragg/Everynightimages/Alamy

My job is my passion

© Granier/Bios

Speaking

- Describe the two photos.
- What jobs do these men do? Are they usual jobs?
- Imagine why they chose them.
- Would you like to do one of these jobs? Why or why?

STREET TALK

The cyclone cowboy

© Warren Faidley/Hachette

1 Listen to these word from the interview.

- storm chaser • tornadoes
- shoot • lightning • hailstorm
- adventure • uncertainty
- challenge • achieving
- intriguing

2 Listen to Warren and fill in your questionnaire.

Photo by **Warren Faidley**, USA

I The dream job

© P.Bourrier/Maxppp

It may be every little boy's and girl's dream job–eating chocolate and sweets all day. But chocolate tasters are serious and passionate about chocolate.

Chloe Doutre-Roussel, confectionery[1] buyer for Fortnum and Mason, the London luxury store, starts work at 5 a.m. each day to ensure that her taste buds[2] are in perfect condition.

"After I wake up, I sit with my laptop, surrounded by chocolate to taste," she says. "To do this properly[3], you need to be slightly hungry. You mustn't eat anything else beforehand and be far away from anything else with strong tastes or smells, like tea or coffee."

This is also not a job for greedy[4] people, she says: "You can't taste more than four to six chocolates properly at the same time. To be good at this job you need a lot of discipline, just like a wine connoisseur. When I was growing up, I spent my pocket money on dark and milk chocolate, tasting the difference. I've been working here for two years but I consider myself to have had 25 years' serious tasting behind me."

WORDS:

1 confectionery : *confiseries*
2 taste buds : *papilles gustatives*
3 properly : *correctement*
4 greedy : *gourmand*

FEEDBACK

1. What is Chloe Doutre-Roussel's specialised in?
2. What is the best time for her to start work? Why?
3. Can you say what her working conditions are like?
4. Can Chloe have a full breakfast before she starts work? Justify.
5. What food would be incompatible with her work?
6. Why is chocolate tasting like wine tasting?
7. How has she become such an experienced taster?

2 My passion for computers

© W. Faidley/Picture Group ; M. Okoniewski/Gamma

I have a passion for computers. It all started when I was ten, and we got our first computer at home.

It was an impressive machine in those days, an XT with a 10 MB hard disk. First, I loved playing games, but soon I started to learn how to program. Very quickly, I got addicted to writing programs, I could make the computer do what I liked!

When I was 15, I discovered the Internet and realised that this network of millions of computers was even better! You can let your own machine do what you like, you can show what you are doing to millions of other people and spread what you write very easily. It's an absolute superior means of communication.

At 22, I've just started my first job which involves the Internet and security. I have no car, but I have four computers, and I hope to start my own Internet business eventually. I follow my passion and have not regretted it yet!

Ward Vandewege, Belgium

FEEDBACK

1 ▸ What happened when Ward was ten?
2 ▸ What did he use the computer for?
3 ▸ Pick out the expression meaning: "I couldn't live without working on my computer".
4 ▸ Why was the Internet a big discovery for Ward when he was 15?
5 ▸ Does his passion play an important part in his life? Justify.
6 ▸ What about you? Do you have a passion? What for?

3 Working with dolphins

© A. Kurt/Jacana

I work on a boat that takes people to the Bahamas to see the wild dolphins.

Swimming with wild dolphins and diving in the Bahamas is an incredible experience, but sharing the excitement and enthusiasm with passengers is even better. One day one passenger was so excited that she almost knocked me over as I came out of the water.

The most difficult thing about working on any boat is the very limited amount of personal space. Our crew shares cabins with passengers.

I've learned to work well as part of a team and to be flexible and adapt to new situations and personalities. This job also gives me the opportunity to meet people from different countries, cultures, and backgrounds. It may sound like a lot of fun, but it is also a lot of hard work. If you offered me all the money in the world to work in an office, I'd still prefer to be here.

www.wilddolphincharters.com. Ben Nerney

FEEDBACK

1 ▸ What is the boy's job?
2 ▸ Does he work on a fishing boat or on a pleasure boat? Justify.
3 ▸ Is he sometimes surprised by the passengers' reactions? Justify.
4 ▸ Pick out the advantages and drawbacks of the job.
5 ▸ Pick out the sentence showing that he is really happy with his job.

Comprehension

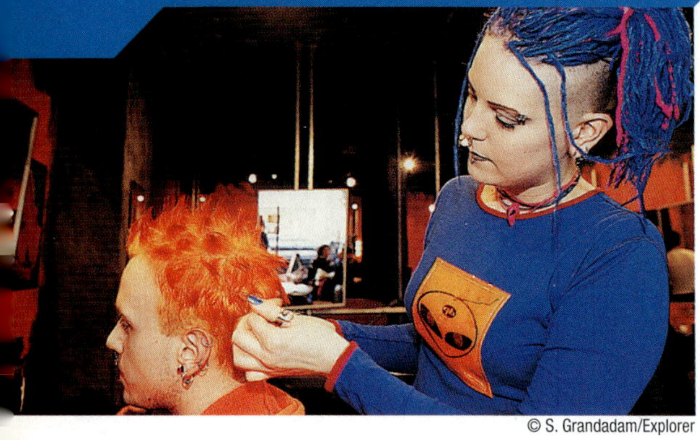

© S. Grandadam/Explorer

Before you read

1. Describe the pictures.
2. Would you like to do this job? Justify.

Read the text

3. Who is who?
   - David Newman
   - Charles Worthington
   - Andrea Watson
4. Say as much as you can about the main character: name, age, birth place, workplace.
5. Locate his native place on a map and say if it is an island, a country, or a town.
6. Put these events of the narrator's life into chronological order:
   - He started working for a stylist in London.
   - He worked in a salon in Surbiton, Surrey.
   - He began a four-year apprenticeship.
   - He travelled round Europe.
   - He moved to England.
   - He became the artistic and training manager.
   - He did the L'Oreal colour degree.

Read down to line 23

7. Pick out elements showing that it was the right job for him.
8. Did his mother want him to be a journalist? Justify.
9. How long did he work in his native place?
10. Pick out the reason why he went to work in London.
11. What do Australians usually do when they leave their country?
12. How did he come to know about the job in London? What is his position in the salon today?

Read the end of the text

13. Pick out the best points, then the worst points of the job.
14. Can a hairdresser make a lot of money? Justify.
15. What is David's advice?
16. Pick out the qualities mentioned by David. Which one do you think is most important for the job?

ALLEZ PLUS LOIN

1 Les mots *originally* (ligne 2), *regarded* (ligne 10) sont des mots transparents. Trouvez une autre traduction que la traduction littérale qui serait maladroite.

2 *I worked my way up in the company* (ligne 17). D'après le contexte (fin de la phrase) et le sens de *up*, le narrateur a-t-il changé de poste dans la société ? ▸ **FICHE** p. 75

3 *Fit your lunch in when you can* (ligne 29). D'après le contexte, cela signifie-t-il qu'il prenait tout son temps pour déjeuner ou au contraire qu'il avait à peine le temps de déjeuner ?

4 *Once you are qualified and have graduated to stylist* (lignes 31/32). *Qualified* est un mot transparent, quel sens peut avoir *graduated* qui en est un synonyme?

5 Le mot *endless* (ligne 33) est un adjectif composé du nom *end* et du suffixe - *less*. Qu'exprime ce suffixe ? Traduisez cet adjectif. ▸ **FICHE** p. 75

RÉSUMEZ

1 **Ecoutez l'enregistrement une fois et résumez en anglais.**

- David Newman - hairdressing - Tasmania
- eight years - moved - England - stayed - salon
- then - job - stylist - London
- worked his way up - company - manager
- although - job - tiring
- six days a week - break - lunchtime
- but - positive - tells himself - going to - great day

2 **Résumez en français.**

1. Que savez-vous de David Newman?
2. Citez les étapes successives de sa formation et de sa carrière.
3. Quels conseils donne-t-il à ceux qui veulent faire de la coiffure leur métier ?

Grammaire en contexte

1. **Repérez les pronoms relatifs dans les segments de phrases suivants :**
   The atmosphere, which was great, made me happy. (l. 1)
   My advice to those who hope to have a career … (l. 34-35)
2. **Donnez l'antécédent de chaque relatif.**
3. **Dites pourquoi les relatifs sont différents.**
4. **Relevez les deux autres relatifs dans le premier paragraphe.**

A brush with glamour

David Newman, 34, who works with Charles Worthington in London, talks to the journalist ANDREA WATSON

The minute I walked into a salon, I knew it was what I wanted to do. The atmosphere, which was great, made me happy. It was in Tasmania, where I was born, and though originally I wanted to be a journalist, my mother suggested I had more of an eye for fashion.

© Eshet/La Photothèque

I began a four-year apprenticeship, going to college one day a week. By my second year, I was cutting hair and started to build up regular clients. After about eight years I moved to England where my grandmother was born.

British hairdressers were regarded as world leaders and although I came from a small town, I liked the idea of big cities and wanted to come over and see what was happening. I did the normal Australian thing and travelled round Europe and then worked for a year in a salon in Surbiton, Surrey.

One year later, a friend told me about a vacancy for a stylist in London. I worked my way up in the company and am now the artistic and training manager. That means I cut and colour hair two afternoons a week and am responsible for all the training and the artistic direction of the team which does our fashion shows. I am also in charge of the colour direction. Last year, I did the L'Oreal colour degree.

The best days are when someone says you've changed their life! And I love the people I work with and meet. The worst side of the job is standing on your feet all day.

Many people work a nine-hour day, six days a week, but there are days when you finish at 8 p.m. and fit your lunch in when you can. I've never worked in a salon where there's an official break - it's a luxury.

The pay for an apprentice is about £75 a week rising to £85. Once you are qualified and have graduated to stylist it jumps to £150, and from there you can earn commission on the amount of clients and the colours, and then the salary opportunities are endless.

My motto is: be positive. I always tell myself I'm going to have a great day. My advice to those who hope to have a career in hairdressing is: get work experience - approach your local salon and ask to do a couple of days' observation. If you are dynamic, patient, creative and willing to learn, this is a job for you.

The Express

Les propositions relatives

Définition

Les propositions relatives viennent compléter un groupe nominal.
Elles sont introduites par des relatifs :
who / whom / which / whose / that ou Ø.

Choix du relatif

Le choix du relatif dépend :

- **du groupe nominal (l'antécédent peut être humain ou non humain)**
- **de la fonction du relatif (sujet ou complément)**

Antécédent humain

- **Fonction sujet : *who***

Ex: *The woman **who** is sitting next to the door is a regular customer.*
▸ La femme qui est assise près de la porte est une cliente fidèle.

- **Fonction complément : *who(m)* / *that* / Ø**

Ex: *The little girl **who(m) / that / Ø** you've just seen is pleased with her new haircut.*
▸ La petite fille que tu viens de voir est très contente de sa nouvelle coupe.

Antécédent non humain

- **Fonction sujet : *that* / *which***

Ex: *This is the kind of colour **that / which** lasts one month.*
▸ C'est le genre de couleur qui dure un mois.

- **Fonction complément : *that* / *which* / Ø**

Ex: *This is the kind of haircut **that / which / Ø** I like.*
▸ C'est le genre de coupe que j'aime.

Emploi de *whose*

Whose **indique une relation de possession entre l'antécédent et le nom qui suit.**

Whose **n'est jamais suivi d'un déterminant mais directement d'un nom (Ø + nom).**

Ex: *This is the little girl **whose Ø mother** is a singer.*
▸ C'est la petite fille dont la mère est chanteuse.

Emploi de *what* et *which*

Ils permettent de traduire "ce que", "ce qui".

- ***What*** **annonce ce qui suit.**

Ex: *What I like best is hairdressing.*
▸ Ce que je préfère, c'est la coiffure.

- ***Which*** **reprend ce qui précède.**

Ex: *I got a job in a hairdressing salon, **which** pleased my parents.*
▸ J'ai obtenu un emploi dans un salon de coiffure, ce qui fit plaisir à mes parents.

Emploi de *where*, *when* et *why*

Ils s'emploient lorsque l'antécédent est :

- **un lieu (*where*)**
- **un moment (*when*)**
- **une cause (*why*)**

Ex: *Tasmania is the country **where** I was born.*
▸ La Tasmanie est le pays où je suis né.

Ex: *You were late the day **when** you started working.*
▸ Tu étais en retard le jour où tu as commencé à travailler.

Ex: *That's the reason **why** you were dismissed.*
▸ C'est la raison pour laquelle tu as été renvoyé.

ENTRAÎNEZ-VOUS

1 Donnez : la fonction du pronom relatif (sujet ou complément) et dites si l'antécédent est humain ou non humain.

a. The man who came yesterday is one of your friends.
b. Bob, who is my best friend, wants to give up his job.
c. This is the kind of job which can be very tiring.
d. This job, which I liked a few years ago, is awful now!

2 Complétez avec *who* ou *which*.

a. Betty is exactly the person … can help you. She can come every day.
b. Her mother, … disapproved of her decision, called me yesterday evening.
c. This job, … is in a trendy salon, is well-paid.
d. The flat … is next to the salon is nice. She could rent it.

3 Reliez les deux énoncés avec le relatif entre parenthèses.

a. The man left without paying. He was in a hurry. (*who*)
b. I haven't seen the job advertisement. It was in the evening newspaper. (*which*)
c. The man is my brother. He wants to leave the salon before 10. (*who*)
d. His timetable would frighten you. It is very full. (*which*)

4 Reliez les énoncés avec *whose*.

a. The girl would like to work in my salon. Her C.V. is excellent.
b. The hairdresser is a man. His salon is next to my house.
c. The little boy does not want a haircut. His mother has just left.

5 Traduisez.

a. Ce n'est pas ce que je voulais.
b. Il m'a dit que j'aurais un emploi bien payé, ce qui n'est pas vrai.
c. Connais-tu la raison pour laquelle elle n'a pas cet emploi ?
d. Je me souviens seulement du jour où elle est allée à son entretien d'embauche.

JEUX DE MOTS

1 Le suffixe *-less* transforme un nom en adjectif et a un sens privatif. Complétez les phrases.

Ex: A story without an end is endless.
A person without money / a job / a father / a car / a child is…

2 Décrivez les mots ci-dessous avec le suffixe *-ship*.

citizen - apprentice - relation - partner - friend
Ex: citizen - citizenship
Complétez les phrases avec les mots obtenus.

a. The student learnt a lot during his ... to a plumber.
b. He works well with his boss. They have a good …
c. John and Bill are inseparable. Their … has lasted for years.
d. David and Martha opened a hairdresser's together. Their … has been very successful.
e. His sense of ... is excellent. He is always helping his community.

3 Complétez avec la préposition appropriée :

for (2 fois) – around – from – to

a. David came ... an island in the south of Australia.
b. After college, he travelled ... Europe.
c. He moved ... England at the age of 20.
d. As soon as he arrived, he asked ... a job in hairdressing.
e. He became responsible ... the colour work.

Language skills

D'UNE LANGUE À L'AUTRE

1 Lisez les phrases suivantes et dites :

- **dans quelles phrases *what* et *which* sont des pronoms interrogatifs, puis observez leur traduction;**
- **dans quelles phrases ce sont des relatifs ayant pour antécédent un nom ou une proposition et observez leur traduction.**

a. *What made him change his mind?*
▸ Qu'est-ce qui lui a fait changer d'avis ?

b. *What was his motto?*
▸ Quelle était sa devise ?

c. *Hairdressing was what he wanted to do.*
▸ La coiffure était ce qu'il voulait faire.

d. *Which of these two colours do most customers prefer?*
▸ Laquelle de ces deux couleurs la plupart des clients préfèrent-ils ?

e. *He soon got regular clients, which was quite encouraging.*
▸ Il eut bientôt des clients réguliers, ce qui était très encourageant.

f. *His working days, which last nine hours, are exhausting.*
▸ Ses journées de travail, qui durent neuf heures, sont épuisantes.

2 Traduisez en français.

a. Which school did she go to?
b. What diploma has she got?
c. She has always known what she wanted to do.
d. She dreamt of becoming a stylist, which meant working very hard for several years.

ATELIER D'ÉCRITURE

1 Look at the drawing and say who is doing what. Use *who / which / where / when / whom / whose / why*

Ex: *Mrs Benson, the woman who is sitting next to the green-haired boy, would like a haircut. The man whose hair you dyed yesterday*

2 What do you think will be more important for you: your career or your personal and family life? Give your reasons. (60 to 80 words).
Follow these steps:

- First introduce the subject.
- Then, give the reasons why your career is important.
- Next, say why your personal life cannot be neglected.
- Finally, give your personal opinion: how you will try to keep a healthy balance between your career and your personal life.

CONSEILS D'ÉCRITURE

Utilisez le lexique suivant

- **pour parler de votre vie professionnelle :**
  earn money - have responsibilities - do something you like - use your skills - be part of a community - share your ideas with your colleagues…
- **pour parler de votre vie personnelle :**
  have time for yourself - have children - look after them - spend time with your family or friends - go on holiday - travel…
- **pour introduire votre opinion :**
  I think that… - personally…

Rédigez des propositions relatives en vous aidant de Language skills page 92.

ADJECTIFS

dark	*foncé*
dream	*de rêve*
endless	*interminable*
hard	*dur*
great	*exceptionnel*
wild	*sauvage*
hungry (be)	*faim (avoir)*
addicted (be)	*dépendant de (être)*
mad about (be)	*fou de (être)*

NOMS

advice	*conseils*
amount	*montant*
background	*milieu*
buyer	*acheteur*
career	*carrière*
crew	*équipage*
diving	*plongée*
sweets	*sucreries*
apprenticeship	*apprentissage*
fashion show	*defilé de mode*
foot (feet)	*pied(s)*
luxury	*luxe*
laptop	*ordinateur portatif*
means	*moyen*
side	*côté*

VERBES

build up	*se constituer*
cut	*couper*
earn	*gagner*
ensure	*assurer*
fit in	*intégrer*
follow	*suivre*
grow up	*grandir*
involve	*comporter*
jump	*sauter*
knock over	*renverser*
taste	*goûter*
move	*déménager*
need	*avoir besoin*
share	*partager*
spend	*dépenser*
spread	*faire circuler*

AUTRES

eventually	*finalement*
slightly	*légèrement*
still	*toujours*
though	*bien que*
yet	*encore*

Exercices

1 Associez les débuts de phrases 1 à 6 aux fins de phrases a à f.

1. Children…
2. The internet allows you to…
3. Music lovers…
4. Large families…
5. Fast drivers…
6. House prices…

a. … may knock someone over in their cars.
b. … move to bigger houses.
c. … grow up fast.
d. … spend a lot of money on cds.
e. … spread information.
f. … jumped last year.

2 Complétez avec l'adjectif approprié.

a. A beautiful house that everyone wants is a … house.
b. An exam which is difficult is a … exam.
c. An animal which is not domestic is a … animal.
d. A programme which goes on and on is an … programme.
e. A fantastic film is a … film.

3 Trouvez les noms correspondant aux indications suivantes.

a. The series of jobs you do in your life: …
b. Swimming under water: ...
c. Quantity: …
d. Purchaser: …
e. A portable computer: …
f. A team of people on a boat: …

4 Complétez avec un mot choisi dans la liste de la catégorie "Autres".

a. … he loved doing people's hair he wanted a rest.
b. He was … tired of working on his feet all day long.
c. He looked at lots of holiday brochures but … didn't know where to go.
d. … he decided to stay in London.

The life of a chef

Gary Rhodes, the presenter of "Masterchef" on BBC2, talked to Janine Hazlewood.

Gary is a workaholic who has an incredibly disciplined routine. It begins with a 4.30 a.m. alarm call, followed by half an hour's exercise before he zips off in his Porsche to City Rhodes or one of his three other restaurants in London, Manchester and Edinburgh. He's rarely home before 11 p.m. And on top of this there are the TV series to make and the books to write.

Gary didn't have a privileged childhood. He grew up on a council estate in Rainham, Kent, and is proud to have got where he is today through sheer hard work. He's devoted to his mum who raised him, his older brother and his sister, after their father walked out when Gary was six years old.

"When I was 14, Mum went back to work and I helped her by looking after and cooking for my little sister. It sounds funny but it was the best thing that happened to me. Having that responsibility made me stronger and I discovered something I was good at."

After leaving school with a few O levels, he got a place at a catering college[1]. He started work as a junior chef at the Hilton in Amsterdam. Highly ambitious, he set about working his way up the pecking order[2] and, at 26, became Head Chef at The Castle Hotel in Taunton, where he won a Michelin star. Later, he moved to The Greenhouse Restaurant in Mayfair where he gained a second Michelin star.

By then he and TV had discovered each other. "I've always loved TV and hope it goes on forever," says Gary but "the most important job for me is the restaurants. That's where I get my inspiration, and cooking with the lads in the kitchen keeps my feet on the ground."

At 41, he still feels he has much to prove. "If I can maintain the two Michelin stars at my London restaurants for another ten years, I hope I'll have respect from my peers[3] within the industry. That would be the highest compliment of all."

Family Circle, *June 2001*

WORDS:

1 catering college: *école hôtelière*
2 pecking order: *hiérarchie*
3 peers: *pairs (personne exerçant la même activité)*

A Répondez en français aux questions suivantes et justifiez vos réponses. 8 pts

1. Pourquoi l'emploi du temps quotidien de Gary Rhodes est-il si chargé ? **1 pt**
2. Gary ne vient pas d'un milieu aisé. Comment a-t-il néanmoins réussi ? **1 pt**
3. Dans quelles circonstances a-t-il découvert qu'il était doué en cuisine ? **1 pt**
4. Quelles sont les trois étapes qui ont marqué le début de la carrière de Gary ? **3 pts**
5. Qu'est-ce qui est le plus important pour Gary : son émission à la télévision ou son travail dans le restaurant ? Pourquoi ? Donnez deux raisons. **2 pts**

B Traduisez en français le dernier paragraphe. 4 pts

C Complétez avec le pronom relatif qui convient. 4 pts

1. That man, ... didn't have a privileged childhood, is now the manager of three restaurants in London.
2. He never returned to the restaurant ... he started as a junior chef.
3. Since 2000 he has been the presenter of "Masterchef,"... is a cooking programme on BBC 2.
4. This chef, ... life is very busy, tries to spend the weekends with his family.

D Write about 80 words to answer the following question. 4 pts

Do you prefer eating in a traditional restaurant or in a fast-food restaurant? Give your reasons.

Le stage en entreprise

En classe de baccalauréat professionnel, les stages en entreprise prennent une place importante dans votre formation.

On pourra vous demander de décrire en anglais *"a typical day at work during your training period"*.

A. Servez-vous de cette fiche comme guide pour rédiger votre essai.

***Step one:* Introduction**

1. *When did you do your work experience?*
2. *Which company did you do it in?*

***Step two:* Your company**

3. *What was the name of the firm?*
4. *Where was it located?*
5. *What type of business was it?*
6. *Number of employees? (size of the company)*
7. *How did you get there? How long did it take?*

***Step three:* The department you worked in**

8. *Name of the department?*
9. *Your tutor, his position in the company?*
10. *Did you get on well with the people you worked with?*
11. *What were your working hours?*
12. *Did you have any breaks in the morning or in the afternoon?*
13. *What facilities were there in the company? (a cafeteria, a vending machine…)*

***Step four:* Your tasks**

14. *What different things did you do in the company? Make a list of the tasks. (Check your vocabulary in a dictionary!)*
15. *Did you stay in the same department or not?*
16. *What equipment did you use?*

***Step five:* Your assessment**

17. *Did you have any problems during your work experience?*
18. *What benefits did you draw from it?*
19. *Would you recommend this firm to another student?*

***Step six:* Conclusionn**

20. *What do you think about your work experience?*

B. Rédigez votre compte rendu.

- *Rédigez votre essai au prétérit en suivant les étapes ci-dessus.*
- *Utilisez des marqueurs de temps. (**Step three and four**)*
- *Pensez aux adverbes de fréquence. (**Step four**)*
- *N'employez pas un lexique trop spécialisé : le lecteur doit comprendre ce que vous avez fait.*
- *Essayez de donner un avis personnel éclairé sur votre stage.*

EXERCICE

1 Les paragraphes de ce compte rendu ont été mis dans le désordre. Retrouvez l'ordre indiqué en A p.97.

1. My tasks were quite varied. In the morning, I usually entered data into the computer. I also checked invoices and put them in different files. Then, in the afternoon, I always did some photocopying and sent faxes. I occasionally answered the phone, which I didn't like very much. Anyway, I became proficient in using a computer, the photocopier and the fax machine.

2. My place of work was situated in a small town in the suburbs of Rouen. It was a chemical factory of about 40 employees. Every day I had to take the train. The journey took about 20 minutes, and then I walked to the company. The train arrived early so I had plenty of time to get to work.

3. From November 2nd to December 23rd 2006, I did my work experience in a small company called Socomat.

4. I think I was lucky because my work experience wasn't a waste of time and it gave me a good idea of what real work is in a firm.

5. In my opinion, my work experience was really worthwhile and useful. I put into practice the things I had learned at school and I also learned how to deal with new accounting software. I feel I fitted quite easily into the team and they were very friendly.

6. I worked in the accounts department which was not very large. There were four people working there and my supervisor Mrs Couder was the chief accountant. I got on very well with her because she always gave me clear instructions and she was patient. She didn't mind answering my questions. In the morning, I started at 8.30 and I finished at 4.30 pm. We had two twenty-minute breaks during the day. We sometimes went to the cafeteria and it gave me the opportunity to meet other people and to chat with younger colleagues.

2 Lisez les expressions suivantes et indiquez par + celles que vous utiliseriez pour faire ressortir les points positifs et par – celles que vous utiliseriez pour indiquer les points négatifs de votre stage.

1. It was a waste of time.
2. I feel more confident.
3. I enjoyed the way…
4. I was left alone.
5. I didn't appreciate…
6. It was useful.
7. I wouldn't recommend it.
8. Everybody helped me.
9. I found it difficult to…
10. I learned a lot.

kit 9

© Stone/Getty

Write the right way

© Rex/Sipa

Speaking

- Describe the two photos (where, what, how)
- Compare the ways the three people are working.
- Which way do you usually write and why?
- Do you prefer sending letters or emails? Justify.

Are you reliable?

STREET TALK

© Judy Martinez/Hachette

1 Listen to these words from the interview.

- hire journalism • spirit
- covering • letter • dull
- formal • lack • industrious
- conscientious • articulate
- ingredients

2 Listen to David and fill in your questionnaire.

David, *The Sunday Times*, London, U.K.

1 Job ads

© SPL/Cosmos

WORDS:

1 consultancy: *cabinet d'expertise*
2 hardware: *machines*
3 allowance: *indemnité, allocation*
4 within commuting distance: *accès possible par transport en commun*

MOTORWAY MAINTENANCE TECHNICIANS AND ENGINEERS

Working for the country's leading consultancy[1] you will be an experienced Motorway Maintenance Engineer/Technician with significant experience in this field.
It is expected that you will be au fait with all hardware[2] aspects of motorway cabling, signals, control centres and motorway equipment. It is also hoped that you will be working in the South East and that you will be flexible on the work location.
Good rewards are on offer.

ASSISTANT MAINTENANCE SUPERVISOR

Electrical, Mechanical, Plumbing, and good Painting / Decorating skills required, to work in a 7-storey clothing retail store.
Basic salary £24,000 per annum, plus overtime, 25 days holiday, pension, travel season ticket allowance[3], health care, etc.
Please only apply if you live within commuting distance[4] of Piccadilly, SW London.

FEEDBACK

1. What job is advertised in the first ad?
2. Pick out the sentences referring to the advantages of the job?
3. Where in England will the applicants work?
4. Will they always work in the same place? Justify.
5. Will the workers get a high salary?
6. Which job is advertised in the second ad?
7. What place will the employee have to work in?
8. Which people should apply for the job?

2 On-line Forum

Delete | Answer | Answer all | Forward

What are your worst job interview experiences? Any mistakes you really regret making?

Girl-From-Mars - 08:05 PM
I had an interview for Safeway[1] a couple of years ago and I didn't get the job. I was so bad! I wasn't prepared for answering difficult questions like "why do you want to work here?" and "why do you think you'll be suitable[2] to work here?" I talked really fast and very quietly. I kept mumbling[3] and that's never a good thing to do! I was very shy. I need a list of all these things NOT to do in interviews!

Helly - 08:15 PM
Don't go in thinking you know everything. Act as if you are willing to learn, even if you do know everything ;-). Dress properly and do not go in looking scruffy[4]. Prepare questions to ask them so you sound as if you are interested. Don't sit there completely quiet or answer with just "yes / no" answers.

WORDS:
1 Safeway: *chaîne de supermarché britannique*
2 Be suitable: *convenir*
3 mumbling: *marmonner*
4 scruffy: *débraillé*

FEEDBACK

1 ▸ What are the people speaking about on this forum?
2 ▸ Why was the Girl-From-Mars "so bad"during her interview for Safeway?
3 ▸ Pick out the two questions asked by the interviewer.
4 ▸ What happened then? Why?
5 ▸ Why wasn't she satisfied with the way she spoke?
6 ▸ What would be useful for her next interviews?
7 ▸ According to Helly, what do you have to show your interviewer?
8 ▸ Does she think clothes are important? Justify.
9 ▸ How should the applicant behave?

© F.Wartenberg/Picturepress/StudioX

3 Washington Post survey

The Washington Post asked top personnel executives for stories of unusual behavior by job applicants. Here are some of their best (or worst) examples.

1. Stretched out on the floor to fill out the job application.
2. Brought her large dog to the interview.
3. Chewed bubble gum and constantly blew bubbles.
4. Wore a Walkman and said she could listen to me and the music at the same time.
5. Announced she hadn't had lunch and proceeded to eat a hamburger and French fries in the interviewer's office.
6. Wouldn't get out of the chair until I would hire him. I had to call the police.
7. Stood up and started tap dancing around my office when I asked him about his hobbies.
8. Pulled out a Polaroid camera and snapped a flash picture of me. Said he collected photos of everyone who interviewed him.
9. Came to the interview with a moped and left it in the reception area. He didn't want it to get stolen, and stated that he would require indoor parking for the moped.

WORDS:
1 executives: *cadres*
2 behavior: *comportement*
3 tap dancing: *faire des claquettes*

FEEDBACK

1 ▸ Who took part in the Washington Post survey?
2 ▸ What were they asked to do?
3 ▸ What can't applicants take to interviews?
4 ▸ What did one interviewer have to do to get rid of (*se débarrasser*) an applicant?
5 ▸ What did an applicant do with his camera? Why?
6 ▸ What would the last person require from the company if he were recruited?
7 ▸ Which is the funniest story? Why?

Comprehension

© M.Gaillard/REA

Look at the letter

1. Which of the two job ads, on page 100, is Patty interested in?
2. Find out:
   - the sender's name and address;
   - the addressee's name and address;
   - the date;
   - the reference.
3. Match the paragraphs of the letter with the headings:
   - the applicant's qualifications and abilities;
   - the purpose of the letter;
   - hopes for an appointment.

Read paragraphs 1 and 2

4. How did Patty know that the store needed someone with a variety of skills?
5. Why does she know the workplace so well?
6. Pick out elements showing that she really wants to work with this company.
7. What is her main qualification?
8. What does she expect from this job?
9. Is she an expert at electrics?
10. Pick out the two qualities she mentions about herself.

Read paragraphs 3 and 4

11. Pick out the reasons showing that working in the store is not a problem for Patty.
12. What does she plan to do: carry on working with her father or try something new?
13. Does she think she is physically fit for the job? Justify.
14. What does she expect from the appointment with the company employer?
15. Is she just going to wait for the employer to call her?

ALLEZ PLUS LOIN

1 Une des traductions de *fields* (ligne 7) est "champs". D'après le contexte, quelle traduction pourriez-vous proposer ici ?

2 Sachant que le nom *wire* signifie fil électrique, que signifie le verbe *wire* ? Proposez maintenant une traduction pour le verbe *rewire* (ligne 9).

3 Dans le § 3, quel est l'adjectif qui montre que l'on ne s'attend pas à voir une femme postuler pour ce type d'emploi ? Décomposez-le et proposez une traduction.
▶ **FICHE** p. 76

RÉSUMEZ

1 Ecoutez l'enregistrement et résumez en anglais.

- Patty Moore - 20-year-old girl - qualified - plumber
- apply - maintenance job - clothing retail store
- electrical - mechanical - plumbing - painting - decorating - skills - needed - part - team
- letter - explains - can - many things
- for instance - rewire - decorate - house
- practises - many - sports - strong - enough - hard
- hopes - get - appointment - persuade - employer - right

2 Résumez en français.

1. Comment Patty a-t-elle su que le magasin recherchait quelqu'un ?
2. Dans quels secteurs d'activité a-t-elle de l'expérience ?
3. Quels atouts met-elle en avant dans sa lettre ?

Grammaire en contexte

1. Relevez les formes verbales dans ces segments de phrase :

a) *... I have done a vocational course.*

b) *...I have picked up so many skills.*

2. De quoi sont-elles composées ?

3. Trouvez deux autres formes verbales similaires dans le paragraphe 2.

4. Choisissez une des propositions permettant de justifier l'emploi de ces formes :

a) action se situant dans le présent

b) action se situant dans le passé

c) lien entre le passé et présent

An application letter

Patty Moore
7, Wembley Hill
Wembley,
HA9 0WS
Mobile : 0786 564 345

© M. Gaillard/Réa

Action Technical Services Ltd
Recruitment Administration
Action House,
35 - 41 Montagu Street,
Kettering Northamptonshire
NN16 8XG

Thursday, July 21st 2005

Job ref: RAC0954506

Dir Sir,

I was really interested to see your advertisement for someone with Electrical, Mechanical, Plumbing, and Painting / Decorating skills to work in a 7-storey clothing retail store in London. I know your store well as I live within commuting distance in Wembley and often go shopping there. The building is beautiful and I would feel honoured to be part of the team looking after it.

I think I am just the person you are looking for. You see, I have just qualified as a plumber (City and Guilds 6089, NVQ[1] level 2) and before going on to qualify at level 3, I would like to gain experience in other fields. That is why I am answering your ad. I am not a qualified electrician but I have done a vocational course in basic electrics and I have already helped my uncle, a NICEIC[2] registered electrician, rewire several houses. So, I can assure you I know what I am doing. If I do not know how to do something I always say so and I am not afraid of hard work. In fact, I thrive on it. I am a fast learner, which is why I have picked up so many new skills.

I realize it is unusual for a woman to want to do work like this, but I have always done handy jobs[3], both around the house and professionally. My father has his own house-decorating business and I have been helping him out since the age of 15. However, I am now 20 years old and want to make my own way in life. Physically I am strong and in tiptop condition thanks to all the sport I do: boxing, marathon running and weightlifting.

I would greatly appreciate your agreeing to see me. That way I can persuade you first hand how well I would fit into your project. Do not hesitate to get in touch with me if you need any more information. I will call you up in a few days to see if we could arrange an appointment. I do hope you will seriously consider my application.

Looking forward to hearing from you soon,

Yours sincerely,

Patty Moore

WORDS:

1 NVQ: *National Vocational Qualification*
2 NICEIC: *National Inspection Council for Electrical Installation Contractor*
3 handy jobs: *petits travaux*

Have + V-en (ou present perfect)

Have + V-en

Cet aspect permet de faire le lien entre le présent (*have*) et le passé (*V-en*). *V-en* symbolise le participe passé.

Il exprime le résultat d'une action passée et en fait un bilan.

Ex: *Come and have a look!*
*Patty **has painted** the kitchen.*
▸ Viens voir ! Patty a peint la cuisine.
(Je peux voir maintenant le résultat du travail de Patty.)

Il exprime une continuité de l'action commencée dans le passé et se poursuivant dans le présent.

Ex: *Patty's father **has worked** in London for years.*
▸ Le père de Patty travaille à Londres depuis des années.
(Le fait qu'il travaille à Londres est toujours vrai au moment présent.)

Have been + V-ing

L'énonciateur fait un commentaire sur le sujet grammatical.

Ex: *Patty's uncle **has been rewiring** his house.*
That is why he looks so tired.
▸ L'oncle de Patty a refait l'installation électrique de sa maison. C'est la raison pour laquelle il est si fatigué.
(Il ne s'agit pas d'une information neutre. Je m'intéresse à l'oncle de Patty.)

Comparons avec la forme "simple".

Ex: *Patty's uncle **has rewired** his house.*
▸ L'oncle de Patty a refait l'installation électrique de sa maison.
(Il s'agit d'une simple information. Je m'intéresse au résultat de son travail.)

Emploi de *since* et *for*

***Since* est utilisé pour indiquer un point de départ.**

Ex: *She has worked at the agency **since** June.*
▸ Elle travaille à l'agence depuis juin.
(Elle a commencé en juin et y travaille toujours.)

***For* est utilisé pour indiquer une durée.**

Ex: *She has been at the agency **for** 6 months.*
▸ Elle est à l'agence depuis 6 mois.
(Elle est arrivée il y a 6 mois et s'y trouve toujours maintenant.)

Vous remarquez que dans ces deux cas, *have + V-en* se traduit en français par le présent.

ATTENTION

***For* s'utilise également avec *V-ed* (prétérit). Il indique toujours une durée mais sans lien avec le présent et dans ce cas il se traduit par "pendant".**

Ex: *She **worked** with her father **for** 5 years*
▸ Elle a travaillé avec son père pendant 5 ans.
(Elle ne travaille plus avec son père.)

ENTRAÎNEZ-VOUS

1 Complétez avec *for* ou *since*.

a. She has been working … last night.
b. I have lived here … 20 years.
c. I have been waiting for my appointment … 2 o'clock.
d. I have been waiting for my appointment … 3 hours.
e. I have not seen my uncle … a couple of weeks.

2 Mettez les mots suivants dans l'ordre en mettant les verbes à la forme *have* + *V-en*.

a. send / letter / I / just / application / my / . /
b. retail / I / never / store / work / a / in / . /
c. answer / I / just / receive / an / . /
d. long / retail / how / you / store / work / in / this / ? /

3 Utilisez *have* + *V-en*, ou *V-ed*.

a. Patty (decide) to study plumbing a few years ago.
b. When she arrived at school, she (meet) another girl.
c. Patty and Jane (be) friends since they first met.
d. Last year, both of them (work) with plumbers for two weeks.
e. They are real friends; they (know) each other for two years.

4 Traduisez.

a. Le frère de Patty est électricien depuis 2 ans.
b. Il a travaillé en Australie pendant 3 mois. Puis il est rentré à Londres.
c. Il travaille chez Macy's depuis janvier. Et il étudie la plomberie depuis 3 semaines.

JEUX DE MOTS

1 Trouvez les synonymes des mots suivants dans le texte page 103.

a. big shop
b. search
c. be frightened
d. uncommon
e. convince

2 Trouvez les noms de métiers se rapportant aux activités suivantes.

a. electrics
b. mechanics
c. plumbing
d. painting
e. decorating

3 Reliez les éléments 1 à 4 aux éléments a à d pour faire des mots composés cohérents.

1. maintenance	a. application
2. job	b. distance
3. commuting	c. technician
4. retail	d. store

4 Associez les débuts de phrases 1 à 5 aux fins de phrases a à e.

1. Please do not hesitate...
2. I look forward...
3. I saw your advertisement in today's newspaper and...
4. I would be grateful if...
5. As you will see from my CV...

a. …I can speak two foreign languages.
b. …to hearing from you.
c. …you could send me more information about the job.
d. …to contact me.
e. …I would like to apply for the post of secretary.

D'UNE LANGUE À L'AUTRE

1 Lisez les phrases suivantes et dites par quels temps on peut traduire *have* + *V-en*.

a. *Patty has been forced to move.*
▶ Patty a été obligée de déménager

b. *Patty has been working in the store for 6 months.*
▶ Patty travaille dans le grand magasin depuis 6 mois.

c. *She has met very nice people.*
▶ Elle a rencontré des gens très sympathiques.

• ***Have* + *V-en* et *have been* + *V-ing* se traduisent généralement de la même manière en français.**

2 Lisez les phrases suivantes et dites :

• Par quel temps on traduit *have* + V-*en* lorsqu'il est précédé de l'expression : *it's the first / second / third time…*

• Par quelle expression on le traduit lorsqu'il est accompagné de l'adverbe "*just*" ;

a. *It's the first time she has come to work here.*
▶ C'est la première fois qu'elle travaille ici.

b. *She has just finished her studies.*
▶ Elle vient de terminer ses études.

3 Traduisez les phrases suivantes en français.

a. How long have you been helping your father?
b. It's the first time I have earned my living.
c. I have just bought a new CD player with my first salary.
d. She has moved to a larger flat.
e. She has been living there for a few weeks.

4 Traduisez en anglais.

a. Elle habite à côté du magasin depuis un mois.
b. Elle vient de refaire l'installation électrique de son appartement.
c. Ses collègues ont décidé de l'aider.
d. C'est la première fois qu'elle prépare un repas dans sa cuisine.
e. Elle est très fatiguée parce qu'elle a beaucoup travaillé.

ATELIER D'ÉCRITURE

1 Look at Patty in her new flat page 104. She is exhausted. Say why.

Wordbox:
• clean – rewire – paint – tidy up – wash – decorate
• floor – flat - walls – books – dishes – cup of tea

2 You have just read this advertisement in THE GUARDIAN and you are interested in the job. Write a letter of application.

> ***WANTED:*** *Sales Assistant*
> ***Organisation****: Harout Barin - Telephone: +44 (0) 20 7731 0546*
> *Street Address - 57A New King's Road - Fulham - London SW6*
>
> **JOB AD - ANTIQUE SHOP**
> Oriental antique shop in Fulham requires part-time sales assistant to work 2-3 days per week increasing to 5 days later in the year to cover Manager's maternity leave. Suitable applicants should have retail experience in a similar field, be motivated, energetic and computer literate.
>
> We are looking for a flexible person, who has a "hands on" approach, good customer skills and an interest in antiques.

Follow these steps:
• Be careful about the layout of the letter.
• Say who you are writing to.
• Write a short introduction (Say where you saw the advert)
• Then, give details about yourself (age, subjects studied at school, training period…)
• Add details of your interests, especially those related to the job advertised.
• Don't forget the signing off!
• Sign your letter.

CONSEILS D'ÉCRITURE

• **N'hésitez pas à chercher parmi les documents du kit pour vérifier et parfaire votre lettre.**

ADJECTIFS

flexible	*flexible, souple*
quiet	*calme*
scruffy	*débraillé*
shy	*timide*
strong	*fort*
tiptop	*excellent*
willing	*prêt, disposé*

NOMS

ad	*petite annonce*
allowance	*indemnité*
annum	*année*
answer	*réponse*
applicant	*candidat*
application	*candidature*
appointment	*rendez-vous*
behavior	*comportement*
cabling	*câblage*
clothing	*vêtements*
field	*domaine*
health	*santé*
mistakes	*erreurs*
overtime	*heures supplémentaires*
plumber	*plombier*
skills	*compétences*
store	*grand magasin*
reward	*récompense*
tap dancing	*claquettes*
weightlifting	*haltérophilie*
hardware	*matériel*

VERBES

answer	*répondre*
apply	*demander, postuler*
bring	*apporter*
chew	*mâcher*
fill out	*remplir*
gain	*gagner*
hire	*embaucher*
hope	*espérer*
mumble	*marmonner*
require	*nécessiter*
rewire	*refaire l'installation électrique*
snap	*prendre un instantané*
thrive	*réussir*

AUTRES

already	*déjà*
even	*même*
greatly	*beaucoup*

Exercices

1 Complétez avec des adjectifs.

a. Ask questions in the interview. Don't stay … .
b. Be careful about your clothes. If you look …, you won't be hired.
c. Finally, say that you are very … . You can work any time day or night.
d. She is very … because she does a lot of weightlifting.
e. I am in … condition because I practise kickboxing.

2 Complétez avec des verbes.

a. This ad looks interesting. You should ... for the job.
b. Could you … the job application, please?
c. A company will … you if you show you are the right person.
d. Don't … bubble gum during the job interview.
e. Finally, don't … . Speak clearly!

3 Complétez avec des noms.

a. ... is very important. Don't wear dirty jeans.
b. The basic salary is £24,000 per ....
c. I made a few … . For instance, I forgot to say goodbye.
d. Working in a retail … would be great!
e. I have an … with the employer today at 2 p.m.

4 Complétez avec des mots du lexique.

a. What … are required for this job?
b. None. But your … must be good.
c. When did you send in your ...?
d. A week ago. I … I'll get the job.
e. They say they will … 5 people.
f. If I am recruited, I'll do some … to stay in good shape.

A job interview

I went for an interview at one of the Technical Colleges in New York City. The job was to handle the college and departmental websites[1]. I brought everything with me, a CD with my web files, a back up[2] copy on a USB key, and handouts[3] outlining[4] my presentation. I arrived an hour before the meeting, so I stopped on the 8th and 9th floors to check out the classrooms and views outside the windows.

Approaching the time for the meeting, I went up to the 10th floor where the interview was going to be held. A woman asked me if I was there for the interview and commented, "What a day to have an interview." It was a very hot day.

In the interview room there were long tables facing a wide screen. I seated myself and prepared my materials. Then, the panel of seven started to come in one by one. I was getting nervous and self-conscious[5]. I was wondering what they were silently thinking of me.

The panel was completed and seated together with myself in front. The interview process began. I thought that we would talk about my work history first and then do my presentations, but it was the other way; the panel would ask questions as the interview went along. So, I put my CD in drive A. I looked at the screen and looked for a mouse. My thought was saying, "Oh no, No mouse! No regular keyboard!" I had to use a movable keyboard[6], which didn't seem to be working; I was not familiar with its functionality. It took me a while to figure out[7] how to work it and one of the members kindly assisted me. To make matters worse, I wasn't listening to the suggestion to just touch the screen to make it work. I wanted to have a good presentation without major problems. I still continued with my presentation, showed them my design. Only three of the panel asked questions.

After my presentation, I was given the opportunity to ask questions. I was still feeling upset and I could not think of a sensible one immediately. I asked only two, but I didn't think they were enough to complete the expected time for the interview process. The meeting ended.

WORDS:

1 departmental websites: *sites des départements*
2 back up: *sauvegarder*
3 handouts: *documents (à distribuer)*
4 outlining: *qui donnent un aperçu*
5 self-conscious: *gêné, intimidé*
6 movable keyboard: *écran tactile*
7 figure out: *réussir à comprendre*

A Répondez en français aux questions suivantes. Composez des phrases complètes et justifiez vos réponses. 8 pts

1. Quel est le sujet de ce document ?
2. Dites ce que vous savez de l'emploi pour lequel la jeune femme a postulé.
3. S'est-t-elle bien préparée à l'événement dont il est question?
4. Comment la pièce où a eu lieu cette rencontre a-t-elle été agencée ? Combien de personnes étaient présentes ? Dans quel état d'esprit la jeune femme se trouvait-elle ?
5. Quelle particularité de l'équipement informatique a perturbé la présentation de la postulante ? A-t-elle obtenu de l'aide ?
6. Après sa prestation sur l'ordinateur, que lui a-t-on demandé de faire ? Est-elle tout à fait satisfaite de ce qui s'est passé?

B Traduisez en français : "*I arrived an hour… it was a very hot day*". (lignes 6 à 13). 4 pts

C Mettez le verbe entre parenthèses au temps qui convient. 4 pts

1. How long ago you *(apply for)* this job ?
2. The personnel manager *(give)* her an appointment yesterday .
3. She *(write)* her covering letter for more than one hour now.
4. She *(not finish)* her CV yet.

D Write about 70 to 80 words in English to answer the following questions. 4 pts

- Have you ever had a summer job interview?
- How did you prepare yourself for it?
- Who did you meet?
- What did you have to speak about?
- How instructive was this experience?

© G. Girard/Contact Press Images

Getting to work

© Pictor International

Speaking

- When and where do you think the large photo was taken?
- Compare it to the small picture.
- List the vehicles you can see, then quote other ways of travelling.
- In which of these two places would you prefer to live? Say why.

STREET TALK

Driving is a bit silly

© H. Donnezan/Rapho

1 Listen to these words from the interview:

- slow moving • safe • visible
- Day Glo clothing • fluorescent
- lanes • by no means • fitness
- routine • cycle panniers • presentable

2 Listen to Sara and fill in your questionnaire

Sara, picture researcher, News International, London, U.K.

I BBC forum

Welcome to the BBC Forum

On the 17th of February, 2003, the London Congestion Charge was introduced by the Mayor, Ken Livingstone. London is the largest city in the world to have adopted congestion charging. Today it costs £8 to move around within the congestion charge zone between 7 a.m. and 6.30 p.m., Monday to Friday. Drivers can pay by telephone, text message, post, Internet, or in person at a retail outlet. Drivers are also able to purchase daily, weekly, monthly or annual passes. However, some vehicles like taxis and emergency services are exempt from the charge. Ken Livingstone says the scheme has been a great success and traffic has been cut by 18% and delays are down 30%.

© SPL/Cosmos

Your comments:

I totally disagree with the congestion charge. It only serves the purpose of the rich who can afford to drive their large gas-consuming cars freely around the zone while the rest of us have to suffer on crowded public transport.

Janet, London

The charge is great. I can now get around London far quicker than beforehand. The buses are much improved as well. This is the kind of measure that we should thank politicians for.

Tony, London

news.bbc.co.uk February, 2004

FEEDBACK

1 Do you think the London Congestion charge is:
- the amount of pollution Londoners suffer from;
- the amount of money every driver has to pay to get into London centre?

2 Find out information about the charge.
- How much? Where? Time of day? Days of the week?

3 Right or wrong? Justify.
- Drivers can pay in different ways.
- Drivers can buy different types of passes.

4 According to K. Livingstone, what are the benefits of the congestion charge?

5 Match the words with their French equivalents:
- serves the purpose — *ont les moyens*
- can afford — *fait l'affaire*
- freely — *librement*

6 Janet disagrees with the charge. Why? How has it made her life worse?

7 Tony agrees with the new measure. Pick out all his positive words.

8 What do **YOU** think? Is it a good idea to introduce a congestion charge in big cities? Justify.

2 An angry teen on driving

© Kervella/Hoaqui

In this country you have to be 18 to vote, 21 to drink. But at age 14, in some states, and 16 in most, kids are given keys to 2-ton people killers. That makes me angry. I am 17. I have my license and love to drive. Honestly, I don't follow all the traffic rules. I speed, I tailgate. I have never had an accident. But I am a teenager, and like all teenagers, I am immature at times.

Teenagers don't always wear safety belts, they do not respect the speed limit and that causes accidents, injuries and sometimes death. The gravest danger of all is drunk driving which has already killed so many – young and old. According to doctors and researchers at John Hopkins University in Baltimore, 36% of all deaths between ages 15-19 year-olds are the result of automobile accidents. And 42% of all fatal alcohol related crashes are caused by people aged 16-24 according to statistics from the U.S. Department of Transportation and the N.H. Department of Safety. Teenagers must learn about responsibility and consequences before becoming potential killers.

Stefanie Zimmers www.ihigh.com

FEEDBACK

1. Which country is Stefanie talking about?
2. Compare the laws in her country to French laws concerning the age to vote, to drink, to drive.
3. What does the expression "2-ton people killers" refer to?
4. Pick out 2 examples of violation of the Highway Code.
5. What is the main cause of death among 15-19 year olds?
6. Is the narrator for or against the right to drive at the age of 16? Justify.

3 Who drives better? Guys or girls?

- "Girls are more conservative in their driving, guys are reckless. Girls think things through."
  Lindsay Oldroyd, 15
- "Girls, because they mature faster than boys and I think that applies to driving too."
  Brandy Mauel, 16
- "Guys are better drivers cause girls are always putting on makeup."
  Melissa Snow, 15
- "Girls are better drivers because boys are egotistical, macho, and want to show off their driving ability."
  Tino Sanchez, Campus Monitor, 19
- "I have two sisters and they both drive like crazy people. Guys are definitely better."
  Lucas Curelas, 18

Adapted from Bonnie Edgeman and Mike Fink, *Teenage Drivers, menaces or merely misunderstood?*

FEEDBACK

1. Pick out the good and bad qualities that apply to girls and boys concerning their driving ability.
2. Do you think there is a difference in the way boys and girls drive? If so, why do they behave differently?

Comprehension

© N. Wheeler/Corbis

Before you read

1. Describe the picture on the left.
2. Do you think that it is possible to live without a car today? Justify.

Read the text

3. Pick out words referring to cars. Then say if the text deals with:
   - the advantages of owning a car;
   - the joys of not owning a car.
4. Say as much as you can about the narrator: his name, his wife's name, the town, state, country where he is living, why the couple went to Rome.
5. The text can be divided into two parts. Pick out the adverb that helps you find where the second part begins.
6. In which paragraphs do you find information about:
   - the drawbacks of cars,
   - the couple's decision not to own a car,
   - people's reaction,
   - the problems of living without a car,
   - the advantages of carsharing,
   - a definition of carsharing?

Read paragraphs 1 to 4

7. Give the reason why the couple feels marginalized.
8. In which places is it easy to live without a car? Say why.
9. Pick out the drawbacks of driving to work.
10. Did the couple move around Rome by car? Justify.
11. Find the English equivalents of: *en plaisantant (§2), cravate (§2), perdent leur temps (§3), paysages (§3), fardeau (§3)*

Read the end of the text

12. Which sentence shows that the couple could not stick to their decision?
13. On what occasions did they wish to have a car?
14. Pick out the continent where people do carsharing.
15. Pick out the financial and environmental advantages of carsharing.

ALLEZ PLUS LOIN

1 Trouvez (§ 1 et 3) trois expressions en anglais équivalant à : “vivre sans voiture” ▸ **FICHE** p. 75

2 Traduisez la phrase ligne 14-15.
- *Freedom* est un substantif dérivé de *free*. Observez la phrase *Driving is a burden* (ligne 14) et essayez de déduire le sens de *get rid of the car.* ▸ **FICHE** p. 75.

3 Trouvez dans le § 6 les expressions qui font référence :
- au passé du conducteur
- à sa situation financière

RÉSUMEZ

1 Ecoutez l'enregistrement et résumez en anglais.
- Steve - wife - own - car
- were working - Rome - felt - happy - free - without
- get around - city - bike - train - subway
- went back - Portland - realize - often needed
- did not want - buy
- carsharing - solution
- rented - hour
- saved - money - didn't pollute - atmosphere

2 Résumez en français.
Citez :
- les inconvénients de la voiture mentionnés par le narrateur,
- les raisons pour lesquelles il a failli céder à l'achat d'une voiture,
- les avantages de cette formule de location de voiture.

Grammaire en contexte

Cherchez dans le texte les mots se terminant en *–ing* et dites à quoi ils correspondent :

a) ***be* + V–*ing***
b) fonction de nom
c) préposition suivie de **V–*ing***
d) ***V* + V–*ing***

Carsharing in Portland

PORTLAND – Amanda and I have always felt a little bit marginalized by our decision not to own a car. Car-free living may be perfectly normal in cities like London, New York or San Francisco, where good transit systems are in place. But choosing to live without wheels in Portland, Oregon, is not particularly common.

Most Portlanders assume that they need a car, and our choice not to have one is hard for them to understand. A colleague at work jokingly calls me a "wacky[1] biker guy," and many who see me riding to work in a coat and tie probably have similar thoughts.

We see it differently. To us, unmotorized living is liberty. People who fight rush hour traffic in fancy cars waste their time. Some commuters spend over ten hours a week hurtling[2] through unpleasant landscapes. No, thanks! Driving is a real burden; true freedom begins when you get rid of the car.

You may wonder where we got that strange idea. Well, several years ago, Amanda and I taught in Rome. We discovered the joys of urban living by making our way through one of the world's great cities by bike, bus, subway and train.

But Portland isn't Rome. There are plenty of roses here, but there's minimal sunshine. It also isn't particularly easy to navigate by bus. We quickly found that there were times when we really wished we had a car. We usually needed one for short trips: to pick up a piece of furniture, to visit my parents in the suburbs, to buy plants for the balcony or to go to a party.

© Sipapress

We hesitated for a while, should we buy a car or not? A company which offers carsharing saved the day. Modeled after similar programs in Europe, it is an hourly car rental service. Here's how it works: after collecting a $25 application fee, the company checks the driving records and credit histories of all new applicants. Membership costs $10 per month. Once you join, you receive a key that fits every car in the fleet. Carsharing offers a wonderful combination: living with less and having more.

Amanda and I joined immediately. We share 18 vehicles with 282 people. In a typical month the two of us drive a total of about 100 miles and our combined transportation bill is about $60. Is our attitude provincial? Maybe, but, we are doing our best to keep tons of pollution out of the atmosphere.

Steve Gutmann
(volunteer on the board of Portland's Bicycle Transportation Alliance)

WORDS:
1 wacky: *farfelu*
2 hurtle: *circuler à toute allure*

La terminaison *-ing*

BE + V-*ing*

Elle permet de décrire un événement perçu à un moment de son déroulement.

Dans le présent

Présent *be* + *V-ing*

Ex: *Look! The little girl is crossing the street! Slow down!*

▶ Regarde ! La petite fille traverse la rue ! Ralentis !

Dans le passé

Prétérit *be* + *V-ing*

Ex: *The little girl was crossing the street when a car came from the right.*

▶ La petite fille traversait la rue quand une voiture est arrivée de la droite.

Fonction de nom

***V-ing* a toutes les fonctions du nom.**

Il peut tenir la place d'un nom.

Ex: *Reading is their favourite pastime.*

▶ Lire (la lecture) est leur passe-temps préféré.

Music is their favourite pastime.

▶ La musique est leur passe-temps préféré.

Il peut entrer dans un nom composé.

Ex: *Car-renting is a great idea. You can do it on the Internet.*

▶ Louer une voiture est une bonne idée. Vous pouvez le faire sur Internet.

Adjectifs se terminant en *-ing*

Ce sont des adjectifs ayant un sens actif (contrairement aux adjectifs se terminant en *-ed*).

Ex: *Traffic congestion is tiring.*

▶ Les embouteillages sont fatigants.

Drivers are tired when they get home.

▶ Les automobilistes sont fatigués quand ils rentrent chez eux.

Adjectifs composés

On trouve aussi la terminaison *-ing* dans les adjectifs dits composés, c'est-à-dire comportant deux ou plusieurs termes.

Nom + *V-ing*

Ex: *Pollution is a health-devastating problem.*

▶ La pollution est un problème qui nuit à la santé.

Adjectif + *V-ing*

Ex: *Fast-moving vehicles should be banned.*

▶ Les véhicules rapides devraient être interdits.

Après les verbes *like, love, hate, prefer...*

Après ces verbes la forme -ing montre que l'activité est déjà connue par le sujet grammatical.

Ex: *I hate living in polluted towns.*

▶ Je déteste vivre dans les villes polluées. (L'énonciateur a l'expérience des villes polluées et peut donc dire qu'il déteste y vivre.)

ATTENTION

Quand l'activité n'est pas connue mais envisagée dans l'avenir, on emploie *to* + *V*.

Ex: *I would like to live in London. It's such a great town!*

▶ J'aimerais vivre à Londres. C'est une ville tellement fantastique ! (L'énonciateur envisage l'avenir : il ne vit pas à Londres.)

Préposition + V-*ing*

***V-ing* est obligatoire après toutes les prépositions.**

Ex: *After living in a house, it is difficult to move to a flat.*

▶ Après avoir vécu dans une maison, il est difficile de s'installer dans un appartement.

ENTRAÎNEZ-VOUS

1 Complétez avec la forme en *-ing* les verbes donnés entre parenthèses. Dites à quoi cette forme correspond: fonction de nom, adjectif, forme *be* + *V-ing* (dans ce cas, n'oubliez pas d'ajouter be conjugué).

a. A lot of lorries still... the ferry to get to England (*use*).
b. Our transport system ... worse (*get*).
c. The ... effects are dramatic (damage).
d. A website ... to reduce road congestion (*try*).
e. Car fumes ... the nation's health (*damage*).
f. ... our website can be very useful (*read*).

2 Complétez avec les verbes entre parenthèses *(to* + *V* ou *V-ing)*.

a. Car-sharing will allow you … a car when you need it. (*have*)
b. When you want … one, just go online and reserve it. (*use*)
c. … other means of transport and … car usage are the two effects of car-sharing. (*increase - reduce*)
d. In the long term, companies would like … carsharing by … low prices. (*encourage - offer*)

3 Traduisez en anglais.

a. Steve et Amanda ont hésité avant d'acheter une voiture.
b. Habiter dans une grande ville leur permet de voyager facilement.
c. Ils n'utilisent pas de moyens de transport polluants.
d. Pour se rendre à leur travail, ils aiment marcher ou aller à bicyclette.

JEUX DE MOTS

1 Complétez les phrases avec le verbe qui convient.

Ex: If you go to work by bike, you cycle to work.
a. If you go by car, you ... to work.
b. If you go on foot, you ... to work.
c. If you go by plane, you ... to work.
d. If you go on roller skates, you ... to work.

2 Trouvez autant de verbes que possible pour compléter la phrase suivante.

Ex: You can ... a car.

3 Trouvez dans le texte p. 113 les noms correspondant aux verbes suivants.

apply – commute – decide – think – free – choose – combine

4 Complétez les phrases avec les verbes suivants.

need – use – rent – choose – waste – own – congest
a. In Europe nearly 50% of adults who can drive ... a car.
b. Everybody knows that cars ... the roads.
c. People should try not to ... their cars every day.
d. We can ... to live without a car.
e. We refuse to ... our time in traffic jams.
f. It is true that sometimes we really ... a car.
g. The solution is to ... a car when we need it.

Language skills

D'UNE LANGUE À L'AUTRE

1 Observez la traduction de la forme V-*ing* dans les phrases suivantes.

a. *At the moment many cars are converging towards the town centre.*
▸ En ce moment beaucoup de voitures se dirigent vers le centre-ville.

b. *Driving through the city at rush hour can be very stressful.*
▸ La traversée de la ville aux heures de pointe peut être très stressante.

c. *Downtown, pedestrians often hear car drivers hooting.*
▸ En ville, les piétons entendent souvent les conducteurs de voiture klaxonner.

d. *Free parking is more and more difficult to find.*
▸ Il est de plus en plus difficile de trouver à se garer gratuitement.

2 Traduisez les phrases suivantes après avoir déterminé la fonction des mots en V-*ing*.

a. The authorities have improved the situation by developing public transport.
b. Londoners spend long hours commuting every day.
c. He doesn't mind riding his bike in town.
d. Air-polluting emissions from vehicles cause many problems.
e. My friend, who lives in London, much prefers taking the tube to driving.
f. The station waiting-room is always crowded.

3 Faites la liste des différentes possibilités pour traduire les mots en V-*ing*.

ATELIER D'ÉCRITURE

© F. Achdou/Urba Images

1 Describe the photo. Use the word box below.

Wordbox
- in the foreground - in the background - on the right - on the left - in the middle, etc.
- drive - cross - try - wait - walk.

2 Write 80 words in English about the advantages and the disadvantages of living without a car. Follow these steps.
- Introduce the subject by giving one or two reasons why, today, some people choose to live without a car.
- Then, give the advantages of car-free living (peace and quiet, no pollution, exercise, health...) and the disadvantages of life without a car (when it rains, when public transport is unreliable...)
- Finally, say what you will probably choose: life with a car or life without a car.

CONSEILS D'ÉCRITURE

- **Équilibrez les deux paragraphes en donnant à peu près le même nombre d'arguments dans chaque partie.**
- **N'oubliez pas d'utiliser des mots de liaison pour présenter les deux aspects du problème.** **Page 169.**
- **Impliquez-vous dans la conclusion :** *Personally I ... - As far as I am concerned I... - I think that...*

ADJECTIFS

angry	*en colère*
car-free	*sans voiture*
main	*principal*
narrow	*étroit*
nearest (the)	*le plus proche*
reckless	*intrépide*
several	*plusieurs*

NOMS

ability	*capacité*
applicant	*candidat*
biker	*motard*
bill	*note (facture)*
burden	*fardeau*
choice	*choix*
commuter	*banlieusard*
fees	*honoraires, frais*
fleet (of cars)	*parc automobile*
freedom	*liberté*
injuries	*blessures*
keys	*clefs*
landscape	*paysage*
license	*permis de conduire*
rush-hour	*heure de pointe*
safety-belt	*ceinture de sécurité*
speed	*vitesse*
suburb	*banlieue*
subway	*métro*
traffic rules	*code de la route*
trip	*voyage*
waste	*gaspillage*

VERBES

carry	*porter*
cost	*coûter*
fit	*ajuster, aller*
follow	*suivre*
get back	*retourner*
get rid of	*se débarrasser de*
hire	*louer*
keep out	*empêcher d'entrer*
kill	*tuer*
pick up	*ramasser*
reach	*atteindre*
ride a bike	*faire du vélo*
save	*économiser*
spend	*passer*
tailgate	*coller à la voiture de devant*

AUTRES

according to	*selon*

Exercices

1 Complétez les conseils donnés aux automobilistes d'une petite ville historique en ajoutant un adjectif.

a. No trucks in our town. Our town is old and some of the small streets are very …
b. Large cars and caravans should use the … roads only.
c. No dangerous and … drivers in our town.
d. No cars in the town centre. It is …
e. Park in the … car park.

2 Complétez avec des mots du lexique.

a. **Jamie**: Why don't you come on a … with me to Rome?
b. **Lina**: Of course, I will. You know I will … you anywhere, Jamie.
c. **Jamie**: Great! Now I'd like to drive there as the … are so beautiful in Italy.
d. **Lina**: It's a … of money to drive there. It's cheaper to fly.
e. **Jamie**: I hate flying. But we could take the train and … a car once we get there.

3 Associez les mots de la ligne A aux mots de la ligne B pour former des mots composés que vous utiliserez pour compléter les phrases a à d.

A. rush - sub - traffic - safety
B. belt - hour - way - rules

a. The time when there's the most traffic on the roads: …
b. What you use to protect yourself in the car: …
c. Trains that work underground in the city: …
d. What you must obey when you drive: …

Exam Work

Give up your car and walk

Lazy Britons are travelling more and more, but by car or train. According to a recent survey[1], people in Britain are walking less than they did in the past. The average Briton is making 22 fewer journeys[2] a year on foot and 203 extra car journeys.

According to the Transport Minister, the situation is worrying[3]: "We cannot continue as we are now, with increasing pollution from traffic damaging our health and our environment. We must use the car less and walk more. We all need to think what we can do as individuals to reduce air pollution. We could all start by trying to walk to work or school, and walking to the local shop – it might start a new way of life."

According to the survey, those who rarely walk are schoolchildren and middle-aged men. Only 44 per cent of 11 to 15-year-olds walk to school, compared to 53 per cent 10 years ago. The principal reasons why parents prefer to drive their kids to school are fear of traffic and 'stranger danger'. Car-driving middle-aged men are the other culprits[4], with those aged 30-59 making around 25% fewer walking trips than women of the same age.

However, except for schoolchildren and forty-something men, most Britons are walking where they can. According to the Pedestrians' Association, 29 per cent of all journeys in this country are on foot, three times as many as are made by all public transport and 18 times as many as trips made by cyclists. For shorter journeys the figures[5] are even better: more than 80 per cent of journeys under a mile are on foot, despite[6] the bad condition of pavements in most cities. Perhaps most surprisingly, Londoners score highest for walking, with 45 per cent of all journeys made in the capital done on foot. The conditions for walking are not ideal in London, but walking is often preferable to the problems of traffic, parking or public transport.

According to the Pedestrians' Association, the bad walking conditions are one of the main reasons why people choose any other mode of transport over walking. Over a fifth of all pavements in England and Wales suffer from deterioration: they are broken or covered in rubbish.

Adapted from
The Daily Telegraph

WORDS:
1 *a survey:* une enquête
2 *a journey:* un trajet
3 *worrying:* inquiétant
4 *a culprit:* un coupable
5 *a figure:* un chiffre
6 *despite:* en dépit de

A Répondez en français en utilisant uniquement les informations contenues dans le texte. Composez des phrases complètes et justifiez vos réponses. 7 pts

a. Pour quelle raison les Britanniques sont-ils qualifiés de « paresseux » ?
b. Pourquoi les écoliers marchent-ils de moins en moins ?
c. Les femmes et les hommes de 30 à 59 ans pratiquent-ils la marche dans les mêmes proportions ?
d. Le quatrième paragraphe du texte confirme-t-il les observations plutôt négatives des trois premiers paragraphes ?
e. Les Londoniens marchent-ils uniquement pour leur plaisir ou leur santé ?
f. Que critique la Pedestrians' Association ?

B Traduisez en français le deuxième paragraphe. 4 pts

C Recopiez ces phrases en utilisant *be* + V*-ing* ou V*-ing* ou *to* + base verbale. 5 pts

a. Traffic (*increase*) pollution and health problems everywhere in Europe.
b. Authorities would like (*alert*) all car users about pollution.
c. More and more people spend some time (*exercise*) at weekends.
d. The roads used (*be*) more dangerous but the situation has improved.
e. Let's start (*imagine*) pleasant, safe and noiseless cities!

D Write 6 to 8 lines in English about the problems of traffic and pollution in big cities. Give a few examples and try to suggest solutions. 4 pts

Conseils pour l'examen : l'épreuve écrite

All work, no play

Is your boss the first in the office and the last to leave? Is it so long since you have had a holiday that you have forgotten they exist? If your job is regularly **intruding**[1] on your home and social life, then you're probably employed by a **workaholic**[2]. Workaholics may be energetic, enthusiastic and inspiring, but they can often be demanding and difficult.

The Working Time Directive from Brussels stipulates that the maximum working week must not exceed 48 hours but a **survey**[3] conducted last year found that the average number of hours put in by employees was 44, with 20 per cent working up to 55 hours a week. Employers reached an average 51, with 16 per cent working up to 61 hours a week.

"Both employers and employees feel under constant pressure to prove their abilities in the workplace" says psychologist Jack Taylor. "They feel they can do this by working longer hours and expect everyone else to work as hard as they do". Something that Mandy Jaeger, who was employed by a workaholic in 1998, knows well. "No matter how hard I worked - which commonly meant evenings, while lunch breaks were non-existent - I just couldn't keep up with the amount of work he was producing. I was doing the work of three people, but he just assumed that if he was able to do it, so should I," she says. But one day, when Mandy was asked to cancel her pre-booked, long-arranged holiday to work on a last minute job, she said she had just had enough and resigned. "He had had weeks to organise things but **put it off**[4] until two days before I was due to go away, and then expected it to be done immediately." After she left, Mandy heard he had **hired**[5] - and lost - three secretaries in three months.

Says Taylor: "The difficulty for workaholics is to understand how **selfish**[6] they are. Because they're so work-obsessed, they come to expect others to follow **suit**[7]. The poor secretary or **PA**[8] soon realises the situation she is in, and will consequently leave."

The Evening Standard

A. Compréhension

Répondez en français aux questions suivantes. 9 pts

1. Quelles qualités et quels défauts l'auteur de ce texte attribue-t-il aux bourreaux de travail ?
2. Quelles sont, selon Jack Taylor, les raisons qui poussent certaines personnes à travailler trop ?
3. Quel est, selon les directives de Bruxelles, le nombre maximal d'heures de travail par semaine ? Les salariés et les employeurs se conforment-ils à ces recommandations ?
4. Décrivez avec précision la vie professionnelle de Mandy Jaeger pendant l'année 1998 et les raisons de sa démission.

B. Traduction

Traduisez en français de la ligne 16 à la ligne 18. 3 pts

C. Compétences linguistiques

Recopiez les phrases 1 et 2 en les complétant au style indirect. Effectuez les transformations nécessaires. 2 pts

1. Mandy said:
   "My boss is always the first in the office."
   Mandy said that…
2. The boss asked me:
   "Can you type the report immediately?"
   The boss asked me if…

WORDS

1 intrude on: *empiéter sur*
2 a workaholic: *un bourreau de travail*
3 a survey: *une étude*
4 put something off: *reporter quelque chose à plus tard*
5 hire: *embaucher*
6 selfish: *égoïste*
7 follow suit: *faire de même*
8 PA: *Personal Assistant, assistante de direction*

Recopiez les phrases 3 et 4 en les complétant au style direct. Effectuez les transformations nécessaires. 2 pts

3. Mandy answered that she didn't want to cancel her holiday.
   Mandy answered: "I …"
4. Mandy said that Peter would be late.
   Mandy said: "Peter …"

D. Production écrite

Answer the following question in English (80 words). 4 pts

"All work, no play."
Is it your preference in your present or future professional life? Justify your answer.

Fiche 5

Marche à suivre

- Observez attentivement le document : son titre, son origine, la date, pour découvrir le thème du texte.
- Les mots en gras renvoient au lexique traduit et vous éviteront des recherches dans le dictionnaire.
- Les lignes du texte sont numérotées. Cela vous aidera à repérer les informations demandées.
- Lisez le texte avec soin pour en saisir le sens global. (Ne vous précipitez pas sur le dictionnaire !)
- Le travail à faire comporte quatre parties :

A La compréhension

B La traduction

C Les compétences linguistiques

D La production écrite

- Lisez les consignes et revenez au texte.

A La compréhension

a. Lisez bien les consignes

- Il faut répondre en français.
- Les informations sont à rechercher uniquement dans le texte.
- Les réponses doivent être rédigées et justifiées.
- Le barème totalise 9 points. Ce n'est pas négligeable !
- Lisez les questions et essayez de voir quel paragraphe contient la réponse, même si vous ne comprenez pas tout ! Inscrivez dans la marge Q1, Q2, etc...

b. Question 1

La réponse se trouve au début du texte, mais pas dans le premier paragraphe. Donc, il faut vous reporter au paragraphe 2. Traduisez les qualités et les défauts mentionnés et commencez à rédiger votre réponse :

L'auteur pense que les bourreaux du travail sont ..., mais ils ont aussi des défauts : ils sont ...

c. Question 2

Vous repérez rapidement que le journaliste fait parler Jack Taylor dans le paragraphe 4. Cherchez donc ici les raisons :

Les employeurs et les employés travaillent trop parce que ...

d. Question 3

Elle comporte deux sous-questions.
Vous avez noté que "Brussels" apparaissait dans le paragraphe 3.
La première information chiffrée est facile à trouver.
La deuxième est plus délicate.

Il vous faudra peut-être vérifier *average* et *reached.*
Attention : ne confondez pas *employers* et *employees* !

e. Question 4

La question évoque Mandy Jaeger.
Reportez-vous au paragraphe 5.
La question stipule "avec précision" ; il faut donc bien décrire sa vie professionnelle. Pour trouver les raisons de sa démission, quelques vérifications dans le dictionnaire seront nécessaires : par exemple *cancel, due to...*

B La traduction

Relisez le paragraphe en le découpant en unités de sens.
L'identité de la personne qui parle est donnée au début.
Décomposez les phrases en propositions en vous appuyant sur les groupes verbaux.
Dans la phrase 1, attention à *how* devant un adjectif !
Dans la phrase 2, la traduction de *because* n'est pas indispensable en français :
«Ils sont tellement obsédés par le travail» suffit.
Dans la phrase 3, il faut rétablir en français le pronom relatif manquant dans l'expression : *the situation she is in:*
«la situation dans laquelle elle se trouve».

C Les compétences linguistiques

Respectez les amorces qui sont données, recopiez-les sur votre brouillon et effectuez les modifications nécessaires.

Style indirect

Phrase 1 : changez *my*, et le temps *is.*
Phrase 2 : changez la place du sujet et le temps de *can.*

Style direct

Phrase 1 : changez le temps de *didn't want* et changez *her.*
Phrase 2 : changez le temps de *would be.*

D Production écrite

"Answer in English": **Il s'agit de commenter l'expression** *"All work, no play"*: **ne faire que travailler, sans se détendre. On vous demande si vous êtes d'accord avec cette conception, maintenant ou pour l'avenir. Vous devez justifier votre position.**

- **Pensez à structurer votre production : introduction, deux paragraphes et une conclusion.**
  - Introduisez le sujet en partant d'une idée générale qui pose le problème.
  - Ensuite, dites si vous avez adopté cette devise dans votre vie de lycéen et dites pourquoi.
  - Puis, continuez en précisant ce que vous ferez quand vous aurez une vie professionnelle.
  - Concluez par une phrase de synthèse ou une question.
- **Cherchez les mots de liaison pour articuler vos idées en vous aidant du dictionnaire.**

kit 11

© Lebrun/Photo News

You and your boss

© Network Photographers/Rapho

Speaking

- Guess who the two people in the photo above are. How do you know?
- Say where the boss in the smaller picture is. What can you say about the atmosphere in this firm?

STREET TALK

Four bosses and me

© Photonica/Gettyimages

1 Listen to these words from the interview.

- bill • expense reports • separate
- prompt • chaotic • overworked
- flustered • individual • rude
- sarcastic • management
- profound • mellow.

2 Listen to Deborah and fill in your questionnaire.

Deborah Spencer from New-York, U.S.A.

I Young and ambitious

© C.Karnov/Corbis

Australia's working youth are ambitious and eager[1] to learn — but they are quick to leave a company if they don't like it.

A new survey[2] of Australia's working youth has shown that young people are increasingly[3] entrepreneurial[4]. They are attracted to a friendly workplace and are not very influenced by the level of pay. It shows they are not tied[5] to a single employer and are ready to go abroad for the right job. They are attracted to a sociable work environment and many young Australians want to run their own businesses or be self-employed.

As they are big users of online communications they are highly mobile and adventurous. Australia's youth do not like to have to work for a single job or employer. When offered the opportunity of a very attractive job and the chance to sign a long-term contract for five years or more, less than a quarter signed.

This means companies with younger workforces are having to find and introduce more strategies to keep young employees satisfied. They offer team building programmes, flexible hours and benefits like gym memberships.

"A stimulating workplace environment where young people have the chance to grow and learn amongst their peers is more attractive than a job with a high salary but none of the developmental benefits," says psychologist Dianne Ward. "Young people are not just there for the money."

WORDS:

1 eager : *avide*
2 survey : *étude, enquête*
3 increasingly: *de plus en plus*
4 entrepreneurial : *entreprenant*
5 tied : *attaché*

FEEDBACK

1 ▸ Choose the right statement:
- Young Australians want to stay in the same firm for life.
- Young Australians have a strong desire to be successful and independent.

2 ▸ When they choose a job does the salary come first? What do they look for?

3 ▸ Give an example showing that young Australians are ambitious.

4 ▸ Pick out a sentence showing that young Australians are technology-friendly.

5 ▸ Why do most young Australians refuse to sign a long-term contract with an employer?

6 ▸ Pick out the strategies companies use to keep their young staff.

7 ▸ What is a stimulating workplace for a young Australian?

8 ▸ Say what it is for you.

2 I love my job

I love my job
I love the pay!
I love it more and more each day.

I love my boss; he is the best!
I love his boss and all the rest.

I love my office and its location
I hate to have to go on vacation.

I love my furniture, drab and gray,
and the paper that piles up every day!

I love my chair in my padded cell!
There's nothing else I love so well.

I love to work among my peers
I love their leers and jeers and sneers.

I love my computer and its software;
I hug it often though it doesn't care...

I love each program and every file,
I try to understand once in a while!

I'm happy to be here, I am, I am;
I'm the happiest slave of my uncle Sam.

I love this work: I love these chores.
I love the meetings with deadly bores.

I love my job - I'll say it again -
I even love these friendly men -
These men who've come to visit today
In lovely white coats to take me away!!!!

Anonymous

© Cat's collection

FEEDBACK

1 ▸ Read the poem and say if the general tone is sad or happy.
2 ▸ Which expression contradicts: "I love my office"?
3 ▸ Does the narrator feel free there? Justify.
4 ▸ Pick out two words referring to the other workers.
5 ▸ Does he appreciate his colleagues? Justify.
6 ▸ Who does uncle Sam refer to: his boss, the American government or his computer?
7 ▸ Match these words with their French equivalents:
- sneers - chores - once in a while - drab - leers
- *de temps en temps - terne - railleries - regards mauvais - corvées*

8 ▸ How does the poem end? Choose the right version:
- the narrator is taken away by policemen,
- the narrator is fired by his bosses,
- the narrator is taken away to an asylum.

9 ▸ Among the following adjectives, say which ones apply to the poem: serious – dramatic – ironic – romantic – funny – sarcastic

Comprehension

© C.Karnov/Corbis

Before you read

1. Describe the picture. Would you like to work in a company like this one? Justify your answer.

Read the text

2. Does the document mainly deal with:
   - the working conditions of the employees;
   - the high productivity of the company;
   - the employees' favourite food?
3. Choose one of these sentences to complete the title: Pets are allowed...
   - to help the blind working in the company.
   - to come into the company building.
   - to wait for their masters outside the building.
4. Give information about Google:
   - London address;
   - activity and value;
   - vice president's name and age;
   - number of employees;
   - names and origin of the people who started the company;
   - date of creation of the company.

Read paragraphs 1 to 5

5. Which part of the company premises (*locaux*) is described here?
6. Pick out all the elements that you don't usually find in a conventional company.
7. Choose the adjectives that best qualify the atmosphere in this company: cold - relaxed - austere - cool - tense
8. Which sentence in paragraph 3 gives the reason for the company's attitude.

Read the end of the text.

9. Which parts of the premises does the rest of the document deal with?
10. What is unusual in these places?
11. Which sentence shows that the company cares about its employees' health.
12. Pick out the sentence meaning the same as: "fun is not necessarily opposed to work".
13. Now pick out all the elements referring to "fun".

ALLEZ PLUS LOIN

1 Trouvez (ligne 5) l'expression anglaise équivalant à "différent".

2 Regardez (ligne 11) les mots qui suivent *buckets* et déduisez le sens de ce mot. ▸ **FICHE** p. 53

3 *Unremarkable* et *disregard* comportent tous les deux un préfixe. Qu'expriment ces préfixes? *Remarkable* est un mot transparent. *Regard* signifie égard. Déduisez le sens de *unremarkable* et *disregard*. ▸ **FICHE** p. 75

4 Trouvez le sens possible de ces noms composés. *web search engine – childminder – workforce – workplace.* ▸ **FICHE** p. 75

5 Dans quel but *General Motors* et *Walt Disney* sont-ils mentionnés dans le document?

6 Dans quel cas l'entreprise accepte-t-elle d'accueillir les enfants du personnel ?

RÉSUMEZ

1 Ecoutez l'enregistrement et résumez en anglais.

- Google - very important - search engine - Internet
- way - people - work - unusual
- can - eat - drink - sing - video games - workplace
- Google - welcomes - children - pets - necessary
- Google - encourages - people - hard - enjoy themselves - same time - because - happy - workers - more productive

2 Résumez en français.

1. Que savez-vous de la société Google ?
2. En quoi est-elle différente des autres sociétés ?
3. Qu'est-ce qui incite la direction de Google à adopter ce comportement à l'égard de son personnel ?

Grammaire en contexte

1. Repérez dans le paragraph 4 la phrase ayant pour sujet *dogs*.
2. Commentez la construction de sa forme verbale.
3. Nommez la forme utilisée.
4. Qui subit l'action?
5. Qui la fait ?
6. Le responsable est-il nommé ?
7. Pourquoi l'énonciateur a-t-il choisi cette forme verbale ?
8. Relevez dans le paragraphe 6 une forme verbale ayant la même construction.

Pets are allowed

It's an unremarkable building on London's Charing Cross Road - but inside a revolution is taking place that could change the way we all work. Welcome to the Googleplex – an office like no other you've ever seen. Stroll into the reception area of web search engine Google's UK headquarters and the first things you notice are the bright beanbags[1] sitting under a palm tree. Then there's the fridge, where staff can help themselves to free smoothies[2], and the buckets full of drinks and chocolate bars.

© C.Karnov/Corbis

It's a way of work that's paying big dividends. Yesterday, Google became the most valuable media company in the world, worth £44billion. That's more than General Motors and Walt Disney combined.

Vice president Nikesh Arora, 37, says: "It's the little things that make for a happy workforce, and happier people are more productive. It's the Google way of doing things - we're pet-friendly and make sure people get to eat when they work. We've fresh fruit and cereals here for everybody every morning."

Google has a healthy disregard for convention. Dogs are welcomed into the workplace as are the children of staff if a childminder can't be found.

Russ Cohn, 34, who's worked at the office for two years, says: "Google believes that work and play don't have to be separated, so we try to blend them together. Why shouldn't they have fun in the office?"

It's not just the reception area that's different to the standard office block – the rooms are also distinctly offbeat[3], named after British rock musicians including Freddie Mercury, Mark Bolan and Mick Jagger. Googleplex is open-plan and staff – or Googlers – sit at their computers on large, mobile rubber balls or chairs which have been especially designed to suit users' backs. In the canteen, which provides two free lunches a week, there are video games and even a karaoke machine while nearby are electric massage chairs.

Nikesh Arora goes on to say: "There's no reason why we can't work hard and play hard. We go on an annual trip to Lake Tahoe, Nevada, where there's a conference with Google's 3,500 workers. Afterwards, we take over the resort to go skiing."

It's a way of working that comes from California, where founders Larry Page and Sergey Brin began the business in September 1998.

By David Edwards

WORDS:

1 beanbags: *fauteuils poire*
2 smothies: *jus de fruits frais*
3 offbeat: *cocasse*

Le passif

Construction du passif

Un verbe à la voix passive est constitué de deux éléments :
- *be* qui porte la marque du temps ou de l'aspect.
- *V-en* (ou participe passé) qui est invariable.

Be (présent) + V-en

Ex : *I think employees are well paid here.*
▸ Je pense que les employés sont bien payés ici.

Be (prétérit) + V-en

Ex : *He wanted to work with Google because employees were well paid.*
▸ Il voulait travailler chez Google parce que les employés étaient bien payés.

Have (présent) + be-en + V-en

Ex : *Employees have always been well paid in this company.*
▸ Les employés ont toujours été bien payés dans cette entreprise.

Will + be + V-en

Ex : *I am sure employees will always be well paid in this company.*
▸ Je suis sûr que les employés seront toujours bien payés dans cette entreprise.

Be + being + V-en

Ex : *Look! He is being congratulated by the boss.*
▸ Regarde ! Le patron le félicite.

Emploi du passif

En mettant le destinataire (l'objet, la cible) de l'action en tête d'énoncé, l'énonciateur le met en valeur.

Ex: *Dogs **are welcomed** into the workplace.*
▸ Les chiens sont acceptés sur le lieu de travail.
(L'énonciateur s'intéresse aux chiens.)

Comparons avec l'exemple suivant. La forme active montre que le point de vue est différent.

Ex: *The company **welcomes** dogs.*
▸ La société accepte les chiens.
(L'énonciateur parle de la société et la place donc en tête d'énoncé.)

Le responsable de l'action (c'est-à-dire la source ou l'origine) peut être mentionné. L'information complémentaire est introduite par *by*.

Ex: *Dogs are welcomed **by** the company.*
▸ Les chiens sont acceptés par l'entreprise.
(L'énonciateur nous précise l'identité de l'agent qui accepte les chiens.)

Le responsable de l'action peut ne pas être mentionné lorsque l'énonciateur ne le connaît pas ou bien s'il est évident ou encore sans importance.

Ex: *More comfortable chairs were brought into the workplace.*
▸ On a apporté des fauteuils plus confortables sur le lieu de travail.
(Le fait que l'identité de l'agent qui a apporté les fauteuils ne soit pas mentionnée ne gêne pas la compréhension de l'énoncé.)

Traduction du passif

Le passif est plus utilisé en anglais qu'en français. Lorsque le responsable de l'action n'est pas mentionné, il faut souvent avoir recours à "on" dans une traduction en français.

Ex: *The staff were told that the company was going to create a branch in Australia.*
▸ On a dit au personnel que l'entreprise allait créer une succursale en Australie.
(L'énonciateur ne dit pas qui a informé le personnel de l'expansion de l'entreprise.)

ENTRAÎNEZ-VOUS

1 Repérez les formes verbales au passif, puis identifiez leur construction.

a. Russ Cohn has worked in this company for two years.
b. The company was created in 1998.
c. He has always been very well paid.
d. He says that all employees are well treated.
e. The company makes good profit.

2 Mettez les verbes entre parenthèses au passif au temps et à la forme appropriés. Aidez-vous du marqueur de temps.

a. Years ago work *(never mix)* with play.
b. Today they *(no longer separate)*.
c. Last year the staff *(offer)* a trip to Australia.
d. As the company is expanding, around 100 staff *(recruit)* next year.

3 Voici l'histoire de Rupert. Mettez les verbes entre parenthèses au prétérit à la forme active ou passive.

A few years ago, Rupert *(apply)* for a job at Google company but he *(refuse)* the job. He *(tell)* that he *(not have)* the qualifications that *(require)* for the job. So he *(decide)* to go to university and study more. A year later, he *(send)* a new application form and *(wait)* for an answer.
The answer *(arrive)* fast. He *(call)* for an interview.
He *(ask)* why he *(want)* to work for Google.
He *(explain)* that Google *(know)* all over the world and its employees *(very well pay)*.

4 Traduisez.

a. Aujourd'hui on accueille les enfants des employés.
b. L'année dernière des fauteuils spéciaux ont été fabriqués pour le personnel.
c. A la cantine deux repas gratuits sont fournis chaque semaine.

JEUX DE MOTS

On peut transformer un nom en adjectif en lui ajoutant une terminaison *- y (funny), - able (valuable), - al (national) ou - ive (productive) ...*

1 Donnez les adjectifs dérivés de ces noms.

a. health
b. reason
c. tradition
d. action
e. person
f. politics
g. luck
h. attraction
i. anger
j. change
k. nation

2 Complétez avec un adjectif choisi dans la liste ci-dessous.

free – adventurous – flexible – sociable – valuable – single

a. If you are ..., you are not married.
b. If you are ..., you enjoy meeting people.
c. If you are ..., you don't mind changing jobs.
d. If you get something ..., you don't pay for it.
e. If you are ..., you don't mind taking risks.
f. If something is ... , it costs a lot of money.

3 Complétez avec des mots du texte p.125

Google is one of the biggest companies in the ....
The ... enjoy the working conditions there.
Employees can both work and have ... .
This ... of work is quite unusual.
Thanks to special chairs employees never complain about their ... .

D'UNE LANGUE À L'AUTRE

1 Observez les phrases suivantes et donnez les différentes manières de traduire la forme passive.

a. *Google was created by two Californians.*
▸ Google a été créé par deux californiens.

b. *A second karaoke machine is being installed at the moment.*
▸ On est en train d'installer un deuxième karaoké.

c. *He was given a prize.*
▸ Il reçut un prix.

d. *Something must be done to improve the heating.*
▸ Il faut faire quelque chose pour améliorer le chauffage.

e. *What is the manager called?*
▸ Comment s'appelle le directeur ?

f. *Today, computers are sold in supermarkets.*
▸ Aujourd'hui les ordinateurs se vendent dans les supermarchés.

2 Traduisez en français.

a. Everybody knows that workers are well treated in this company.
b. According to the vice president, work and play must not be separated.
c. For the tenth anniversary of the company the staff was offered laptops.
d. A young Japanese is being trained at the moment.
e. Computers are equipped with special screens.

ATELIER D'ÉCRITURE

1 A young trainee is talking about his first day at work. He is sending the e-mail below to his best friend. Complete it using the following verbs in the passive.
be taken round the ..., be introduced to…, be offered ..., be provided with…, be placed under the authority of… .

E-mail

Hi Max,
I'm so glad everything went well!
First I was welcomed by the department manager and…

Philip

2 When you get back to work after a long holiday you find that lots of changes have been made to your workplace. Write 70 to 80 words about these improvements (*améliorations*).
Follow these steps:
- Describe the poor condition of your office before you went on holiday.
- *Say what has been changed (the decoration, the computers, the photocopiers, the cafeteria.)*
- *Conclude by saying how the workers feel about what has been done by the boss.*

CONSEILS D'ÉCRITURE

- **Vous allez devoir utiliser des formes verbales différentes dans cet essai :**
  - le prétérit aux formes active et passive pour décrire votre lieu de travail avant la rénovation. (sol, plafond, meubles, équipement informatique...)
  - le *present perfect* à la forme passive pour constater les changements intervenus.
  - le présent pour évoquer l'état d'esprit des employés maintenant.
- **Pensez aussi à utiliser un mot de liaison exprimant l'opposition entre la première et la deuxième étape de votre essai.**

ADJECTIFS

annual	*annuel*
bright	*vif*
healthy	*sain*
long-term	*long terme*
open-plan (office)	*paysagé (bureau)*
pet-friendly	*qui aime les animaux*
self-employed	*travailleur indépendant*
single	*célibataire*

NOMS

abroad	*à l'étranger*
back	*dos*
benefit	*avantage*
billion	*milliard*
bucket	*seau*
chance	*possibilité*
childminder	*nourrice, assistante maternelle*
file	*fichier*
founder	*fondateur*
furniture	*meubles*
headquarters	*siège*
level	*niveau*
office block	*bureaux*
peer	*pair*
resort	*station (de vacances)*
search engine	*moteur de recherche*
software	*logiciels*

VERBES

allow	*permettre*
believe	*croire*
blend	*mélanger*
disregard	*ignorer*
find	*trouver*
keep	*garder*
leave	*quitter*
mean	*vouloir dire*
notice	*remarquer*
pile up	*empiler*
stroll	*se balader*
suit	*convenir (à)*
take away	*enlever*
take over	*prendre le contrôle*

AUTRES

afterwards	*après*
among / amongst	*parmi*
each	*chaque*
inside	*dedans*
nearby	*proche*
none	*aucun*

Exercices

1 Faites des mots composés en prenant un mot de chaque liste.

a. work - office - head - child - search - soft

b. block - quarters - engine - ware - force - minder

2 Trouvez les adjectifs composés correspondant aux indications données.

a. A large office where everyone works together in one room is …

b. A job which you keep for many years is …

c. Someone who works for themselves is …

d. A company which allows you to bring your dog to work is …

3 Complétez avec des mots de la catégorie "Autres".

a. Billy got a job working … young computer scientists in Australia.

b. He lived … his office and went to work on foot.

c. He didn't have to work … if the weather was good. He could work in the garden.

d. … time he invented a new programme he got a bonus.

e. … he always went on great vacations around the world.

4 Remplacez les mots en gras par des verbes équivalents choisis dans le lexique.

a. Good bosses **see** when their staff is uncomfortable.

b. They make sure their secretaries' chairs **are perfect for** their backs.

c. Lots of papers **collect** on their desks.

d. The cleaners **remove** the papers in the evening.

e. When secretaries go on holiday, other people **do** their jobs.

f. Good bosses never **ignore** their staff's requests.

Mobile telephones

Trudi Smith, a London PA[1], laughs when she recalls her naïve excitement on receiving a mobile from her boss. But when the phone started to ring every time she was in a pub or at a party, the thrill[2] soon turned to resentment. When Smith protested at the invasion into her private time, her boss just answered: "No phone, no job." Smith immediately resigned.

According to Karen Bishop, another PA, the answer is to choose the right boss: her boss is Anita Roddick, chairman of The Body Shop. "For Anita, the mobile phone must not be a burden[3]," says Karen Bishop. "Just as she never expects me to work past 6 p.m. unless[4] there's a crisis, Anita calls only in a true emergency. She respects the fact that my free time is my own." Like many astute employers, Anita Roddick believes that allowing her staff quality free time means that they are happier at work, and that a happy worker is a good worker.

Increasing the demands on secretaries should lead to an increase in their status and salary, because giving a PA a mobile phone is often like requesting free overtime. Some companies, such as British Airways, pay their secretarial staff a bonus if they need to telephone them out of hours - a recognition that they are demanding overtime.

If you own a personal mobile phone, you are under no obligation to reveal its number to your boss. Beaky Evetts, another London PA, should have known she was asking for trouble when she passed her number on to her boss. Now she regrets it because her boss often calls her from places all over the world, at 6 a.m. or 10 p.m.

A sensible thing to do is to establish with your boss exactly why you need a mobile telephone and suggest drawing up together written guidelines on how it will be used. These should determine regularity and hours of use of the telephone, and reasons for its use. Establish which colleagues and clients really need to have access to the telephone number. If it's your own phone, remember that you have the same rights to it as to your home telephone line.

Adapted from *The Independent*,

WORDS:
1 PA: *assistant(e)*
2 thrill: *émotion*
3 burden: *fardeau*
4 unless: *à moins que*

A Répondez en français aux questions suivantes. Composez des phrases complètes et justifiez vos réponses. 8 pts

1. Trudi Smith est-elle satisfaite ou mécontente de son téléphone mobile ?
2. L'attitude d'Anita Roddick est-elle comparable à celle de l'employeur de Trudi Smith en ce qui concerne l'utilisation du téléphone mobile ?
3. Quelle est la raison de l'attitude d'Anita Roddick envers son personnel ?
4. Quelles sont les dispositions favorables adoptées par certaines sociétés vis-à-vis de leurs salariés contraints d'utiliser le téléphone en dehors de leurs heures de travail ?
5. Quelles sont, en matière d'utilisation du téléphone mobile, les règles à établir entre employeur et employé ?

B Traduisez en français le 4e paragraphe. 4 pts

C Complétez avec le mot qui convient : *in spite of - still - until - if.* 2 pts

1. The personal assistant hasn't come back yet: she is ... on holiday.
2. The temporary secretary will replace her ... she comes back.
3. Her colleagues will help her ... she has a problem.
4. She likes the job in this firm ... all the difficulties.

D Mettez le verbe entre parenthèses au temps qui convient. 2 pts

1. Yesterday the boss ... *(call)* her PA three times on the mobile phone during the evening.
2. Karen Bishop ... *(work)* at the Body Shop for five years now.
3. Two years ago British Airways ... *(decide)* to pay their secretarial staff a bonus.
4. It's the third time in the week that the boss ... *(ask)* her to work overtime.

E Write about 70 words in English about the advantages and disadvantages of mobile telephones. Give a few examples to justify your answer. If you have one, tell us why you bought it and what you use it for. 4 pts

kit 12

© P. Charliat/Rapho

Safety and risks

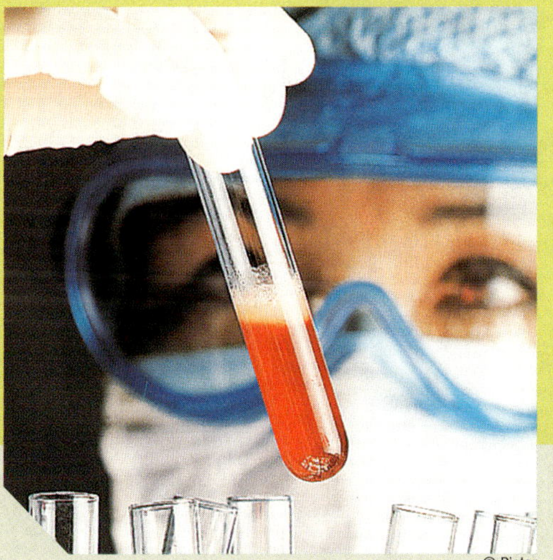

© Pictor

Speaking

- Say where these people are and what they are doing.
- What are they wearing?
- What sort of jobs do they have, and what do they have in common?

Keeping everybody safe

1 Listen to these words from the interview.

• printing plant • machinery • health • environment • minimize • well guarded • chemical • slipping accident • issue • ear muffs • overalls • steel toe caps • vocational • occur • trapped • crushing • injury

2 Listen to Louise and fill in your questionnaire.

Louise, *New International*, London, U.K.

© Judy Martinez/Hachette

I Stories from injured teens

© B. Thomas/Getty/Stone

17-year-old restaurant worker

I'm 5'3" tall. The pans I needed to cover the dough[1] were piled to the ceiling so I stood on a large dough mixer to reach them. As I was getting down, I twisted my leg, fell, and fractured my right leg and my knee. I had asked for a step stool[2] a number of times.

16-year-old nurse's aide

A co-worker and I were transferring a patient from his bed to a wheelchair. I thought the patient was going to fall, so I turned quickly. I felt a sharp pain in my back. I continued to work 5 more hours to finish my shift. I went to the hospital the next day because my back hurt and I had lost feeling in my left leg.

15-year-old gas station attendant

I was pumping gas on the 3-10 pm shift. It was about zero degree out and the wind was blowing. Around 5:00, I couldn't feel my fingers and toes: I told my boss about it twice. I worked the rest of the shift and then went home. I woke up in the middle of the night and still couldn't feel my fingers or toes. I went to the emergency room the next morning. I had second and third degree frostbite[3] on all my fingers and three of my toes.

WORDS:

1 dough: *pâte à pain*
2 step stool: *escabeau*
3 frostbite: *gelure*

FEEDBACK

1 Say what you know about the three narrators: ages, workplaces.
2 For each worker say which part of their bodies was hurt.
3 Say how they got injured.
4 Who was responsible for the accidents?
5 In your opinion which case is the most serious?

2 Teenage boy loses part of his finger

A 17-year-old boy had to have part of the third finger on his left hand (the wedding ring finger) amputated. His fingers were crushed in a pie making machine at the bakery where he worked. The teenager had been employed for the Easter holiday. He had only been working for one hour before the accident happened. His left hand was pulled into the machine after he had tried to remove a pie from the machine.

Magistrates found these faults in the machine the boy used:

- the safety brake which should have stopped the machine was faulty,
- the teenager had not received adequate training on the machine,
- his supervisor was not aware that he was using the machine until the accident happened,
- there was no planned maintenance programme at the bakery before the accident.

The employer pleaded guilty to not ensuring the safety of his employees and was fined £3,000.

© Benoit Decout/REA

© R. Pharaoh/International Stock/Cosmos

FEEDBACK

1. Say what happened.
2. How old is the boy? Where was he working?
3. What sort of machine did he use?
4. Had he been working there for a long time before the accident took place?
5. Was the boy responsible for the accident? Justify.
6. Did the employer respect the safety rules? Justify.
7. What was the conclusion of the case?

Comprehension

© A. Keer/Cosmos

Before you read

1. What is the man in the photo on the right doing? Is it an easy job? Justify.
2. What sort of information do you think you will find in the text?

Read the text

3. Say what you know about the company, ABFAD.
   - Who created it? And when?
   - How many people does it employ?
   - Where is the company based?
   - What turnover is expected in the future?

Read paragraphs 1 and 2

4. What equipment do the Fada brothers use?
5. Match these words with their equivalents:

- ropes	- *nacelles*
- mountaineering kit	- *échafaudages*
- cradles	- *cordes*
- scaffoldings	- *matériel d'alpinisme*

6. What sectors are they involved in?
7. What special piece of equipment has the firm invented to help the employees?

Read paragraphs 3 and 4

8. How many people manage the company?
9. Complete: ABFAD's managers were successful because of two qualities, their ... and their ... They will take part in the Daily Express ... contest
10. Pick out the three important structures they have already worked on.
11. Find the words in the text corresponding to the following definitions:
    - a boat carrying goods in large quantities
    - a long instrument used to watch distant things

Read the end of the text

12. Pick out two trades involved in ABFAD business.
13. What were the ABFAD managing directors' jobs before they started their business?
14. Where did the two Fada brothers meet Chris Hariton?

ALLEZ PLUS LOIN

1 Quel est le sens de *like* (§ 1) ? S'agit-il du verbe *like* "aimer" ou de la préposition *like* "comme" ?

2 Quel est le sens de *close* (§2) ? S'agit-il du verbe *close* "fermer" ou de la préposition *close to* "tout près de" ?

3 Trouvez (§2) le nom composé signifiant "système aimanté breveté" ▸ **FICHE** p. 75

4 Quel est le sens de *judges* (§ 3) ? S'agit-il du pluriel de *judge* "juge "ou du verbe *judge* "juger" à la troisième personne du singulier du présent? Pour le savoir demandez-vous quel est le sujet de la phrase subordonnée introduite par *that* et quel est le verbe.

5 Quel est le sens de *backed* (§ 3) ? Demandez-vous quelle est la nature de *backed* dans la phrase. Aidez-vous de la racine *back* et du contexte.

RÉSUMEZ

1 Ecoutez l'enregistrement et résumez en anglais.

- Abfad - 1996 - two brothers - managing director
- use - mountaineering equipment - ropes - instead - scaffoldings - maintenance - structures
- has invented - magnet - keep - employees - close to - structures - are working on
- employs - 25 to 40 people - successful - plans - offices - abroad - near future

2 Résumez en français.

- Comment la compagnie a-t-elle été créée ? A quoi doit-elle son succès ?
- Cette compagnie est-elle en bonne santé ? Qu'est-ce qui le prouve ?
- Quels travaux exceptionnels cette compagnie a-t-elle réalisés ?

Grammaire en contexte

1. **Observez les trois dernières phrases du texte et identifiez le type de discours employé.**
2. **Quelle ponctuation est toujours utilisée dans ce type de discours ?**
3. **Réécrivez la première phrase en commençant par : *Ian says (that)* ...**
4. **Quels changements constatez-vous ?**

Rope magic

Ian and Alan Fada, two brothers, took to the ropes[1] to start their successful business, ABFAD. They use mountaineering kits instead of cradles and scaffoldings for the construction and maintenance of huge structures like ships, refineries and oil platforms.

The firm's patented magnet device[2] keeps them and their employees close to the structure they are working on – very useful for precision work and on ships, where they sometimes have to work 30ft above water.

© K. Wood/International Stock/Cosmos

ABFAD was founded by Ian and Alan Fada when they teamed up in 1996 with Chris Hariton. Its immediate success was largely due to the vision and tenacity of the trio. These skills are among the qualities that judges will look for among the candidates for the Start-up Stars contest backed by the Daily Express.

ABFAD has won work on projects ranging from[3] the Jodrell Bank telescope and PowerGen chimneys to a massive carrier ship and Abu Dhabi offshore work.

The Sunderland-based firm employs between 25 and 40 people – from painters to senior welding inspectors. This year, as it expands and opens offices abroad, it expects a £1.5 million turnover[4].

Ian Fada, 36, a pipe-fitter, and Alan Fada, 38, a paint sprayer, worked in various shipyards and offshore. Fellow director Chris Hariton, an oil and gas planning engineer, is 44. "We got an opportunity to try out rope access work when it was very new," says Ian. "We saw the potential, thought it wasn't being exploited properly, and developed our own techniques. We met Chris when we worked on the same oil platform and decided to set up the business together."

The Daily Express

WORDS:

1 ropes: *cordes*
2 device: *appareil*
3 ranging from: *allant de, couvrant...*
4 turnover: *chiffre d'affaires*

Le discours direct et le discours indirect

Il existe deux façons de rapporter les paroles de quelqu'un :

- le discours direct : les paroles sont entre guillemets.

  Ex: *He said, "I am proud of my firm."*

- le discours indirect : les guillemets disparaissent et l'énonciateur utilise un verbe introductif.

  Ex: *He said (that) he was proud of his firm.*

Les verbes introductifs

L'énonciateur peut rapporter les paroles de quelqu'un. Les verbes introductifs les plus courants sont : *say, tell, declare, explain, reply …*

ATTENTION

Attention à l'emploi de *say* et *tell*.
- ***Tell* est obligatoirement suivi d'un nom ou d'un pronom ;**
- ***Say* est suivi d'une proposition. S'il est suivi d'un nom ou d'un pronom, *to* est obligatoire.**

Ex: *He told the boss / him (that) he was tired.*
▶ *He said to his boss / to him (that) he was tired.*

Temps et aspects au discours indirect

Lorsque le verbe introductif est au présent *V(-s)*, il n'y a pas de changement de temps ou d'aspect.

Ex: *He says: "I never arrive after 8 a.m."*
▶ *He says (that) he never **arrives** after 8 a.m.*

Ex: *He replies: "I have told him to arrive later."*
▶ *He replies (that) he **has told** him to arrive later.*

Lorsque le verbe introductif est au prétérit *(V-ed)*, les temps et les aspects changent.

V(s) ▶ *V-ed*

Ex: *Alan said: "It's interesting."*
▶ *Alan said (that) it **was** interesting.*

V-ed ▶ *had + V-en*

Ex: *Chris told Alan: "I saw Bob yesterday!"*
▶ *Chris told Alan (that) he **had seen** Bob the day before.*

have + V-en ▶ *had + V-en*

Ex: *Ian said: "I have tried another technique."*
▶ *Ian said (that) he **had tried** another technique.*

will ▶ *would*

Ex: *Chris said "I will come".*
▶ *Chris said (that) he **would** come.*

Changements obligatoires

Les pronoms personnels et les déterminants possessifs.

Ex: *Bob said: "**I** am pleased with **my** new job."*
▶ *Bob said (that) **he** was pleased with **his** new job.*

Les adverbes de temps et de lieu varient lorsque l'énonciateur rapporte les paroles à un autre moment et à un autre endroit.

Ex: *Roger said: "I met my new boss **yesterday**."*
▶ *Roger said that he had met his new boss **the day before**.*

Discours direct		Discours indirect
now	▶	*then*
today	▶	*that day*
yesterday	▶	*the day before*
tomorrow	▶	*the next day*
last week	▶	*the week before*
next week	▶	*the week after*
here	▶	*there*
this	▶	*that*
ago	▶	*before*

Les questions

Au discours indirect, l'ordre des mots est celui d'un énoncé affirmatif ; il n'y a pas de point d'interrogation.

- Présence d'un mot interrogatif au style direct. Ce mot interrogatif est conservé au style indirect.

Ex: *He asked me: "Where did you read this?"*
▶ *He asked me where I **had read** that.*

- Absence de mot interrogatif au style direct. On utilise *if*.

Ex: *He asked me: "Have you seen this job ad?"*
▶ *He asked me if I **had seen** that job ad.*

Les ordres

- Pour rapporter un ordre, on utilise *to + V*.

Ex: *Brian told them: "Close the door"*
▶ *Brian told them **to close** the door.*

- Pour rapporter une interdiction, on utilise *not + to + V*.

Ex: *The boss told us: "Don't arrive after 8 a.m."*
▶ *The boss told us **not to arrive** after 8 a.m.*

ENTRAÎNEZ-VOUS

1 Transformez les énoncés suivants au discours indirect.

a. Chris said: "I will be late tonight."
b. Brian answered: "We will start at 8 a.m."
c. Ian declared: "I have just finished my job."
d. Chris replied: "We can leave."

2 Rapportez les questions que vous a posées votre nouvel employeur.

He asked me…
a. Do you like working high up?
b. When did you arrive in England?
c. How long have you been working on oil platforms?
d. Can you weld and paint?

3 Complétez avec *say* ou *tell* à la forme voulue.

a. Brian … it was too late to work on this telescope.
b. I an … me to weld this piece.
c. Why did you … him to use this rope? It's too short!
d. No, I didn't … such a thing!

4 Rapportez les ordres donnés par votre employeur en utilisant l'amorce suivante :

He told me…
a. Bring your dungarees every day.
b. Don't be late.
c. Check your ropes before using them.
d. Never start working without Alan or Ian.

5 Rétablissez la ponctuation et les majuscules.

a. Roger told me that it was time to go
b. he asked me where did you leave the longest rope
c. he told me to learn a new technique
d. he asked Bob do you really want to work with us

6 Traduisez.

a. Il m'a dit de vérifier les échafaudages.
b. Je lui ai demandé si je pouvais utiliser n'importe quel matériel d'alpinisme.
c. Il a dit que les nacelles n'étaient plus utilisées.
d. J'ai demandé qui était mon patron : Alan ou Ian ?
e. Il a répondu : "Je suis le patron !"

JEUX DE MOTS

1 Trouvez les noms des métiers correspondant aux verbes suivants et traduisez-les.

Ex: *paint* ▸ *painter* (peintre)
a. weld, **b.** clean, **c.** drive, **d.** fit, **e.** spray.

2 Associez les mots de la liste A à leur contraire dans la liste B :

A. useless - badly - lose - find - far from - different - small - under.
B. same - above - close to - huge - look for - properly - win - useful.

3 Choisissez le suffixe *- al* ou *- ful* pour trouver les adjectifs à partir des noms suivants.

a. beauty
b. pain
c. care
d. nation
e. continent
f. stress
g. wonder
h. hope

4 Recherchez dans le texte p. 135 les synonymes des mots et expressions en gras :

a. ***Start*** a business
b. The company ***was created***
c. ***The staff***
d. ***Go into partnership with***
e. ***Have a chance to***

5 Complétez avec des prépositions.

a. Bill was working … a high oil platform.
b. It was 30ft … the water.
c. However he was always afraid… slipping and falling … the sea.
d. The magnet device kept him close … the structure.
e. However, he decided to look … a new job immediatly.
f. He would prefer to work … an office.

Language skills

D'UNE LANGUE À L'AUTRE

1 Observez la traduction du verbe *make* dans les phrases suivantes :

a. *The manager makes his employees work too hard.*
▶ Le directeur fait trop travailler ses employés.

b. *His attitude makes them furious.*
▶ Son comportement les rend furieux.

2 Traduisez en français.

a. Their device has made work on scaffoldings easier.
b. It made climbing very safe.
c. It also made them rich.
d. Their successful business made them famous.
e. But it made them stay long hours in their offices.
f. The staff complain because their boss makes them work overtime.

3 Traduisez en anglais.

a. Ils m'ont fait écrire une lettre.
b. Ils m'ont fait signer au bas de la page.
c. J'étais embauché et cela m'a rendu heureux.

ATELIER D'ÉCRITURE

1 Look at the drawing.
Report what the people said using indirect speech.
The journalist asked Roy if / why / what …
Roy answered / told / that …

2 Write 60 to 80 words about a workplace accident which happened to you or to a friend of yours.
Follow these steps.

- First, say who was involved in the accident, where and when it took place.
- Then, say exactly in what circumstances the accident happened (job being done, machine being used, environment, people around…).
- Next, say how serious the injury was and how it all ended.
- Finally, give your reactions or your friend's reactions and give some advice so that people could avoid accidents in the workplace.

CONSEILS D'ÉCRITURE

- **Utilisez le prétérit pour le récit et pensez aux marqueurs de temps.**
- **Vous devez rapporter les réactions du patron et des collègues à l'aide du discours indirect**
  They told me that... he asked why....
- **Donnez des conseils en utilisant les structures appropriées.**
  you should…, don't do…, why don't you…?

ADJECTIFS

available	*disponible*
faulty	*défectueux*
guilty	*coupable*
same	*même*

NOMS

brakes	*freins*
emergency	*urgence*
finger	*doigt*
frostbite	*gelure*
knee	*genou*
leg	*jambe*
oil	*pétrole*
opportunity	*occasion*
pain	*douleur*
painter	*peintre*
patient	*malade*
rope	*corde*
shift	*équipe*
step stool	*petit escabeau*
toe	*orteil*
turnover	*chiffre d'affaires*
wheelchair	*fauteuil roulant*

VERBES

be aware	*être au courant*
be fined	*avoir une amende*
crush	*écraser*
expand	*s'agrandir*
expect	*s'attendre à*
fall	*tomber*
feel	*sentir / ressentir*
get injured	*être blessé*
happen	*survenir / se passer*
hurt	*blesser / faire mal*
keep safe	*sécuriser*
look for	*chercher*
lose	*perdre*
need	*avoir besoin*
pulled into	*pris dans*
remove	*enlever*
set up	*monter*
spray	*vaporiser*
take to	*se mettre à*
twist	*tordre*

AUTRES

above	*au-dessus*
abroad	*à l'étranger*
among	*parmi*
still	*toujours / encore*

Exercices

1 Complétez avec les noms du lexique.

a. When you are hurt you feel a …

b. The boy couldn't feel his fingers because he had severe …

c. Handicapped people need … to move around.

d. The doctor visits his … every morning.

e. The nurse needed a … to reach the top cupboard.

f. The trainer fell down and broke his right…

2 Complétez à l'aide de verbes suivis d'une préposition.

a. The manager must … better safety equipment.

b. The accountant has just lost his job. His family hopes he won't … drinking.

c. The apprentice's shirt was … the machine.

d. They are fed up with their working conditions. They want to … their own business.

3 Trouvez les équivalents anglais des expressions en gras dans la liste.

a. The employer was found **responsible**.

b. The tribunal decided he had to **pay**.

c. The painter decided to **take off** the graffiti from the wall.

d. The manager will make a profit of £4,000 on his annual **sales** of £40,000.

e. The business is going to **become bigger**.

f. The young applicant is optimistic and **hopes** to be engaged.

4 Complétez les amorces de la colonne A avec les fins de phrases de la colonne B.

A	B
a. Jimmy fell…	1. …was broken.
b. Part of the platform…	2. … get injured in this way.
c. His leg…	3. … crushed him.
d. His body…	4. … was very intense.
e. He felt…	5. … hurt a lot all over.
f. The pain…	6. … off a high platform
g. Every year lots of people…	7. … terribly miserable.

It pays to keep it clean

There have been some interesting court cases in recent years highlighting the dangers and the absurdities which can result from bad housekeeping[1].

Once two workers were individually fined £40 each for openly smoking in non-smoking areas. When a factory inspector visited the workplace, he discovered the two men smoking next to some cylinders containing highly flammable liquid. And 43 cigarette ends were discovered nearby.

Another extreme case was that of the butcher who broke every hygiene rule[2] that existed. He was fined £240 for amongst other things: dirty and blood-spattered[3] walls and floors; no hot water supply; dirty hand towels; broken cement at the back of the sink, and 755 lbs of bad meat left in the freezer.

Another example of bad housekeeping is when a worker puts a package in a place another cannot see. The second worker then steps back and falls over, possibly while he is carrying a heavy load. This type of incident has led to many accidents and fines.

A variation on this theme occurred in a research laboratory in Redhill. Chemicals were stored underneath the floor in a cellar two feet deep. The entrance was covered by a floor-lid[4]. One man opened the lid to fetch a chemical and left the lid off[5]. When his colleague stepped back from his workbench[6] holding a beaker[7] of hydrofluoric acid, he fell down the cellar, severely burning himself.

Another really strange case involved a woman who came into work early, went into the kitchen area, and slipped[8] on some custard, injuring her back. She successfully sued the company proving that it pays to keep it clean. Accidents can be expensive!

Safety

WORDS:

1 housekeeping: *entretien*
2 break a rule: *violer un règlement*
3 blood-spattered walls: *des murs couverts d'éclaboussures de sang*
4 a floor lid: *une trappe dans le sol*
5 leave the lid off: *laisser la trappe ouverte*
6 a workbench: *un établi, une table de travail*
7 a beaker: *un gobelet*
8 slip: *glisser*

A Relatez en français quatre infractions citées dans le texte et précisez, si possible, le lieu, le risque et la pénalité. 8 pts

B Traduisez en francais le dernier paragraphe. 4 pts

C Mettez au discours indirect. 2 pts

1. The factory inspector said to the two workers:
"It is forbidden to smoke in this area!"
The factory inspector told the two workers …
2. The chef asked his apprentice:
"When did you last clean the fridge?"
The chef asked his apprentice...

D Mettez au discours direct. 2 pts

1. The factory nurse told the manager
that there were too many accidents in the laboratory.
The factory nurse told the manager: " … "
2. The workers' spokesman said
that they would go on strike if nothing was done.
The workers' spokesman said: " … "

E Répondez en anglais en 80 mots environ. 4 pts

Give some of the safety rules in a place where you have worked.
Give an example of what can happen if somebody breaks the safety rules.

Conseils pour l'examen : l'épreuve orale

Vous pouvez vous présenter à un oral d'anglais facultatif lors des épreuves du baccalauréat. Cet oral est avant tout une épreuve de communication. Il s'appuie en partie sur un document étudié pendant l'année et en partie sur votre stage en entreprise. Sa durée est de 20 minutes.

A. Première partie de l'épreuve

Le candidat doit tout d'abord présenter le document choisi (texte, dialogue, etc.).

1 Préparez au brouillon la présentation du document à l'aide des éléments suivants :
type de texte - origine - date - thème - iconographie

1. The document is …
   It was published in …
   It comes from …
   It was written by …
2. The picture shows …
   It is composed of …
   It illustrates …
3. The text is about …
   The text deals with …
   The main idea of the text is …

2 Assurez vous-même la présentation du document à l'aide de phrases simples mais correctes.

B. Deuxième partie de l'épreuve

Le professeur pose ensuite des questions de compréhension sur le texte. Pour saisir rapidement le sens des questions, soyez particulièrement attentif au pronom interrogatif et au verbe.

- Faites des réponses complètes ***(full sentences)***.
- Si on vous pose une yes / no question, on vous demandera de justifier à l'aide du texte (à vous de retrouver rapidement la justification demandée !)
- Le professeur pourra vous demander votre avis sur le problème ou la situation développés dans le texte. Essayez d'y réfléchir pendant le temps de préparation !
- Utilisez : ***I think that…, In my opinion…, Personally…*** et justifiez avec ***Because… This is why…***

On peut vous demander d'évaluer le document. Il faudra dire ce que vous en pensez et justifier :
I find this text interesting because …
I agree with the writer's opinion because …
I find this text surprising because …

C. Troisième partie de l'épreuve

Le professeur pourra vous poser des questions plus personnelles en liaison avec le thème du texte. Par exemple, si vous commentez un texte sur Londres, il vous demandera si vous connaissez cette ville. Essayez de prévoir les questions possibles !

D. Quatrième partie de l'épreuve

Le professeur vous interrogera sur votre stage en entreprise. Il est donc indispensable de relire le rapport que vous avez rédigé au cours de l'année. Il pourra aussi vous poser des questions plus générales sur votre avenir.

Voici quelques questions possibles :

- When did you do your work experience?
- Where did you do it?
- What did you have to do?
- Did you enjoy it? Why?
- What job would you like to find?
- Have you got any plans for the summer, for the future?

NOTE

En cas de problème pendant l'entretien, vous pouvez intervenir en anglais en utilisant :

- *I'm sorry. Could you repeat, please?*
- *Could you speak more slowly, please?*

EXERCICE

Complétez les amorces de réponses.

1. What country have you already visited?
   I have been to…
   I visited… in 20…
2. How did you like it?
   It was… The country… The people I met… The weather…
3. Would you like to go there again and what for?
   Yes, I would… to work... and... a summer job.
4. What means of transport do you usually use?
   I usually take…
   I travel by…
   I drive to…
5. Do you mind using public transport?
   No, I…, I think it... … and safe.
6. Why did you enjoy your work experience?
   Because I… with adults. I learned how to… and I… a lot of confidence.
7. Are you going to pursue your studies?
   No, I'd like to enter the... world because...
8. What are you going to do to find a job?
   I… the ads, then… send… to firms… go to the local job centre.
9. What job would you like to get?
   I'd like to… in... because... and as I am qualified in..., I think...
10. Would you prefer to work in a small firm or in a big one and why?
    I'd prefer... a big firm because... … a modern equipment, and… more opportunities

kit 13

© PROD DB

Spying

© SPL/Cosmos

Speaking

- What is the man in the large picture doing?
- What is special about the shoe? Imagine what the man can do with it.
- What sort of a film does the photo come from? Which famous character does the man make you think of?
- Look at the small picture. What do you think it is?
- Who uses these devices? What for?

STREET TALK

A dream of mine

◂ Lindsay Moran, USA.

© Photonica/Getty
© couverture livre de L.Moran Penguin Group (USA)

1 **Listen to these words from the interview.**

- actually • involve • paramilitary
- extreme • defensive
- surveillance • recruitmen
- misconceptions • convince
- assumed • in actuality.

2 **Listen to Lindsay and fill in your questionnaire.**

I Is he really a pilot?

Frank Abagnale Jr passed millions of dollars in bad checks. He successfully passed himself off as a pilot, a doctor and a lawyer, and travelled the globe - all before he was 21. After serving jail time, Abagnale started working with the FBI to help catch other forgers.

Could a kid today do what you did?

Frank: It's so much easier today because of technology. It would take ten minutes to create a forged check with a laptop and a printer. We could make up IDs and airline identification cards and all sorts of things with the color copiers, scanners, digitizers, ink jet printers, all the technology that's available today.

© Amblin-Magellin-Bungalow 78/DR/TCD

Do you think that even with police databases it would be possible for someone to do what you did, crisscrossing the globe?

Frank: Yeah. Unfortunately there are much more brilliant criminals than I was who have not been caught yet. The truth is today we live in an extremely unethical society. We don't teach ethics at home, we don't teach it in school. Ironically, I teach ethics at the FBI Academy because of who I am. I teach young agents about character and ethics. I stress the importance of that over everything else.

Interview: Franck Abagnale, jr
www.spielbergfilms.com

FEEDBACK

1 ▸ Pick out elements showing that Frank was not an honest man.
2 ▸ What are people who do this "job" called? (see introduction)
3 ▸ When did he start working for the FBI? What does his job consist in?
4 ▸ Why do you think the FBI gave Frank a job?
5 ▸ Why is it easier now to copy all sorts of documents?
6 ▸ According to Frank, is it easier or more difficult to be a criminal today? Justify.
7 ▸ What does *ethics* mean: political ideas / moral principles / scientific rules?
8 ▸ Why does Frank insist on teaching ethics to young FBI agents?

2 *Spy*: A reality show

Have you ever wondered[1] what it would be like to be a spy? *Spy* is a new 10-part series that will show what the secret world of intelligence and espionage is really like. The programme gives ordinary people the chance to become a James Bond. They will leave their old lives behind, relocate to a new city and assume a whole new identity.

© Photo12.com

The selection process

The team of experts looked for people of all ages, and from all walks of life[2] to take part. The candidates had to have the key skills needed to make a good spy. A series of questions and exercises were designed to test all applicants.

Spy school

Spy school HQ[3] was based at a secret location in central London. The two-month training consisted of tests, missions and challenges. Highly specialised lessons covered surveillance and counter-surveillance training, planting bugs, code-breaking, interrogation techniques, assuming a new identity and "going grey" – the ability not to be noticed into any environment.

The series has a competitive element - to see who will make the best spy. At the end of the course, the applicants take part in a full-scale operation, competing against each other. Only then will they know what it truly takes to be a spy. Could you be a spy?

BBC

WORDS:

1 wonder: *se demander*
2 all walks of life: *tous les milieux*
3 HQ (headquarters): *quartiers généraux*

FEEDBACK

1 ▸ What domain will the new BBC reality show explore?
2 ▸ How will the programme change the candidates' lives?
3 ▸ Did the experts select young and rich candidates only? Justify.
4 ▸ How did the experts choose the candidates?
5 ▸ Where and how long did the training take place?
6 ▸ Pick out the expressions meaning: hiding microphones - pretending to be someone else
7 ▸ Find the sentence which explains what "going grey" means.
8 ▸ What did they have to learn on the training course?
9 ▸ Is the TV series challenging? Justify.
10 ▸ How does the course finish?

Comprehension

© SPL/Cosmos

Before you read

1. Describe the pictures.
2. What is Russian Roulette?
   What do you think the text is about?

Read the text

3. Check your answer above.
4. Match the two columns.

• Ivanov	• the place where the company was located
• Chelyabinsk	• Federal Bureau of Investigation
• Seattle	• the place where Ivanov was imprisoned
• Invita security	• Ivanov's friend and colleague
• Gorshkov	• an American company
• FBI	• a Russian computer programmer
• Connecticut	• Ivanov's home town in Russia
• New England	• the place where the two Russians are living now

Read the first two paragraphs

5. Why did Ivanov fly to the USA?
6. What did Invita Security promise him?
7. What "other job" was he very good at?
8. What did Ivanov suggest to the company?
9. In §2, find expressions meaning:
   enter illegally - give work to
10. What did Invita Security need Ivanov and Gorshkov for?

Read the end of the text

11. What were the two Russians asked to do in the Seattle office?
12. How did the interviewers feel the programmers' demonstration?
13. What happened later?
14. Could the two Russians fly back to Russia?
    Say why or why not.
15. What does the journalist think of the hackers' American adventure?
    Was it a complete failure (*échec*)?

ALLEZ PLUS LOIN

1 Quel élément de l'expression *"the doors flew open"* (ligne 31) indique une certaine brutalité dans l'action ?

2 Quel est le champ lexical du paragraphe 5 ? D'après le contexte déduisez le sens des verbes : *were charged - were jailed - be tried.* Pourquoi sont-ils au passif ? ▸ **FICHE** p. 00

3 Qui étaient en réalité les deux hommes d'affaires ? Justifiez votre réponse à partir du texte.

RÉSUMEZ

1 Ecoutez l'enregistrement et résumez en anglais.

- Ivanov - Vasiliy - Russian computer programmers - applied - job - Invita Security - the USA
- company - interested - two Russians - excellent hackers
- Invita security - pretended - needed - two Russians - break into - customers' networks
- in fact - conspiracy - FBI - arrest - hackers
- after spending - prison - now - live - work - legally

2 Résumez en français.

- Dites ce que vous savez des deux jeunes Russes.
- En quoi devait consister leur travail pour la société Invita Security ?
- Pourquoi leur expérience américaine a-t-elle tourné au cauchemar ?

Grammaire en contexte

1. Dans les énoncés suivants :

- *(§ 2) "They wanted* ***them to persuade*** *those companies…"*
- *(§ 3) "The interviewers* ***asked their guests to demonstrate*** *some of their skills…"*

a) Identifiez les éléments en gras.
b) Dans le premier énoncé, remplacez *"them"* par un nom.
c) Devinez comment s'appellent ces propositions.
d) Citez les verbes qui les introduisent.

Russian Roulette

Ivanov, then a 20-year-old computer programmer from Chelyabinsk, Russia, had flown to Seattle in November 2000 to apply for a job with a company called Invita Security. To the young Russian, Invita promised the dream job. The company even promised him they would pay his airfare and pick him up at Seattle airport.

At Ivanov's suggestion, the company encouraged him to bring along a fellow programmer, Vasiliy Gorshkov. When the two Russians arrived, their Invita hosts told them what they wanted them to do. They needed a few good hackers to break into the networks of potential customers. They wanted them to persuade those companies to hire Invita to keep hackers out. Ivanov was familiar with the tactic.

© Taxi/Getty

As Ivanov, Gorshkov and two American business types sat at a table in a Seattle office, Gorshkov regaled the interviewers with tales of his hacking exploits, and Ivanov allowed himself to dream of a better life. He was exhausted. The trip from Chelyabinsk had taken nearly 48 hours. The interviewers asked their guests to demonstrate some of their skills, and the two Russians took turns logging into their own network back in Chelyabinsk. Ivanov knew that he and Gorshkov were good, so when his hosts appeared to be impressed, Ivanov was not surprised.

The big surprise would come later, when the two Russians were being driven to their lodgings. The car stopped suddenly; the doors flew open, and Ivanov heard someone say: "FBI. Get out of the car with your hands behind your back." It was then that he remembered something he had heard about America. It was the kind of place where anything could happen.

Ivanov and Gorshkov were charged with conspiracy, computer fraud, hacking and extortion. Gorshkov was jailed in Seattle and Ivanov was flown east, to Connecticut, to be tried and imprisoned.

Today, the most significant gain from the Ivanov case may be for Alexey Ivanov and Gorshkov themselves. Their goal had long been to come to the United States. And now they are there, living and working in New England.

www.msnbe.com/news

La proposition infinitive

Définition

Une proposition infinitive est une proposition subordonnée qui comporte un sujet et un verbe à l'infinitif.

Ex: *Invita Security wants **Ivanov to work** in Seattle.*
- Invita Security veut qu'Ivanov travaille à Seattle.

*The company wants **the two men to demonstrate** their skills.*
- La société veut que les deux hommes fassent une démonstration de leurs compétences.

Si le sujet est un pronom, ce dernier se met à la forme complément *(me, you, him, her, it, us, you, them)*.

Ex: *Invita Security wants **him to work** in Seattle.*
- Invita Security veut qu'il travaille à Seattle.

*The company wants **them to demonstrate** their skills.*
- La société veut qu'ils fassent une démonstrarion de leurs compétences.

Si la proposition est à la forme négative, *not* se place avant l'infinitif.

Ex: *His parents advised him **not** to rush to Seattle.*
- Ses parents lui ont conseillé de ne pas se précipiter à Seattle.

Les verbes introduisant une proposition infinitive

La proposition infinitive s'emploie après les verbes qui servent à donner des ordres, des conseils, qui marquent une pression du sujet sur autrui.

ask

Ex: *Ivanov asked Gorshkov to be ready to leave.*
- Ivanov a demandé à Gorshkov d'être prêt à partir.

want

Ex: *Ivanov does not want his parents to worry.*
- Ivanov ne veut pas que ses parents s'inquiètent.

advise

Ex: *Ivanov advised Gorshkov to arrive at 7 at the airport.*
- Ivanov a conseillé à Gorshkov d'arriver à 7 heures à l'aéroport.

expect

Ex: *He expects him not to be late.*
- Il s'attend à ce qu'il ne soit pas en retard.

allow

Ex: *Invita Security allowed them to travel for free.*
- Invita Security leur a permis de voyager gratuitement.

tell

Ex: *The two Americans told them to get out of the car.*
- Les deux Américains leur ont dit de sortir de la voiture.

prefer

Ex: *They would prefer Ivanov to come to the USA.*
- Ils préfèrent qu'Ivanov vienne aux Etats-Unis.

order

Ex: *The two Americans ordered them to hold up their hands.*
- Les deux Américains leur ont ordonné de lever les mains.

would like

Ex: *He would like them to give more details.*
- Il aimerait qu'ils donnent plus de détails.

REMARQUE

Lorsque le premier verbe exprime une préférence ou une volonté (*prefer*, *want*, *would like*), la traduction en français fait apparaître "que".

Ex: *They wanted the two Russians to come to Seattle*
- *Ils voulaient que les deux russes viennent à Seattle*

ENTRAÎNEZ-VOUS

1 Relevez les propositions infinitives dans les énoncés suivants.

a. My friends told me to visit Seattle.
b. They said I should go to San Francisco.
c. They also advised me to brush up my English.
d. Finally, they thought I would get the dream job!
e. A few weeks later, I realized they were wrong.

2 Remettez les mots dans l'ordre et découvrez comment devenir un espion.

a. answer / series / questions / of / The / wanted / me / a / to / experts /
b. break / They / codes / told / to / me /
c. identity / advised / have / new / a / They / to / me /
d. They / become / would / like / to / James / me / Bond / a /

3 Ivanov raconte son arrestation. Utilisez les amorces.

a. "Put your hands behind your back." They ordered …
b. "Don't talk to your colleague." They advised …
c. "Give us your passport." They wanted …
d. "Follow the instructions." They expected …

4 Complétez les amorces.

a. Gorshkov was going to leave Russia.
His girlfriend didn't like the idea.
His girlfriend didn't want…
b. He wanted to sell his flat.
His parents didn't agree.
His parents didn't want …
c. Ivanov won't come to his sister's wedding.
The family regrets it.
The family would like ….
d. Ivanov's brother planned to fly to Seattle.
Ivanov did not agree.
Ivanov advised…

5 Traduisez.

a. Nous voulons que tu restes à Chelyabinsk.
b. Mes parents aimeraient que je leur écrive.
c. Je vous conseille de ne pas appeler votre famille.
d. Ils m'ont dit d'attendre le procès.

JEUX DE MOTS

1 Complétez les phrases avec les mots de liaison suivants :
in order to / finally / because / so / in spite of

a. A man was arrested at the airport … his passport was forged.
b. The police took the man to an office … question him.
c. … the presence of his lawyer the man was really scared.
d. The police realised he didn't understand their language, …they called a translator.
e. … they managed to get some useful information from the man.

2 Trouvez le contraire des adjectifs suivants :
worse - earlier - unfamiliar - hard - extraordinary - unskilled

3 Complétez les phrases avec le mot qui vous paraît le plus approprié.
Demandez-vous d'abord à quelle catégorie grammaticale il doit appartenir.

a. When the two Russians saw the American businessmen, they were very ….
b. The … from the airport to the Americans' office was quite long.
c. Please show us some … your skills.
d. Put your hands … your back.
e. The two men were … shocked.

4 Le nom *hacker* se décompose en *hack* + *er*. Trouvez les noms correspondant aux verbes ci-dessous.

- work, programme, keep, interview, design, drive, forge, manage

Utilisez les noms obtenus pour compléter ces mots composés.

- a dress… / a truck… / a bank… / a comput… / a passport… / a radio… / a goal… / an office…

D'UNE LANGUE À L'AUTRE

1 Lisez ces phrases et leur traduction et dites quel mode on utilise en français pour traduire les subordonnées infinitives introduites par *want*, *like*, *love*, *prefer*.

a. *The FBI men would like the young expert to go on a mission.*
▸ Les hommes du FBI aimeraient que le jeune spécialiste aille en mission.

b. *He would prefer them to give him a full-time job.*
▸ Il préfèrerait qu'ils lui donnent un travail à temps complet.

c. *He wanted the manager to give him an appointment.*
▸ Il voulait que le directeur lui donne un rendez-vous.

2 Traduisez en français.

a. He does not want his daughter to take part in the reality show.
b. He would prefer her to keep her job.
c. He expects her boss to fire her.
d. He advised her to think of her future.

3 Traduisez en anglais.

a. Le policier veut qu'ils apportent leur carte d'identité.
b. Il les a autorisés à rentrer chez eux.
c. Il préfèrerait qu'ils ne quittent pas la ville.

ATELIER D'ÉCRITURE

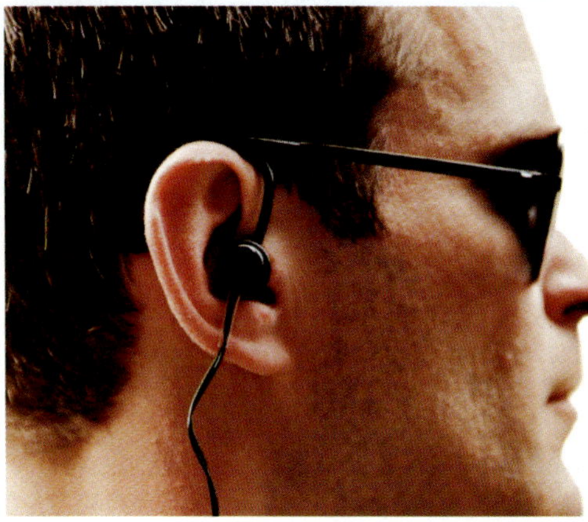

© Photonica/Getty

1 What did the experts want / expect / order / advise / tell / ask.... the applicants to do during their training for the Spy Reality Show?

The experts wanted the applicants ...

Word box:

- learn code breaking, assume a new identity, learn how to plant bugs, compete against each other, feel at ease anywhere, watch their environment, be very careful, develop their own tactic…

2 You are attending a spy course. Your teacher is very strict about the school rules. Write the speech he makes at the beginning of the school year. (Write about 80 words)

Follow these steps:

- First the teacher welcomes the students.
- Then he tells them about the school rules, what he wants them to do and not to do (working hours, breaks, lunch time, clothes, no smoking places, lateness, punctuality…).
- Finally he wishes them a good school year.

CONSEILS D'ÉCRITURE

- **N'oubliez pas que le règlement de l'école est très strict.**
- **Dans la deuxième partie du discours commencez les phrases par :** *I don't want you to, I advise you to, I would like you to, I prefer you to...*
- **Justifiez chaque règle du professeur en utilisant des mots de liaison :** *because, as, in order to ...*

ADJECTIFS

exhausted ▸ *épuisé*

NOMS

ability ▸ *capacité*
airfare ▸ *prix du billet d'avion*
databases ▸ *bases de données*
dream ▸ *rêve*
factory ▸ *usine*
fellow ▸ *type, homme*
forger ▸ *faussaire*
goal ▸ *but*
guest ▸ *invité*
jail ▸ *prison*
laptop ▸ *ordinateur portable*
lawyer ▸ *avocat*
network ▸ *réseau*
printer ▸ *imprimante*
skill ▸ *compétence*
tale ▸ *conte*
training ▸ *formation*
trip ▸ *voyage*
truth ▸ *vérité*

VERBES

apply for ▸ *postuler pour*
be charged ▸ *être accusé*
be like ▸ *ressembler*
be tried ▸ *être jugé*
break into ▸ *entrer par effraction*
catch ▸ *attraper*
design ▸ *créer*
fly ▸ *aller en avion*
hear about ▸ *entendre parler de*
hire ▸ *engager*
keep out ▸ *protéger*
leave ▸ *partir*
need ▸ *avoir besoin*
notice ▸ *remarquer*
pass off ▸ *se faire passer*
pick up ▸ *prendre quelqu'un ou quelque chose*
remember ▸ *se souvenir*
stress ▸ *mettre l'accent, insister*
take turns ▸ *prendre son tour*
wonder ▸ *se demander*

AUTRES

behind ▸ *derrière*
each other ▸ *les uns les autres*
halfway ▸ *à mi chemin*
nearly ▸ *presque*
truly ▸ *véritablement*
unfortunately ▸ *malheureusement*

Exercices

1 Trouvez dans la liste le verbe synonyme des deux verbes donnés.

a. draw, create ▸ …
c. insist, focus on ▸ …
d. engage, employ ▸ …
e. go away, be off ▸ …

2 Complétez avec des noms du lexique.

a. Today with a computer and a printer it is quite easy to become a …
b. But you need some … in computing.
c. Ivanov was able to break into people's ….
d. His … was to make a lot of money and to travel round the world.
e. In Russia the two hackers used to work in an abandoned ….
f. They were invited to go to the USA, so they didn't have to pay their … .
g. As they were found guilty they were sent to ….
h. The ... was that the two Americans were actually FBI agents.

3 Choisissez dans la liste le verbe à particule qui convient pour compléter les phrases suivantes.

a. Don't worry, we'll … you … at the airport!
b. It was not very difficult for the hacker to … the firm's computer network.
c. Did you … this job when you saw the ad?
d. You need antivirus software to … bugs ….
e. Let me know if you … a company that needs a new employee.

Never too young

Andrew Butt, 20, is managing director of Enable Software, a company with an annual turnover[1] of £1 million. He has 16 employees, flies a helicopter, owns two homes and a Mercedes, and travels the world.

The company that Andrew founded three years ago with his partner, Denys Shortt, helps businesses to manage and develop websites, intranet and other areas. The idea was simple."I decided to create software that any company director could use." says Andrew.

He aimed to ensure that if a director wanted to change something on his website or add a new piece of information to his intranet, he could do so without calling in expensive experts. Companies loved it. In a year, Enable has sold more than £1 million of software.

Andrew had a fascination for computers from an early age and spent every evening after school at his PC. At 12, he got his first taste[2] of working with computers in the real world when his father, an accountant, allowed him to help out at a local helicopter company near his home in Coventry.

At 14, he set up a one-man business selling computer hardware and solving computer problems and turnover hit £12,000 within six months. With business booming, he was keen to leave school. His parents agreed, provided that he had a private tutor to help him to pass his school examinations. By then, the internet was taking off[3] and Andrew decided to add website design and development to his business, and was soon working on more than 1,000 sites. At 16 he joined forces with Denys Shortt, a distributor of hi-tech products.

Andrew is an ideal role model for other young entrepreneurs. His message: "Age is not a problem. Just so long as you have total confidence in yourself, your ability and your products, you can succeed."

The Times, Saturday, July 12, 2003 (adapted)

WORDS:

1 a turnover: *un chiffre d'affaires*
2 a taste: *un aperçu*
3 to take off: *décoller*

A Donnez les informations en français. 2 pts

Andrew Butt : âge, domicile, profession du père.
Son entreprise : nom, activité, associé, nombre d'employés, chiffre d'affaires.

B Répondez aux questions en français. 7 pts

1. Décrivez les débuts professionnels d'Andrew Butt.
2. Quelle activité Andrew Butt a-t-il entreprise à l'âge de 14 ans ? Donnez des précisions.
3. Comment son entreprise a-t-elle évolué ?
4. Quel est le message délivré par Andrew Butt ?

C Traduisez le 3 ème paragraphe. *"He aimed to ensure ... £1 million of software"* 3 pts

D Mettez les verbes entre parenthèses à la forme qui convient. 2 pts

If you want to gain the skills your company *(need)* in today's modern world, please *(contact)* EMPOWER TRAINING SERVICES. We guarantee our course *(improve)* your opportunities and make life easier. In the past five years we successfully *(train)* more than 500 students.

E Complétez avec les mots de liaison. 2 pts

in order to - unless - although - but - in spite of - so that.

1. The results last year were bad, ... they could have been worse.
2. The company is now doing better ... its recent problems.
3. ... the new manager has not been in charge for long, a number of changes have already been made.
4. A website has been set up ... make business more efficient.

F Rédigez en anglais une présentation de l'entreprise "BOX OFFICE". 4 pts

COMPANY FACT FILE

Name:	*BOX OFFICE*
Location:	*Birmingham, UK*
Employees:	*18*
Activity:	*Manufacturing (box files for office use)*
Production:	*350,000 files per year*
Turnover:	*£500,000 in 2003*
Future plans:	*Expansion / introduction of on-line sales*

kit 14

© Sevans/AP/Sipa

The grass is greener

Speaking

- Guess what the woman's job consists of and who she is talking to.
- Say as much as you can about the card at the bottom of the page. What is it for?
- Can you think of any reasons why people want to leave their country?

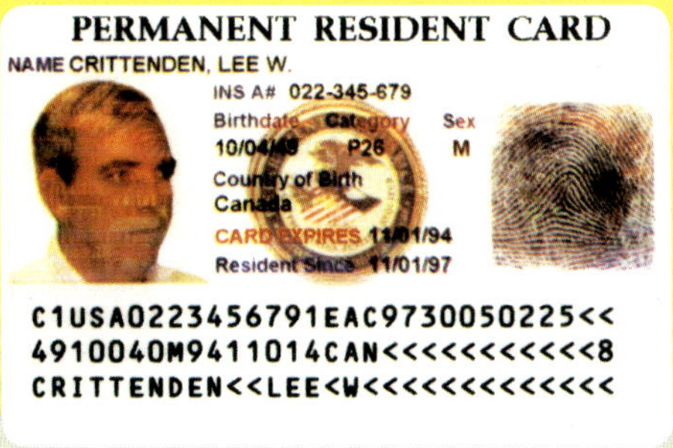

© AP Photo/Khu Bui

STREET TALK

It all started as a joke

© Judy Martinez/Hachette

1 Listen to these words from the interview.

- involves • catering • staff
- guests • running of the restaurant
- encourage • Portuguese
- Madeira • Guernsey • worth it.

2 Listen to Leonardo and fill in your questionnaire.

Leonardo, The Carlton Hotel, Bournemouth, U.K.

I Green card lottery

Each year the U.S. Government, through its diversity visa program, makes 55,000 immigrant visas available to eligible people.

Applicants for the U.S. Diversity Program Immigration Visas are initially chosen through a lottery. Immigrant visas are given to six geographic regions, with a greater number of visas going to regions with lower rates of immigration – and no visas going to countries sending more than 50,000 immigrants to the U.S. in the past five years. No country can receive more than 3,500 diversity program visas in any one year.

The winner can enter the U.S. and exchange the immigrant visa for a green card, given by the Immigration and Naturalization Service (INS). If the winner is already in the U.S., he or she can get a green card from INS without leaving the country.

© R. Crandall/Picture Group

FEEDBACK

1 ▸ Say what the document is about:
- a lottery that allows the winners to visit the USA for free,
- a lottery that allows the winners to work and live in the USA,
- a lottery that is reserved to Europeans.

2 ▸ Which countries cannot enter the lottery?

3 ▸ Which countries will get more visas?

4 ▸ What is the maximum number of visas given to the same country?

5 ▸ What card does a winner get when he arrives in the USA?

2 Tips for green cards winners

© L. Sparham/Matrix/Cosmos

I won the Green Card lottery and came to the United States last year. Since then I have faced a few problems that should be a lesson for anyone.

You need a driver's license to prove you are here legally. Unless you live in New York or Chicago, you definitely need a car to go to work.

You cannot work without a social security card. You have to wait in rain and snow at 4 a.m. in the morning to get one.

But America can really be the land of opportunity if you are a hard worker. Labour is valued in this country.

My life here, as far as money is concerned, is much better than in Kenya. But for the first months, I thought of packing up and going back home. So my advice to anyone who has won the Diversity Visa Programme is that there is life at the end of the tunnel. Good luck in your pursuits.

Concerned Kenyan

FEEDBACK

1 ▸ What is the nationality of the narrator?

2 ▸ How did he come to the USA?

3 ▸ Pick out a piece of advice he gives to people coming to the USA.

4 ▸ Is a social security card necessary?

5 ▸ Has he ever regretted coming to the USA? Justify.

3 At home in America?

Born in Guyana, I came to NY on a student visa in 1990 at 20. I had no relatives here when I came. My first job was as a helper in a mechanic's shop. Then I worked at McDonald's sweeping and mopping before being in charge of security in a clothing store.

A year later, I worked at the neighborhood Key Food supermarket for two years until I finished college. I worked 7 days, 35/hrs a week. I graduated second in my class.

I shared a one-bedroom attic with my three brothers who later joined me over here. It was infested with cockroaches[1] and mice and in winter it was freezing. Upon graduation, things got better. We moved into a first floor apartment with 2 bedrooms. Today, my wife and I own a home and I am working on an MBA[2].

Mine is the story of a successful immigrant. I am so grateful for the opportunities given to me by this country and I was glad to become a citizen. But I don't feel like an 'American', I still feel like a foreigner. I hope one day my son can truly feel at home in America.

Chabi

© AP/Sipapress

WORDS:

1 cockroaches: *cafards*

2 MBA: *diplôme d'études commerciales supérieures*

FEEDBACK

1 ▸ Say:
- which continent Chabi came from;
- if he went to New York to find a job;
- how old he was;
- if he had any family in New York when he arrived.

2 ▸ List the different places he worked in and the jobs he did in each workplace.

3 ▸ Did he work hard? Justify.

4 ▸ Were his living conditions good? Justify.

5 ▸ Pick out elements showing that his story as an immigrant is a successful one?

6 ▸ Imagine the reasons why he still feels like a foreigner.

Comprehension

© C. Brown/SABA-REA

Before you read

1. Describe the pictures.
   Say what these people want to do.
   For what reasons?
2. Look at the title and say what you think the document is about?

Read the text

3. Check your answers.
4. Pick out as much information as you can about Xico: age, possible native country, what he looks like, etc.

Read paragraphs 1, 2 and 3

5. What country does the "promised land" refer to?
6. What does Xico intend to do?
7. Is it the first time that Xico has tried to get into the "promised land"? Justify.
8. Who regularly stops him and his companions?
9. Find three important conditions that will make his crossing successful.
10. Pick out the reason why Xico is determined to cross the border.

Read the end of the text

11. Compare the Hispanic population to the other minorities.
12. Who do migrants have to pay money to? Does the amount of money vary? Justify.
13. Where do Xico and his companions spend the night? What are they determined to do?

ALLEZ PLUS LOIN

1 Où se trouve Xico? Quelle est la ville américaine dont il aperçoit les lumières?

2 Découpez les mots *moonlight* (l.15) et *roadblock* (l.33) pour en trouver le sens. ▸ **FICHE** p. 75

3 D'après le contexte que peut signifier census (l.21) ? Donnez un mot français de la même famille.
▸ **FICHE** p. 53

4 Que pense l'agent James Garvey de la plupart de ces clandestins ?

5 Expliquez la technique appelée "*banzai*" utilisée par les futurs immigrants. Faites preuve de logique pour deviner le sens des mots *spot* (l.36) et *wrapping* (l.35) ▸ **FICHE** p. 53

RÉSUMEZ

1 Ecoutez l'enregistrement et résumez en anglais.

- Xico – trying – once again – border – the USA
- been caught – already – never give up
- the USA – country – sure – find – job – money
- the USA – attracts – various nationalities – such as – Irish – Chinese – Iraquis – Russians
- people – smugglers – enter – promised land
- have – invented – technique – banzai – allows – large number – border

2 Résumez en français.

- Quels faits montrent que les candidats à l'émigration sont vraiment déterminés à franchir la frontière ?
- Quelle est la raison principale qui les pousse à quitter leur pays ?

Grammaire en contexte

1. **Relevez tous les énoncés du texte faisant référence à l'avenir.**
2. **Identifiez les éléments des structures employées.**
3. **Traduisez l'énoncé suivant en français et comparez les formes verbales en anglais et en français.**
   I will be back when the weather is fine.

A new life in a promised land

Xico is just a few steps away from the promised land. He is 24, moustachioed and wearing a small backpack. Below him twinkle the lights of San Ysidro in the United States. Like Xico some 100 other men are also going to try to cross the border.

© UPPA

"I have been caught six times" says Xico, writing his name down in a notebook to ensure that the spelling is correct. But I always say to the border patrol I will be back!"

He is camping in the hills, waiting for the right conjunction of moonlight, shift changes and luck that will take him over the border to a job in construction that will pay him ten times what he earns in his own country.

This month the US census showed that for the first time the Hispanic population in the US makes up the largest of the minorities. Of the different nationalities that have attempted to cross into the US via the Californian border, there have been Irish, Chinese, Iraquis, and, more recently, Russians. Some pay smugglers the normal fee of around $1,500 to $2,000, although one Chinese caught had paid $35,000. "Most of them are decent folks, and if you tell them to stop, they stop," says the agent James Garvey.

WORDS:

1 skirt: *longer*
2 drag: *traîner*
3 tyre: *pneu*
4 smooth: *lisser*
5 foam: *mousse*

But some do not. One technique is known as 'banzai' in which up to 100 would-be migrants gather and rush the border. They know that seven or eight will be caught, but the majority will get through – at least as far as the first roadblock. Every night the border patrol skirt[1] the area in their vehicles dragging[2] a tyre[3] to smooth[4] over the sand so that they can spot any footsteps later. The migrants try to combat this by wrapping their feet in carpet material or foam[5].

Back in Tijuana, Xico and his companions head into the hill for the night. They live to cross another day. In fact, they're crossing tomorrow.

The Guardian

L'expression du futur

RAPPEL
En anglais, il n'y a que deux temps : le présent *(V(-s))* et le prétérit *(V-ed)*.
Pour évoquer le futur, l'énonciateur dispose de structures qui expriment des points de vue différents.

Will + V

Lorsque l'énonciateur emploie will, il fait une déduction d'après ce qu'il sait de la situation.

Ex: *Xico **will be** 25 in July.*
▸ Xico aura 25 ans en juillet.

Forme affirmative : sujet + *will / 'll* + *V*
Ex: *They **will /'ll** be happy in the United States.*
▸ Ils seront heureux au Etats-Unis.

Forme interrogative : *will* + sujet + *V* + *?*
Ex: ***Will they earn** more money?*
▸ Gagneront-ils plus d'argent ?

Forme négative : sujet + *will not / won't* + *V*
Ex: *They **will not / won't** come back.*
▸ Ils ne reviendront pas.

ATTENTION

***When* et *as soon as* sont suivis du présent *V(-s)*, contrairement au français.**

Ex: *I will leave as soon as he **comes back**.*
▸ Je partirai dès qu'il **reviendra**.

Ex: *I will cross when the weather **is** fine.*
▸ Je traverserai quand le temps **sera** clément.

Be going to + V

L'énonciateur fait une prédiction en s'appuyant sur la présence d'indices (d'après ce qu'il voit).

Ex: *It's raining.*
*They **are not going to cross** tonight.*
▸ Il pleut. Ils ne vont pas pouvoir traverser ce soir.

Il peut également exprimer une intention, une décision déjà prise.

Ex: ***I'm going to cross** tonight.*
▸ Je vais traverser ce soir.

ATTENTION

***Be going to + V* ne peut pas s'employer dans les énoncés comportant une condition.**

Ex: *He will be glad if we succeed.*
▸ Il sera ravi si nous réussissons.

Be + V-*ing*

L'énonciateur fait part d'un projet personnel en utilisant *be* + V-*ing* et un marqueur de temps.

Ex: ***I'm leaving** next week!*
▸ Je pars le mois prochain !

Le présent (V-s)

L'énonciateur parle de données brutes (emploi du temps, horaires de trains, etc...) et emploie un marqueur de temps.

Ex: *The train **leaves** at four.*
▸ Le train part à quatre heures.

Be to + V

L'énonciateur fait part de quelque chose qui a été convenu ou prévu.

Ex: *The President **is to talk** about the Californian border tomorrow evening.*
▸ Le Président doit parler de la frontière californienne demain soir.

Be about to + V

L'énonciateur insiste sur l'imminence d'une action, d'un événement.

Ex: *The patrol **is about to leave**. Hurry up!*
▸ La patrouille va bientôt partir. Dépêchez-vous !

ENTRAÎNEZ-VOUS

**1 Repérez comment on renvoie à l'avenir dans les phrases 1 à 4.
Associez les formes relevées à leur définition (a à d).**

1. We are going to live somewhere else. Life has become impossible!
2. He will be frightened when he knows about the situation.
3. We check in at 5 p.m.
4. Our plane is about to leave.

a. déduction
b. horaire imposé
c. imminence d'une action
d. intention

2 Écrivez des énoncés cohérents en reliant les éléments 1 à 5 aux fins de phrases a à e.

1. Xico will have more money
2. Are you going to stay
3. Xico is about to
4. If we don't do anything
5. Will life be easier

a. for all these migrants?
b. when he works in the USA.
c. in this country or somewhere else?
d. give up everything in his country.
e. the people of our country will all leave.

3 Choisissez la forme verbale qui convient pour compléter les blancs.

a. He has walked too much.
He ... reach the border tonight. (isn't to - won't)
b. If you go on making a noise,
the border patrol ... see you. (will - is about to)
c. They have seen Juan. He ... be caught!
(is going to - is to)
d. Everybody has been warned: the mayor ... talk to all the citizens tonight. (is about to - is to)

4 Traduisez.

a. Le Président doit se rendre aux États-Unis la semaine prochaine.
b. Je vais téléphoner à l'aéroport.
Je ne me souviens pas du numéro de mon vol.
c. Je serai content quand je serai loin de ce pays.
d. L'avion va bientôt partir. Dépêchez-vous !

JEUX DE MOTS

1 Choisissez le verbe *do* ou *make* pour compléter les expressions suivantes :

a. You ... an effort
b. You ... a profit
c. You ... something/nothing
d. You ... a plan
e. You ... an offer
f. You ... business
g. You ... a favour
h. You ... a mistake
i. You ... money
j. You ... a job.

2 Ajoutez à chaque mot de la liste A un mot de la liste B pour faire des noms composés puis traduisez-les.

A. border - note - back - entrance - immigration - garden
B. fence - laws - pack - patrol - book - fee

3 Complétez ce texte à l'aide des mots de liaison suivants.

but - in order to (2 fois) - although

Xico is one of the many people who would like to reach the United States ... find better opportunities. ... these illegal migrants are often caught by patrol agents, they keep trying to cross the border. The federal agents use different techniques ... stop them, ... most migrants succeed in getting through.

4 Complétez avec les prépositions ou adverbes ci-dessous :

away - back - over - into - below - at

Xico is standing ... the Mexican border. He wants to cross ... to get ... the USA. He is very frightened because the border patrol is not far .... He can see the town ... him and he hopes he will not be caught. He does not want to go ... to his poor village in Mexico.

D'UNE LANGUE À L'AUTRE

1 Lisez les phrases suivantes et relevez les éléments qui permettent de traduire "jusqu'à" lorsqu'il introduit : un lieu / une quantité / une date

a. *Up to 100 migrants gather and rush the border.*
▶ Jusqu'à 100 personnes se rassemblent et se précipitent vers la frontière.

b. *There were as many as 2,000 people waiting.*
▶ Il y avait jusqu'à 2000 personnes qui attendaient.

c. *He decided to stay there until Sunday.*
▶ Il décida de rester là jusqu'à dimanche.

d. *As he had no mobile phone, he had to go as far as the next village to call his wife.*
▶ Comme il n'avait pas de téléphone portable, il dut aller jusqu'au village le plus proche pour appeler sa femme.

2 Traduisez en français.

a. He climbed up to the top of the mountain.
b. He went as far as the village to buy some food.
c. He will not give up, he will try every day until the end of the week.
d. If he works in the US, he will get as much as ten times his current salary.

3 Traduisez en anglais.

a. Il a vécu dans ce village jusqu'à l'âge de 15 ans.
b. Il dort dans une pièce qui contient jusqu'à 10 personnes.
c. Il travaille tous les jours jusqu'à minuit.

ATELIER D'ÉCRITURE

1 Xico's mother went to see a fortune-teller to find out about her son's future. Imagine the end of the conversation.
Ex: *Will he be able to cross the border?*
Of course he will. The crystal ball says he's going to find a good job in the U.S.

Word box:
get through - catch - be rich - get a good job - find a beautiful wife - have children - send you money - come back

2 Write a conversation between two young people: one would like to go and work abroad, the other wouldn't think of leaving his/her country.
Write about 70 words.

- Start like this: You know what, David? I've just been offered a job in the USA and I think it's great! ...
- Each reply must include a good reason.

CONSEILS D'ÉCRITURE

- **Préparez les arguments que vous allez utiliser pour chaque personne.**
  - learn another language
  - fit in a different society
  - find a more exciting life
  - discover a new way of life
  - no desire to leave family or friends
  - want to stick to traditions...

Pensez à utiliser les expressions du futur.

- **Au début de chaque réplique utilisez des expressions comme :**
  Yes, I see ... - Well, ... - Yes, but ...
  - That sounds interesting ... - Personally, ...
- **Utilisez les mots de liaison :**
  however, although, that's why, in order to ...

ADJECTIFS

available	*disponible*
each	*chaque*
eligible	*éligible*
far	*loin*
glad	*content*
grateful	*reconnaissant*
low	*bas*

NOMS

area	*région*
backpack	*sac à dos*
border	*frontière*
carpet	*moquette*
census	*recensement*
citizen	*citoyen*
end	*fin*
face	*visage*
fact	*fait*
fee	*prix*
foam	*mousse*
footsteps	*pas*
foreigner	*étranger*
graduation	*remise des diplômes*
head	*tête*
land	*terre*
driver's license	*permis de conduire*
lights	*lumières*
mechanic	*mécanicien*
mouse (mice)	*souris*
neighborhood	*quartier, voisinage*
relative	*parent*
sand	*sable*
smuggler	*trafiquant*
spelling	*orthographe*

VERBES

be in charge of	*être responsable de*
catch	*attraper*
choose	*choisir*
cross	*traverser*
freeze	*congeler*
get through	*réussir à traverser*
mop	*laver*
move	*déménager*
prove	*prouver*
share	*partager*
spot	*remarquer*
sweep	*balayer*
wrap	*emballer*

Exercices

1 Complétez les séries avec des mots du lexique.

a. beginning – middle …
b. price - charge …
c. face – hand …
d. area – country …
e. candles – lamps …
f. engineer – plumber …
g. aunt - cousin …
h. robber – pirate …
i. reading – writing …
j. rabbit – cat ...

2 Complétez avec des adjectifs.

a. If you are happy, you are …
b. If you are free to do something, you are …
c. If a price is not high, it is …
d. If a place is not near, it is …
e. If you really appreciate what someone has done for you, you are …
f. If you are qualified for a job, you are …

3 Associez les verbes 1 à 9 à leur complément a à i.

1. be in charge of
2. get through
3. mop
4. move
5. share
6. spot
7. sweep
8. wrap
9. prove

a. a barrier
b. someone is innocent
c. a present in paper
d. food with a friend
e. an illegal immigrant
f. a team
g. the floor with a brush
h. the floor with a cloth and water
i. into a new neighborhood

Working part-time

More than one million of the 1.2 million new jobs in the USA are part-time, and part-time jobs now represent 18 percent of the total job market, the highest level since 1997. Many economists and other experts say that most of the jobs being offered are part-time because of economic uncertainty, changing markets and employers' efforts to save money. Some workers take these jobs because they cannot find full-time work but need some income, while others cite other factors, like a desire to spend more time with family or to have a flexible schedule[1].

Whatever the cause, the high number of part-time jobs today has important implications for job seekers as part-time jobs often come without social benefits. Along with the scarcity[2] of benefits, part-time workers – those working less than 35 hours a week – often have lower hourly wages and little or no paid vacation or sick leave[3].

Joe Catanzaro had no health insurance and suffered for it last year. He endured five days of headaches and visual problems. But instead of seeing a doctor immediately he waited until he could no longer stand the pain and then went to a nearby hospital. The headache turned out to be the result of a serious brain disease. He took two weeks off, without pay, from his part-time job while he recovered.

Chuck Harner, 63, worked for 15 years as a manager before he was laid off[4] in 2001. He has a doctorate in mathematics but spent the next 18 months searching fruitlessly for full-time work. In April 2003 he found a 12-hour-a-week job at a supermarket where he does everything from sweeping the floors to selling books and records. As a manager, he made more than $100,000 annually. Now he earns about $7 an hour.

Some workers like part-time work because of its flexibility. Lana Caywood, 49, a teacher, is happily employed three days a week at an elementary school. She likes it because it gives her time for her family.

Flexibility is important for many workers. In a 2004 survey of 946 full-time professionals, 39 percent said that they would definitely accept a job paying up to 10 percent less but offering more work-life balance. And 87 percent said that they looked for flexible hours in a new job. The part-time marketplace is also more accommodating for the laid-off[4] textile worker who wants to retrain, the baby boomer[5] who wants to spend more time with family and the senior citizen who is not ready to retire.

The New York Times - October 10, 2004 (adapted)

WORDS:

1 schedule: *horaire*
2 scarcity: *le manque de*
3 sick leave: *congé maladie*
4 to be laid off: *être licencié*
5 baby boomer: *personne née lors du baby-boom qui a suivi la fin de la seconde guerre mondiale.*

A Répondez aux questions en français. 8 pts

1. Que nous apprend le début de cet article sur la situation de l'emploi aux Etats Unis ?
2. Quelles sont les raisons avancées par les experts pour expliquer cette situation ?
3. Quelles sont, pour les salariés, les difficultés liées aux emplois à temps partiel ?
4. En quoi le cas de Joe Catanzaro est-il représentatif des difficultés rencontrées par les salariés à temps partiel aux Etats-Unis?
5. Pourquoi Lana Caywood apprécie-t-elle de ne pas travailler à plein temps ?
6. Qu'a révélé l'enquête sur la flexibilité du travail menée en 2004 ?
7. Pour quels salariés le travail à temps partiel présente-t-il des aspects positifs ?

B Traduisez en français le paragraphe 4. 4 pts

C Mettez les verbes entre parenthèses à la forme exigée. 2 pts

Joe *(to work)* in the new supermarket for a year when, last month, he *(to break)* his arm while playing football. As he *(to have)* no health insurance, he *(take)* sick leave, without pay, for several weeks.

D Complétez avec any / some / none / no. **2 pts**

... of the workers who were interviewed said they didn't enjoy their jobs because they felt they didn't have ... spare time. They also told the journalist they had ... choice regarding schedule. ... of them, however, said they would go on strike over this.

E Write 80 words in English about the job you would like to get. 4 pts

(job, employer, working conditions, schedule, pay, days off...)

Sommaire annexes

Be

Forme affirmative

Présent

I **am**	I**'m**
you **are**	you**'re**
he / she / it **is**	he /she / it**'s**
we **are**	we**'re**
you **are**	you**'re**
they **are**	they**'re**

Prétérit

I **was**
you **were**
he / she / it **was**
we **were**
you **were**
they **were**

Participe passé

been

Forme négative → be + not

Présent

I **am not**	I**'m not**
you **are not**	you **aren't**
he / she / it **is not**	he /she / it**'sn't**
we **are not**	we **aren't**
you **are not**	you **aren't**
they **are not**	they **aren't**

Prétérit

I **was not**	I **wasn't**
you **were not**	you **weren't**
he / she / it **was not**	he / she / it **wasn't**
we **were not**	we **weren't**
you **were not**	you **weren't**
they **were not**	they **weren't**

Forme interrogative → inversion

Présent

am I ?
are you ?
is he/she/ it ?
are we ?
are you?
are they?

Prétérit

was I ?
were you?
was he / she / it ?
were we ?
were you ?
were they ?

Have

Forme affirmative

Présent

I **have**	I**'ve**
you **have**	you**'ve**
he / she / it **has**	he /she / it**'s**
we **have**	we**'ve**
you **have**	you**'ve**
they **have**	they**'ve**

Prétérit

I **had**
you **had**
he / she / it **had**
we **had**
you **had**
they **had**

Participe passé

had

Conjugaison des temps simples

Verbes réguliers

Forme affirmative	Forme négative	Forme interrogative
Présent simple		
I look	*I* **do not** *look*	**do** *I look?*
you look	*you* **do not** *look*	**do** *you look?*
*he look***s**	*he* **does not** *look*	**does** *he look?*
we look	*we* **do not** *look*	**do** *we look?*
you look	*you* **do not** *look*	**do** *you look?*
they look	*they* **do not** *look*	**do** *they look?*

Forme contractée : **do not** → **don't**
does not → **doesn't**

Prétérit		
*I look***ed**	**did** *I look?*	*I* **did not** *look*
*you look***ed**	**did** *you look?*	*you* **did not** *look*
*he look***ed**	**did** *he look?*	*he* **did not** *look*
*we look***ed**	**did** *we look?*	*we* **did not** *look*
*you look***ed**	**did** *you look?*	*you* **did not** *look*
*they look***ed**	**did** *they look?*	*they* **did not** *look*

Forme contractée : **did not** → **didn't**

Verbes irréguliers

Le présent simple se conjugue comme les autres verbes

Pour le prétérit simple, voir liste page 166-167

Exemple :	*I* **went**	**did** *I go?*	*I* **did not** *go*
	you **went**	**did** *you go?*	*you* **did not** *go*
	he **went**	**did** *he go?*	*he* **did not** *go*
	we **went**	**did** *we go?*	*we* **did not** *go*
	you **went**	**did** *you go?*	*you* **did not** *go*
	they **went**	**did** *they go?*	*they* **did not** *go*

Forme contractée : **did not** → **didn't**

Conjugaison des formes composées

Forme *be + V-ing*

Présent

he **is** *look***ing**
is *he look***ing***?*
he **is not** *look***ing**

Prétérit

he **was** *look***ing**
was *he look***ing***?*
he **was not** *look***ing**

Modalité - Aspect

he **will be** *look***ing**
will *he* **be** *look***ing***?*
he **will not be** *look***ing**

Present perfect

he **has been** *look***ing**
has *he* **been** *look***ing***?*
he **has not been** *look***ing**

Present perfect

have *+ participe passé*
I **have** *look***ed**
have *I look***ed***?*
I **have not** *look***ed**
he **has gone**
has *he* **gone***?*
he **has not gone**

Futur (expression du)

will *+ V à toutes les personnes*
I **will** *go*
will *I go?*
I **will not** *go*

Forme contractée : **will not** → **won't**

Condition (expression de la)

would *+ V à toutes les personnes*
I **would** *go*
would *I go?*
I **would not** *go*

Forme contractée : **would not** → **wouldn't**

Verbes irréguliers

A

arise	*arose*	*arisen*	s'élever
awake	*awoke*	*awoken*	s'éveiller

B

be	*was*	*been*	être
bear	*bore*	*borne*	supporter
beat	*beat*	*beaten*	battre
become	*became*	*become*	devenir
begin	*began*	*begun*	commencer
bend	*bent*	*bent*	(se) courber
bet	*bet*	*bet*	parier
bind	*bound*	*bound*	lier
bite	*bit*	*bitten*	mordre
bleed	*bled*	*bled*	saigner
blow	*blew*	*blown*	souffler
break	*broke*	*broken*	casser
breed	*bred*	*bred*	donner naissance, élever
bring	*brought*	*brought*	apporter
broadcast	*broadcast*	*broadcast*	transmettre
build	*built*	*built*	construire
*burn**	*burnt*	*burnt*	brûler
burst	*burst*	*burst*	éclater
buy	*bought*	*bought*	acheter

C

can	*could*	-	pouvoir, savoir
cast	*cast*	*cast*	jeter, projeter
catch	*caught*	*caught*	attraper
choose	*chose*	*chosen*	choisir
cling	*clung*	*clung*	s'accrocher
come	*came*	*come*	venir
cost	*cost*	*cost*	coûter
creep	*crept*	*crept*	ramper
cut	*cut*	*cut*	couper

D

deal	*dealt*	*dealt*	distribuer
dig	*dug*	*dug*	creuser
do	*did*	*done*	faire
draw	*drew*	*drawn*	dessiner
*dream**	*dreamt*	*dreamt*	rêver
drink	*drank*	*drunk*	boire
drive	*drove*	*driven*	conduire
dwell	*dwelt*	*dwelt*	habiter

E

eat	*ate*	*eaten*	manger

F

fall	*fell*	*fallen*	tomber
feed	*fed*	*fed*	nourrir
feel	*felt*	*felt*	sentir
fight	*fought*	*fought*	combattre
find	*found*	*found*	trouver
flee	*fled*	*fled*	fuir
fling	*flung*	*flung*	lancer
fly	*flew*	*flown*	voler (avion)
forbid	*forbade*	*forbidden*	interdire
forget	*forgot*	*forgotten*	oublier
forgive	*forgave*	*forgiven*	pardonner
forsake	*forsook*	*forsaken*	abandonner
freeze	*froze*	*frozen*	geler

G

get	*got*	*got*	obtenir
give	*gave*	*given*	donner
go	*went*	*gone*	aller
grind	*ground*	*ground*	moudre
grow	*grew*	*grown*	pousser

H

hang	*hung*	*hung*	pendre
have	*had*	*had*	avoir
hear	*heard*	*heard*	entendre
hide	*hid*	*hidden*	cacher
hit	*hit*	*hit*	frapper
hold	*held*	*held*	tenir
hurt	*hurt*	*hurt*	faire mal

K

keep	*kept*	*kept*	garder
kneel	*knelt*	*knelt*	s'agenouiller
know	*knew*	*known*	savoir

L

lay	*laid*	*laid*	placer
lead	*led*	*led*	conduire
*lean**	*leant*	*leant*	s'appuyer
*leap**	*leapt*	*leapt*	sauter
*learn**	*learnt*	*learnt*	apprendre
leave	*left*	*left*	quitter
lend	*lent*	*lent*	prêter

* Ces verbes ont aussi une forme régulière en *-ed*

let	*let*	*let*	laisser
lie	*lay*	*lain*	être couché
*light**	*lit*	*lit*	allumer
lose	*lost*	*lost*	perdre

M

make	*made*	*made*	faire
may	*might*	-	pouvoir (possibilité, permission)
mean	*meant*	*meant*	vouloir dire
meet	*met*	*met*	rencontrer
*mow**	*mowed*	*mown*	tondre

P

pay	*paid*	*paid*	payer
put	*put*	*put*	mettre

R

read	*read*	*read*	lire
rend	*rent*	*rent*	déchirer
ride	*rode*	*ridden*	aller à cheval (à bicyclette)
ring	*rang*	*rung*	sonner
rise	*rose*	*risen*	se lever
run	*ran*	*run*	courir

S

saw	*sawed*	*sawn*	scier
say	*said*	*said*	dire
see	*saw*	*seen*	voir
seek	*sought*	*sought*	chercher
sell	*sold*	*sold*	vendre
send	*sent*	*sent*	envoyer
set	*set*	*set*	placer
*sew**	*sewed*	*sewn*	coudre
shake	*shook*	*shaken*	secouer
shed	*shed*	*shed*	se défaire de, perdre
shine	*shone*	*shone*	briller
shoot	*shot*	*shot*	tirer
show	*showed*	*shown*	montrer
shrink	*shrank*	*shrunk*	rétrécir
shut	*shut*	*shut*	fermer
sing	*sang*	*sung*	chanter
sink	*sank*	*sunk*	(s') enfoncer
sit	*sat*	*sat*	(s') asseoir
sleep	*slept*	*slept*	dormir
slide	*slid*	*slid*	glisser
*smell**	*smelt*	*smelt*	sentir
*sow**	*sowed*	*sown*	semer
speak	*spoke*	*spoken*	parler
*speed**	*sped*	*sped*	se presser
*spell**	*spelt*	*spelt*	épeler
spend	*spent*	*spent*	dépenser
*spill**	*spilt*	*spilt*	renverser
spit	*spat*	*spat*	cracher
split	*split*	*split*	diviser
*spoil**	*spoilt*	*spoilt*	abîmer, gâter
spread	*spread*	*spread*	étaler
spring	*sprang*	*sprung*	jaillir
stand	*stood*	*stood*	être debout
steal	*stole*	*stolen*	voler (qq chose)
stick	*stuck*	*stuck*	coller
sting	*stung*	*stung*	piquer
stink	*stank*	*stunk*	sentir mauvais
stride	*strode*	*stridden*	marcher
strike	*struck*	*struck*	frapper
swear	*swore*	*sworn*	jurer
sweep	*swept*	*swept*	balayer
*swell**	*swelled*	*swollen*	(se) gonfler
swim	*swam*	*swum*	nager

T

take	*took*	*taken*	prendre
teach	*taught*	*taught*	enseigner
tear	*tore*	*torn*	déchirer
tell	*told*	*told*	dire
think	*thought*	*thought*	penser
throw	*threw*	*thrown*	jeter
thrust	*thrust*	*thrust*	pousser brusquement

U

understand	*understood*	*understood*	comprendre
upset	*upset*	*upset*	renverser

W

*wake**	*woke*	*woken*	réveiller
wear	*wore*	*worn*	porter
weep	*wept*	*wept*	pleurer
win	*won*	*won*	gagner
withdraw	*withdrew*	*withdrawn*	retirer
withhold	*withheld*	*withheld*	retenir
write	*wrote*	*written*	écrire

Prépositions

Les prépositions introduisent une précision concernant le lieu, le moyen, le temps, etc. Voici les plus courantes.

Le lieu

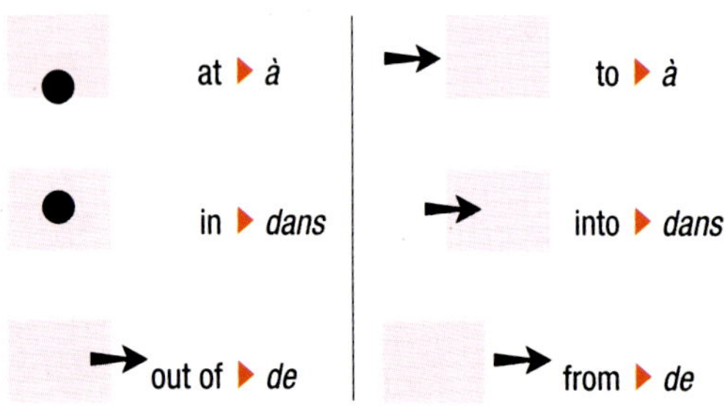

above	*au-dessus de*
across	*à travers, de l'autre côté*
along	*le long de*
among	*parmi*
behind	*derrière*
below	*au-dessous de*
between	*entre*
close to	*tout près*
down	*en bas de*
in front of	*devant*
inside	*à l'intérieur de*
near	*près de*
off / far off	*de / éloigné de*
opposite	*à l'opposé de*
outside	*à l'extérieur de*
over	*par-dessus*
round	*autour de*
towards	*vers*
under	*sous*
up	*vers le haut de*

Le temps

after	*après*
at	*à*
before	*avant*
during	*pendant*
for	*pendant - depuis*
from	*à partir de*
in	*en*
on	*le (+ nom du jour)*
since	*depuis*
until	*jusqu'à*

Autres prépositions

about	*à propos*
because of	*à cause de*
by	*par*
except for	*excepté*
for	*pour*
instead of	*au lieu de*
like	*comme*
thanks to	*grâce à*
with	*avec*

Verbes et prépositions

Verbes transitifs indirects en anglais, transitifs directs en français.

approve of	*approuver*
believe in	*croire*
comment on	*commenter*
cut down on	*réduire*
listen to	*écouter*
look at	*regarder*
look for	*chercher*
put s.o. through	*passer qqn (au téléphone)*

Verbes transitifs directs en anglais, transitifs indirects en français.

address	*s'adresser à*
answer	*répondre à*
expect	*s'attendre à*
lack	*manquer de*
mind	*faire attention à*
need	*avoir besoin de*
obey	*obéir à*
suit	*convenir à*
trust	*faire confiance à*

Verbes suivis d'une préposition différente en anglais et en français.

consist in/of	*consister à*
depend on	*dépendre de*
get on (well) with s.o.	*s'entendre bien avec qqn*
live on	*vivre de*
laugh at	*se moquer de*
look after	*s'occuper de*
look like	*ressembler à*
reproach s.o. with sth	*reprocher qqch à qqn*
talk about	*parler de*
think about / of	*penser à*

Pour exprimer l'opposition

but	*mais*
though, although	*bien que, quoique*
on the contrary	*contrairement à*
while	*alors que*
whereas	*tandis que*
however	*cependant*
in spite of, despite	*en dépit de*
nevertheless	*néanmoins*
on the one hand... on the other hand	*d'une part..., d'autre part*

Pour exprimer la condition

if	*si*
even if, even though	*même si*
on condition that	*à condition que*
provided that	*pourvu que*
unless	*à moins que*
in case	*au cas où*

Pour exprimer la cause

because	*parce que*
because of	*à cause de*
as	*comme, puisque*
since	*puisque*
that is why	*c'est pourquoi*
thanks to	*grâce à*

Pour exprimer la conséquence

so, therefore, consequently, as a result	*en conséquence*

Pour exprimer le but

to, in order to, so as to	*afin de*
so that	*afin que...*

Pour ajouter

besides, moreover, on top of that	*de plus*
in addition	*en outre*
too, as well	*aussi*
not only... but also...	*non seulement ... mais encore*

Pour énumérer

first of all, in the first place	*en premier lieu*
secondly	*deuxièmement*
then	*ensuite*
next	*ensuite*
finally	*finalement*
at last	*enfin*

Les numéraux

Les nombres cardinaux

- Ce sont des déterminants car ils précèdent un nom.

De un à vingt		Dizaines	Grands nombres
one	*eleven*		
two	*twelve*	*twenty*	*dozen*
three	*thirteen*	*thirty*	*hundred*
four	*fourteen*	*forty*	*thousand*
five	*fifteen*	*fifty*	*million*
six	*sixteen*	*sixty*	*billion (milliard)*
seven	*seventeen*	*seventy*	
eight	*eighteen*	*eighty*	
nine	*nineteen*	*ninety*	
ten	*twenty*		

- Ils sont invariables lorsqu'ils sont précédés d'un nombre ou de *a few, several.*

Ex: *Several hundred people. Two dozen eggs.*
Plusieurs centaines de personnes. Deux douzaines d'œufs.

- Ils prennent un *s* lorsqu'ils se comportent en noms et sont suivis de *of.*

Ex: *Thousands of teenagers live on their own.*
Des milliers d'adolescents vivent seuls.

Remarque : On utilise la virgule entre les milliers et les centaines et *and* devant les dizaines et les unités.

Ex: *1,512 one thousand five hundred and twelve.*

Remarque : Les années se lisent de la façon suivante :

1900 : nineteen hundred ;
1945 : nineteen forty-five ;
2002 : two thousand and two

Les nombres ordinaux

Du 1er au 10e	du 11e au 20e	du 30e au 90e
the first	*the eleventh*	
the second	*the twelfth*	
the third	*the thirteenth*	*the thirtieth*
the fourth	*the fourteenth*	*the fortieth*
the fifth	*the fifteenth*	*the fiftieth*
the sixth	*the sixteenth*	*the sixtieth*
the seventh	*the seventeenth*	*the seventieth*
the eighth	*the eighteenth*	*the eightieth*
the ninth	*the nineteenth*	*the ninetieth*
the tenth	*the twentieth*	

Remarque : Les dates se lisent de deux façons. **Ex: 17/08/06**

- August the seventeenth, two thousand and six
- The seventeenth of August, two thousand and six

et s'écrivent de trois façons :

17 August 2006 - 17th August 2006 - August 17, 2006
in the 60s : In the sixties (dans les années 60)

- Les pourcentages

95% : *ninety-five per cent* **2.5% :** *two point five per cent*

- Les fractions

1/5 : *one fifth* **2/3 :** *two thirds*

Attention : 1/4 : *a/one quarter* - **3/4 :** *three quarters* - **1/2 :** *a/one half*

- Les prix

$9.50 : *nine dollars fifty* - **£95.60 :** *ninety-five pounds sixty*

The British Isles

The English speaking world

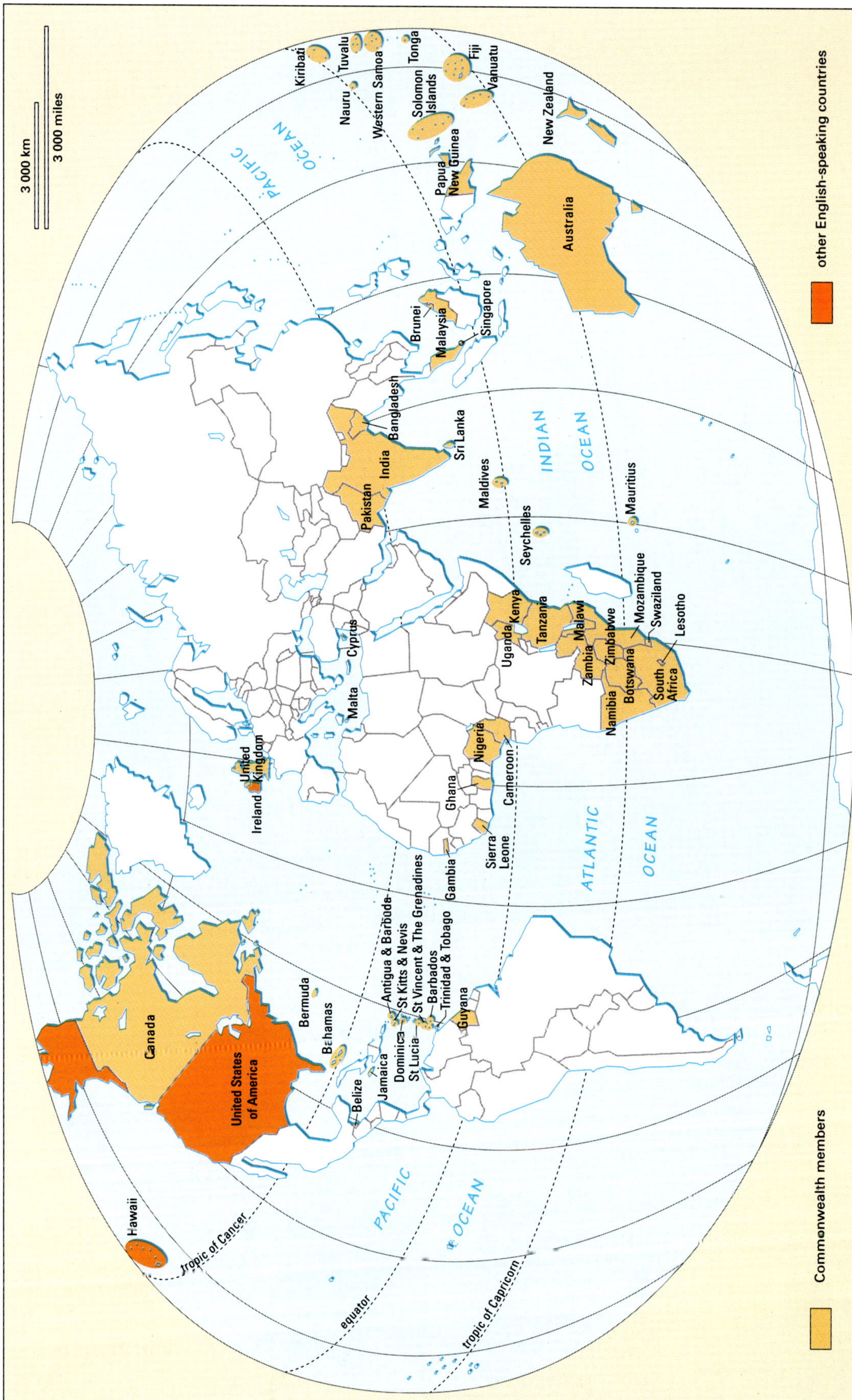

The united states of America

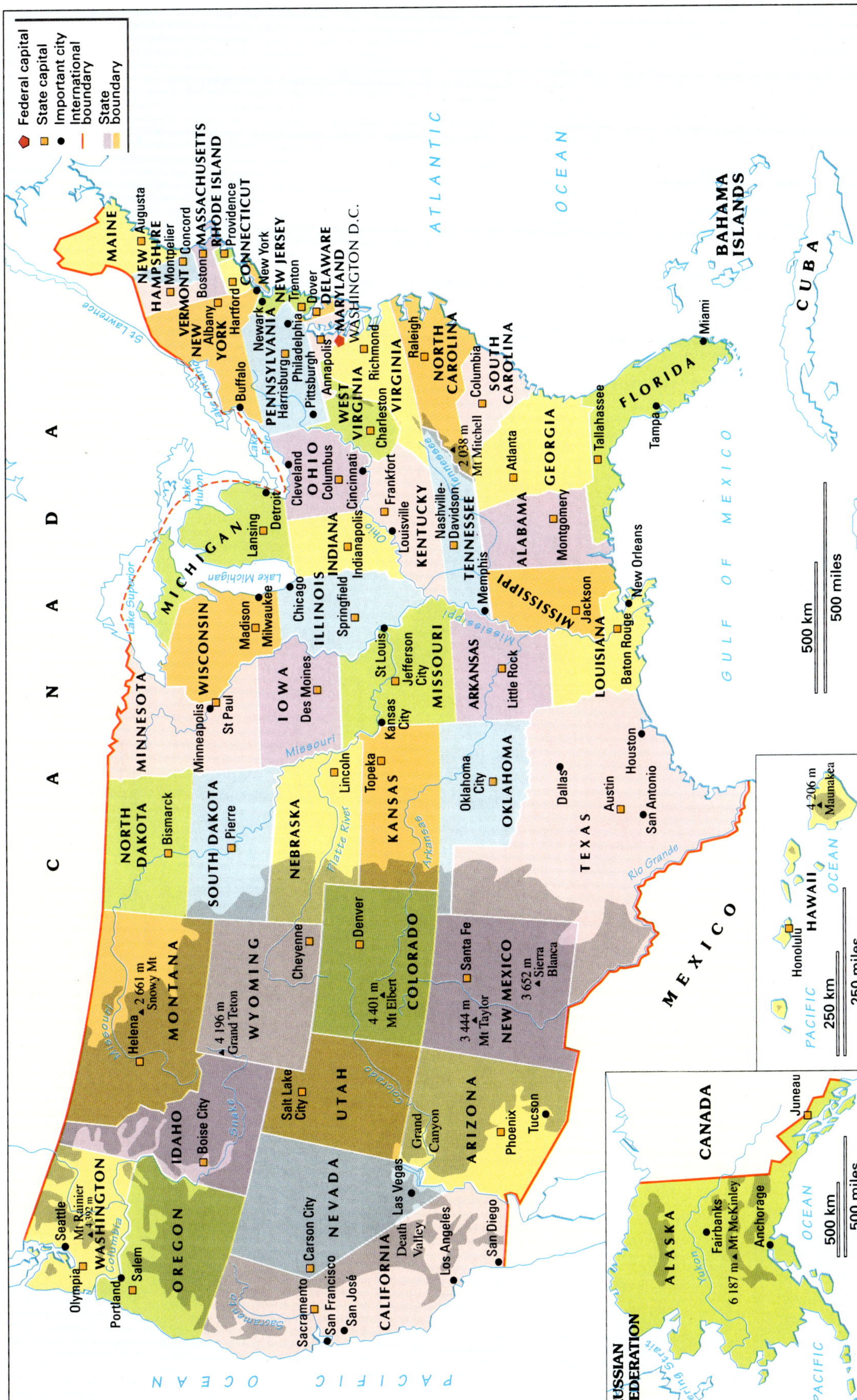

Get to the TOP

You can play this game on your own but it's more fun if you play in pairs.

You want to become director of this famous International Company.

- **First you must answer the following questions. You answer a question and move up one floor.**
- **For each piece of extra information you get an increase in salary.**
- **The winner is the person or group who gets to the top first with the highest salary.**

You are allowed to use the Internet or your dictionary to get the information needed to get to the top.

Good luck!

START HERE

1 **Your aim is to become CEO of this company. What does CEO stand for?**

a. Company Enterpriser Only
b. Chief Executive Officer
c. Crown Opulent Employer

2 **Bravo. You've worked your way up to the second floor. You don't have a secretary yet. How can you answer the phone if you are in an English or American company?**

a. 'Hello, I am Jimmy Smith speaking'
b. 'Yes, what do you want?'
c. 'Jimmy Smith speaking. How can I help you?'

FOR AN EXTRA $1000 DOLLARS A YEAR JUSTIFY YOUR CHOICE.

3 **Well done! Now you are on the third floor. Your new boss is an American, Ellen McDonald. How can you address her?**

a. Ellen
b. Madam
c. Mrs

YOU'LL GET A $1000 RAISE IF YOU CAN SAY WHAT THE DIFFERENCE IS BETWEEN: MS, MRS AND MISS WHEN PUT IN FRONT OF SOMEONE'S SURNAME.

4 **On this floor you have far more responsibility. You are expected to invite your British and American visitors to lunch. What sort of lunches are they used to having?**

a. A long lunch in a restaurant
b. A 20-minute sandwich break
c. No lunch break

5 **You are almost half way up to the top and your salary has gone up $3000 a year. When your American colleague takes a French person to lunch what questions do you advise him NOT to ask?**

a. How much do you earn?
b. How big a family do you have?
c. What are your hobbies?

Get to the

6 **You are on the sixth floor. You train sales people. What is the best reply for a customer who asks, 'Do you have a tuna sandwich left, please?'**

a. 'I'm sorry. We don't have any left. Would you like something else instead? Our ham sandwiches are delicious.'
b. 'No, sorry. Who's next?'
c. 'No, I don't.'

JUSTIFY YOUR CHOICE FOR AN EXTRA 1000 DOLLARS A YEAR.
IF YOU ANSWER THIS QUESTION CORRECTLY, YOU WILL GET A 'TWO-FLOOR-UP' PROMOTION.

7 **You use a lot of abbreviations in a company. Do you know what these abbreviations stand for?**

a. FYI
b. ASAP
c. PA

AN EXTRA $2000 A YEAR IF YOU CAN THINK OF ANOTHER ABBREVIATION THAT'S USED.

8 **Almost there! Divide the following into things that are typically French, those that are typically American and those that could be both.**

- ❑ Going out for a drink with colleagues after work every evening.
- ❑ Shaking hands with everybody in the office in the morning on arrival.
- ❑ Saying 'Hi, how are you doing?' in the morning on arrival.
- ❑ Inviting colleagues home for lunch or dinner.
- ❑ Calling your colleagues and bosses by their Christian names.
- ❑ Inviting the boss home for dinner.
- ❑ Hierarchy is all important.
- ❑ A decision cannot be made without asking the boss.
- ❑ Kissing people you don't know very well on both cheeks.
- ❑ Keeping a lot of space around you when you are with other people and not getting up close.

9 **One more floor to go. But before you get the key to the best office in the company look at the picture and find out what this anagram is:**

I IMMENSE TOY
(It means if you don't work quickly you will not get as much salary.)

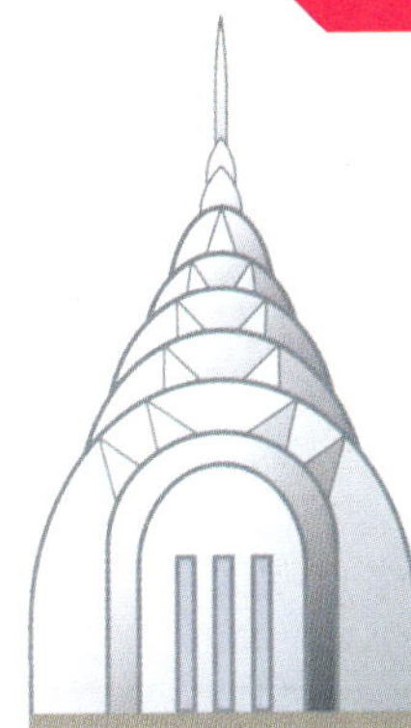

10 **You've got the key! You go into the office and there are a lot of very useful things in there. Name as many as possible and then you can choose the best PA in the company.**

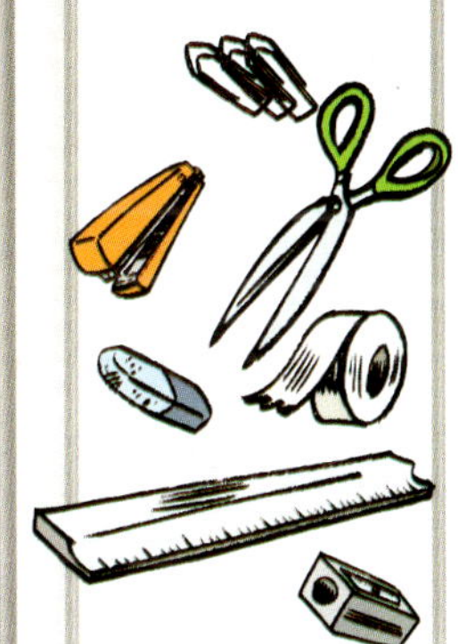

Check the answers with your teacher, the time you did the quiz in, and how much extra money you earned. The winner is the person with most correct answers, the fastest time and the highest salary.

TOP

Imprimé en Italie par ROTOLITO LOMBARDA
Dépôt légal n° 67774 - 03/2006
Collection n° 60 - Édition n° 01
18/0301/4